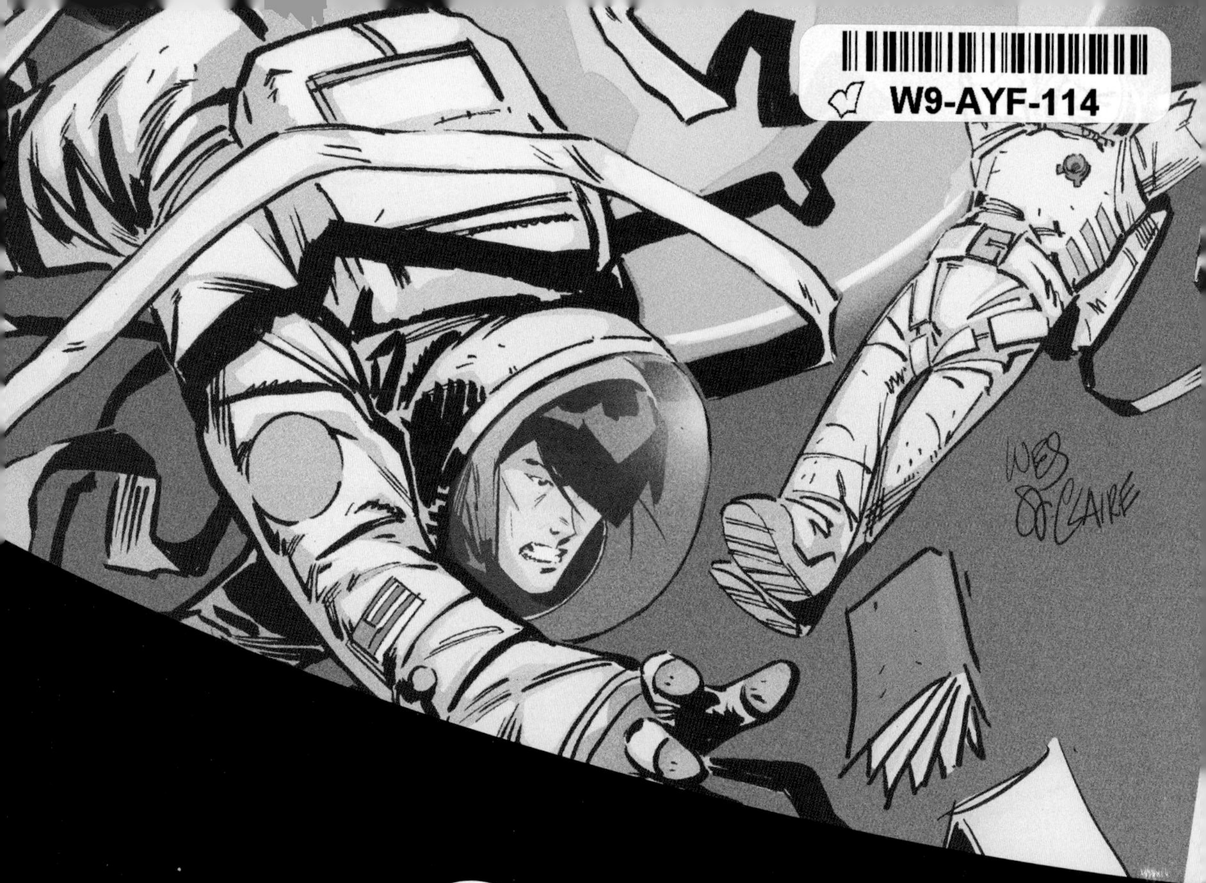

BEYONDERS™

VOLUME 1

THE MAPMAKERS

PAUL JENKINS

WESLEY ST. CLAIRE

MARSHALL DILLON

B E Y O N

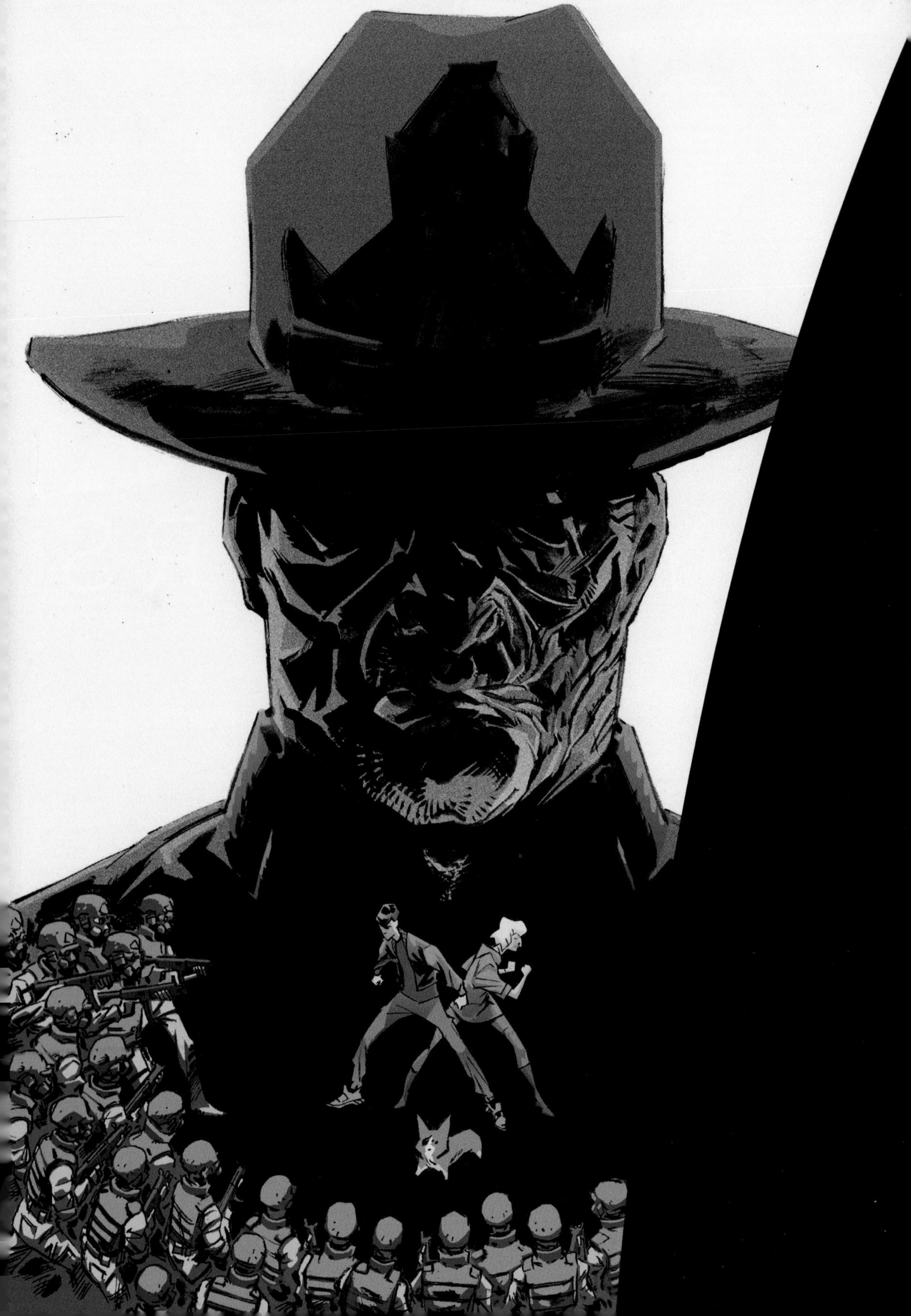

D E R S
VOLUME 1
THE MAPMAKERS

PAUL JENKINS creator & writer

WESLEY ST. CLAIRE artist

MARSHALL DILLON letterer

WESLEY ST. CLAIRE front & original series covers

RAFAEL DE LATORRE w/ **MARCELO MAIOLO, JUAN DOE,**
ANDI EWINGTON, ALE GARZA w/ ORACLE &
WESLEY ST. CLAIRE variant covers

JARED K. FLETCHER logo designer

COREY BREEN book designer

MIKE MARTS editor

MIKE MARTS - Editor-in-Chief • **JOE PRUETT** - Publisher/CCO • **LEE KRAMER** - President • **JON KRAMER** - Chief Executive Officer
STEVE ROTTERDAM - SVP, Sales & Marketing • **LISA Y. WU** - Director, Retailer Relations • **DAN SHIRES** - VP, Film & Television UK
CHRISTINA HARRINGTON - Managing Editor • **BLAKE STOCKER** - Chief Financial Officer • **AARON MARION** - Publicist
LISA MOODY - Finance • **CHARLES PRITCHETT** - Comics Production • **COREY BREEN** - Collections Production
TEDDY LEO - Editorial Assistant • **STEPHANIE CASEBIER** & **SARAH PRUETT** - Publishing Assistants

AfterShock Logo Design by **COMICRAFT**
Publicity: contact **AARON MARION** (aaron@publichausagency.com) & **RYAN CROY** (ryan@publichausagency.com) at **PUBLICHAUS**
Special thanks to: **IRA KURGAN, MARINE KSADZHIKYAN, ANTONIA LIANOS, STEPHAN NILSON** & **JULIE PIFHER**

AFTERSHOCKCOMICS.COM Follow us on social media 🐦 📷 f

Amazing Riches Await Clever Explorers

CAN YOU CRACK THE CODE?

As you read through the first issue of BEYONDERS, I hope you notice that the pages contain a series of little symbols—and perhaps other hidden clues—that lead readers on a path to an **awesome treasure**.

Hidden in the pages of our story is an **actual treasure hunt**, inspired by my lifelong love of secret codes and mysteries. Each issue will contain clues which, when assembled, will lead lucky readers to an awesome revelation.

All you have to do is solve the clues!

The answers can be found on the AfterShock website.

Have fun...and happy hunting!

PAUL JENKINS
March, 2019

The Beyonders

1

EVERYTHING IS A LIE

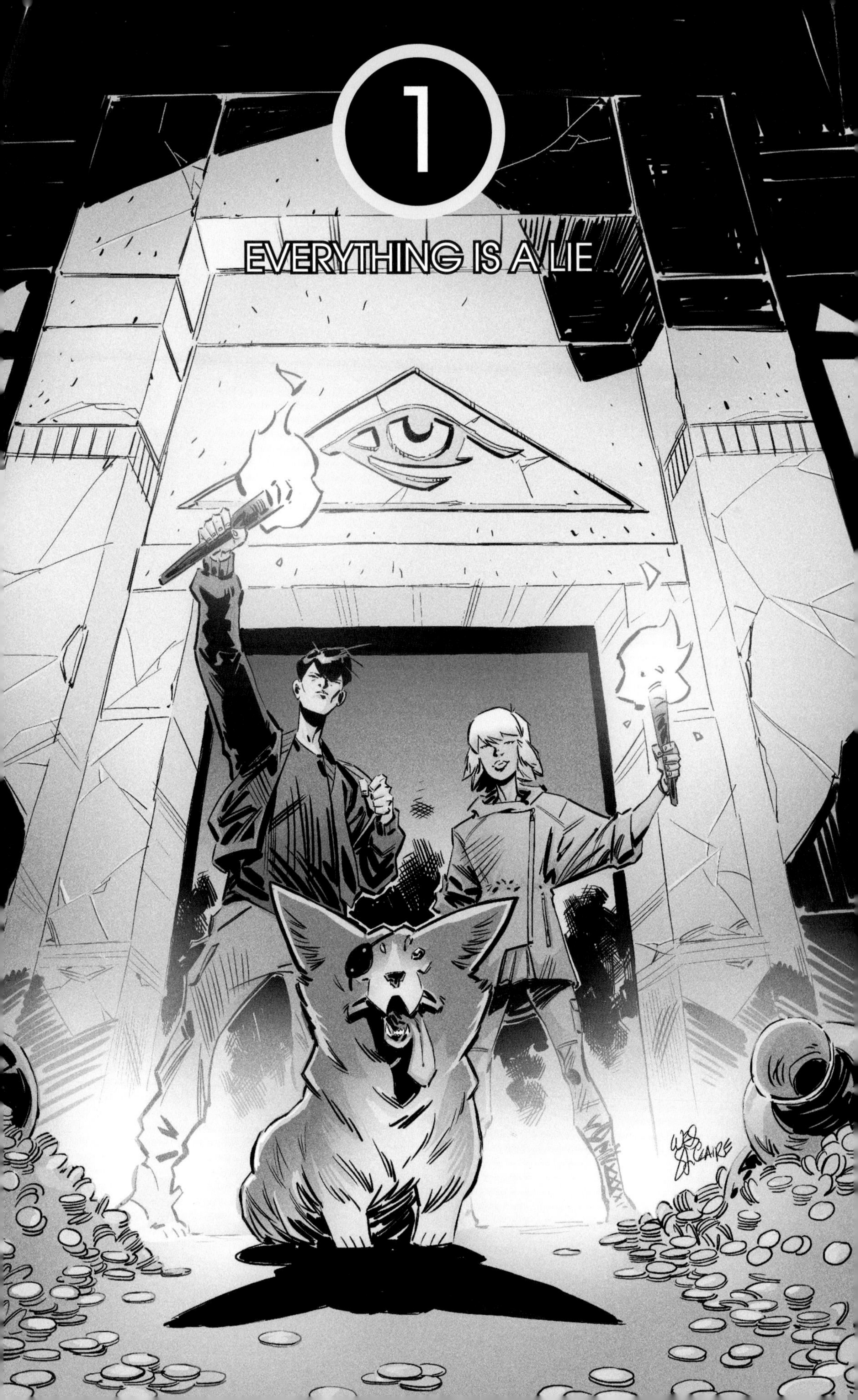

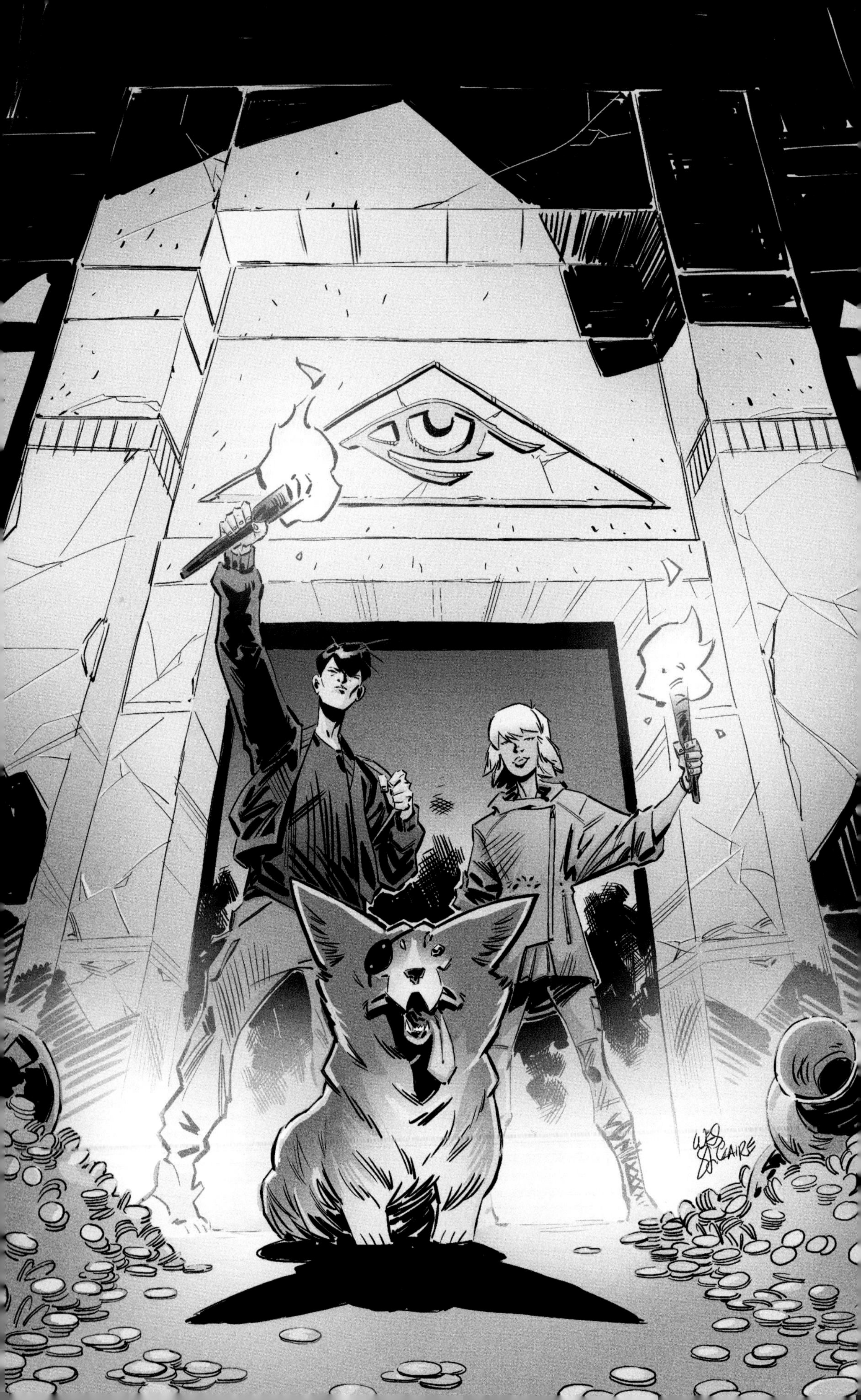

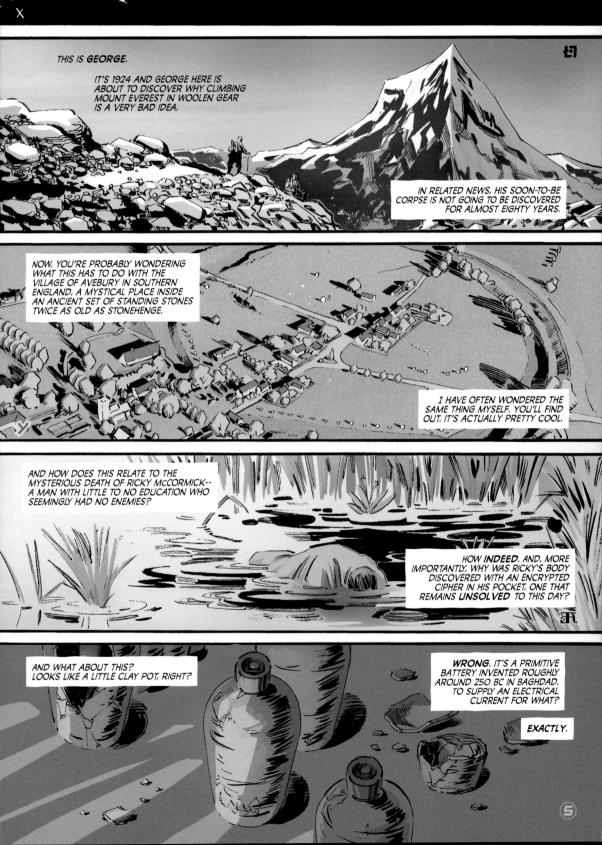

OKAY, PAY ATTENTION BECAUSE THIS IS **COMPLICATED**.

THERE'LL BE A QUIZ AT THE END.

X

THIS IS **GEORGE**.

IT'S 1924 AND GEORGE HERE IS ABOUT TO DISCOVER WHY CLIMBING MOUNT EVEREST IN WOOLEN GEAR IS A VERY BAD IDEA.

IN RELATED NEWS, HIS SOON-TO-BE CORPSE IS NOT GOING TO BE DISCOVERED FOR ALMOST EIGHTY YEARS.

NOW, YOU'RE PROBABLY WONDERING WHAT THIS HAS TO DO WITH THE VILLAGE OF AVEBURY IN SOUTHERN ENGLAND, A MYSTICAL PLACE INSIDE AN ANCIENT SET OF STANDING STONES TWICE AS OLD AS STONEHENGE.

I HAVE OFTEN WONDERED THE SAME THING MYSELF. YOU'LL FIND OUT. IT'S ACTUALLY PRETTY COOL.

AND HOW DOES THIS RELATE TO THE MYSTERIOUS DEATH OF RICKY McCORMICK-- A MAN WITH LITTLE TO NO EDUCATION WHO SEEMINGLY HAD NO ENEMIES?

HOW **INDEED**. AND, MORE IMPORTANTLY, WHY WAS RICKY'S BODY DISCOVERED WITH AN ENCRYPTED CIPHER IN HIS POCKET, ONE THAT REMAINS **UNSOLVED** TO THIS DAY?

AND WHAT ABOUT THIS? LOOKS LIKE A LITTLE CLAY POT, RIGHT?

WRONG. IT'S A PRIMITIVE BATTERY INVENTED ROUGHLY AROUND 250 BC IN BAGHDAD. TO SUPPLY AN ELECTRICAL CURRENT FOR WHAT?

EXACTLY.

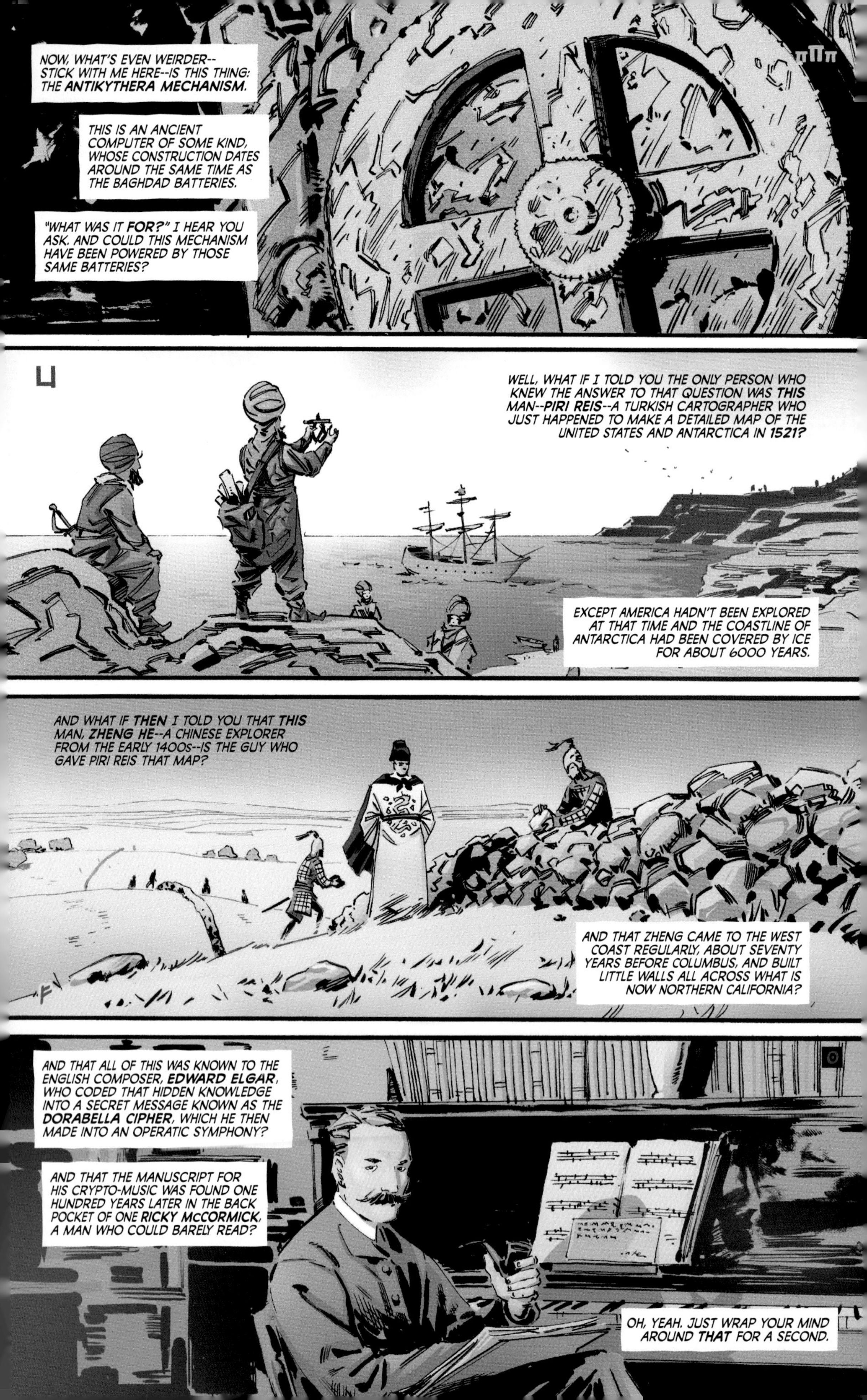
NOW, WHAT'S EVEN WEIRDER--
STICK WITH ME HERE--IS THIS THING:
THE ANTIKYTHERA MECHANISM.
THIS IS AN ANCIENT COMPUTER OF SOME KIND, WHOSE CONSTRUCTION DATES AROUND THE SAME TIME AS THE BAGHDAD BATTERIES.
"WHAT WAS IT FOR?" I HEAR YOU ASK. AND COULD THIS MECHANISM HAVE BEEN POWERED BY THOSE SAME BATTERIES?
WELL, WHAT IF I TOLD YOU THE ONLY PERSON WHO KNEW THE ANSWER TO THAT QUESTION WAS THIS MAN--PIRI REIS--A TURKISH CARTOGRAPHER WHO JUST HAPPENED TO MAKE A DETAILED MAP OF THE UNITED STATES AND ANTARCTICA IN 1521?
EXCEPT AMERICA HADN'T BEEN EXPLORED AT THAT TIME AND THE COASTLINE OF ANTARCTICA HAD BEEN COVERED BY ICE FOR ABOUT 6000 YEARS.
AND WHAT IF THEN I TOLD YOU THAT THIS MAN, ZHENG HE--A CHINESE EXPLORER FROM THE EARLY 1400s--IS THE GUY WHO GAVE PIRI REIS THAT MAP?
AND THAT ZHENG CAME TO THE WEST COAST REGULARLY, ABOUT SEVENTY YEARS BEFORE COLUMBUS, AND BUILT LITTLE WALLS ALL ACROSS WHAT IS NOW NORTHERN CALIFORNIA?
AND THAT ALL OF THIS WAS KNOWN TO THE ENGLISH COMPOSER, EDWARD ELGAR, WHO CODED THAT HIDDEN KNOWLEDGE INTO A SECRET MESSAGE KNOWN AS THE DORABELLA CIPHER, WHICH HE THEN MADE INTO AN OPERATIC SYMPHONY?
AND THAT THE MANUSCRIPT FOR HIS CRYPTO-MUSIC WAS FOUND ONE HUNDRED YEARS LATER IN THE BACK POCKET OF ONE RICKY McCORMICK, A MAN WHO COULD BARELY READ?
OH, YEAH. JUST WRAP YOUR MIND AROUND THAT FOR A SECOND.

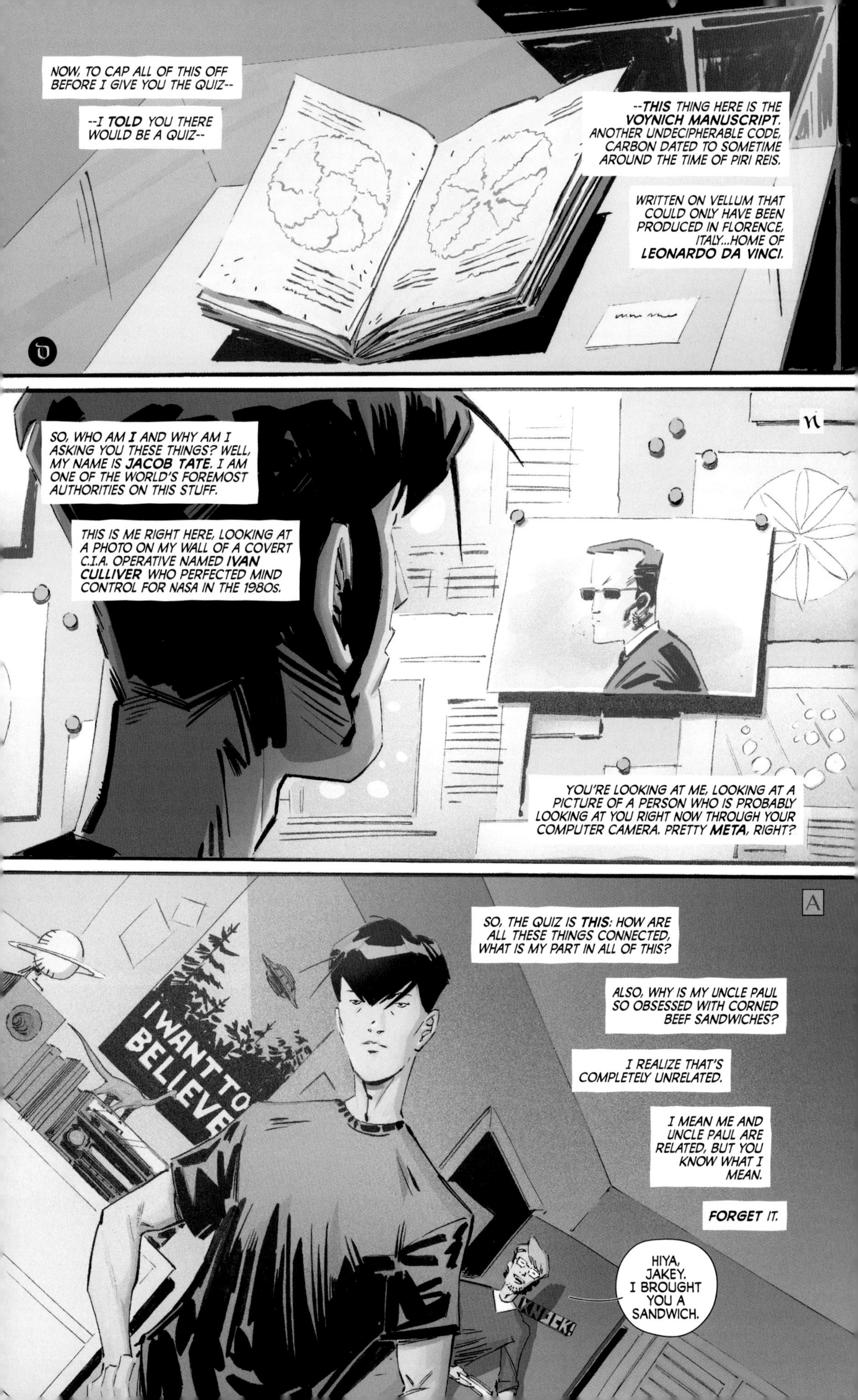
NOW, TO CAP ALL OF THIS OFF BEFORE I GIVE YOU THE QUIZ--
--I **TOLD** YOU THERE WOULD BE A QUIZ--
--**THIS** THING HERE IS THE **VOYNICH MANUSCRIPT**. ANOTHER UNDECIPHERABLE CODE, CARBON DATED TO SOMETIME AROUND THE TIME OF PIRI REIS.
WRITTEN ON VELLUM THAT COULD ONLY HAVE BEEN PRODUCED IN FLORENCE, ITALY...HOME OF **LEONARDO DA VINCI**.
SO, WHO AM **I** AND WHY AM I ASKING YOU THESE THINGS? WELL, MY NAME IS **JACOB TATE**. I AM ONE OF THE WORLD'S FOREMOST AUTHORITIES ON THIS STUFF.
THIS IS ME RIGHT HERE, LOOKING AT A PHOTO ON MY WALL OF A COVERT C.I.A. OPERATIVE NAMED **IVAN CULLIVER** WHO PERFECTED MIND CONTROL FOR NASA IN THE 1980s.
YOU'RE LOOKING AT ME, LOOKING AT A PICTURE OF A PERSON WHO IS PROBABLY LOOKING AT YOU RIGHT NOW THROUGH YOUR COMPUTER CAMERA. PRETTY **META**, RIGHT?
I WANT TO BELIEVE
SO, THE QUIZ IS **THIS**: HOW ARE ALL THESE THINGS CONNECTED, WHAT IS MY PART IN ALL OF THIS?
ALSO, WHY IS MY UNCLE PAUL SO OBSESSED WITH CORNED BEEF SANDWICHES?
I REALIZE THAT'S COMPLETELY UNRELATED.
I MEAN ME AND UNCLE PAUL ARE RELATED, BUT YOU KNOW WHAT I MEAN.
FORGET IT.
KNECK!
HIYA, JAKEY. I BROUGHT YOU A SANDWICH.

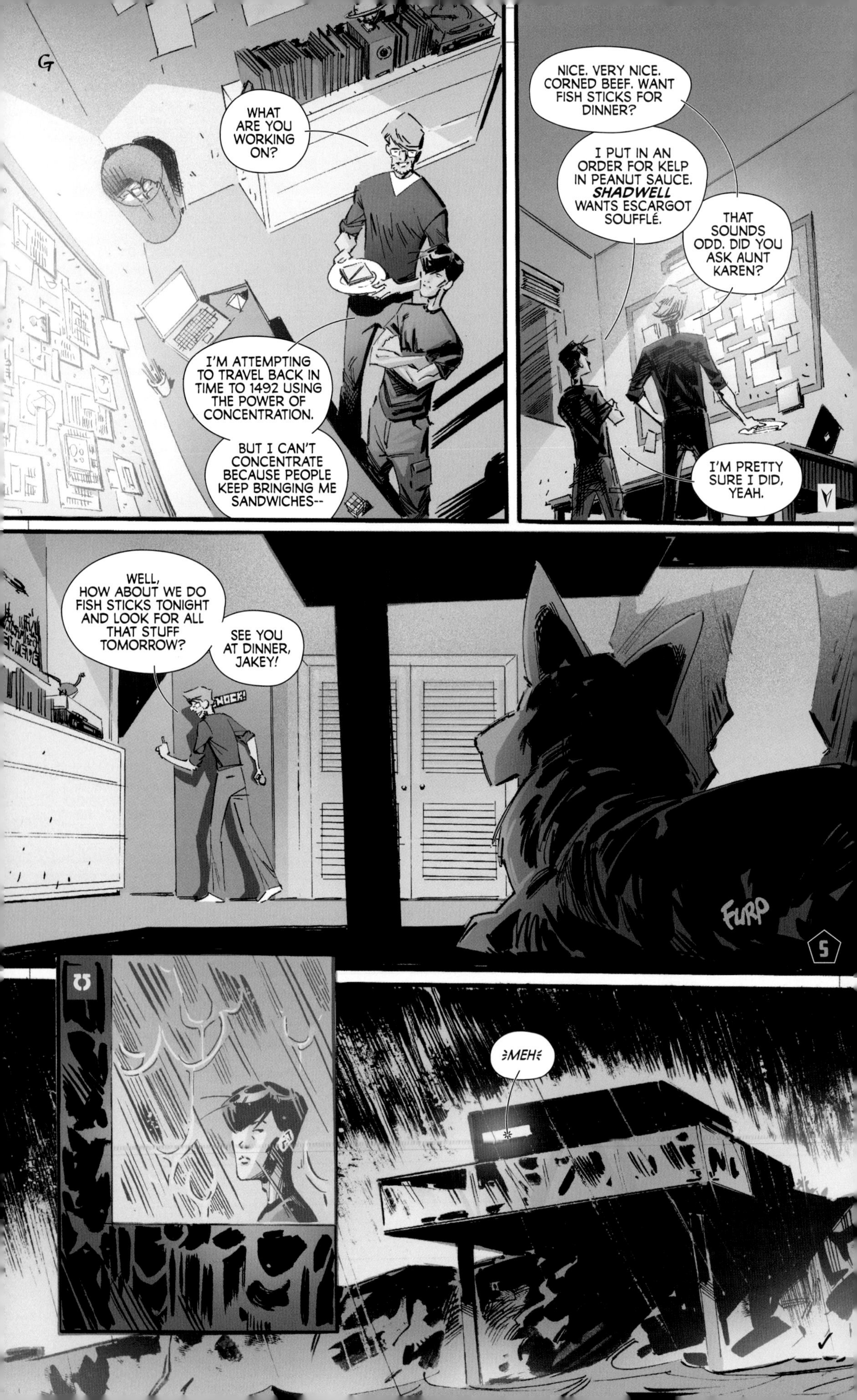

G
WHAT ARE YOU WORKING ON?
I'M ATTEMPTING TO TRAVEL BACK IN TIME TO 1492 USING THE POWER OF CONCENTRATION.
BUT I CAN'T CONCENTRATE BECAUSE PEOPLE KEEP BRINGING ME SANDWICHES--
NICE. VERY NICE. CORNED BEEF. WANT FISH STICKS FOR DINNER?
I PUT IN AN ORDER FOR KELP IN PEANUT SAUCE. SHADWELL WANTS ESCARGOT SOUFFLÉ.
THAT SOUNDS ODD. DID YOU ASK AUNT KAREN?
I'M PRETTY SURE I DID, YEAH.
WELL, HOW ABOUT WE DO FISH STICKS TONIGHT AND LOOK FOR ALL THAT STUFF TOMORROW?
SEE YOU AT DINNER, JAKEY!
WOCK!
FURP
5
MEH

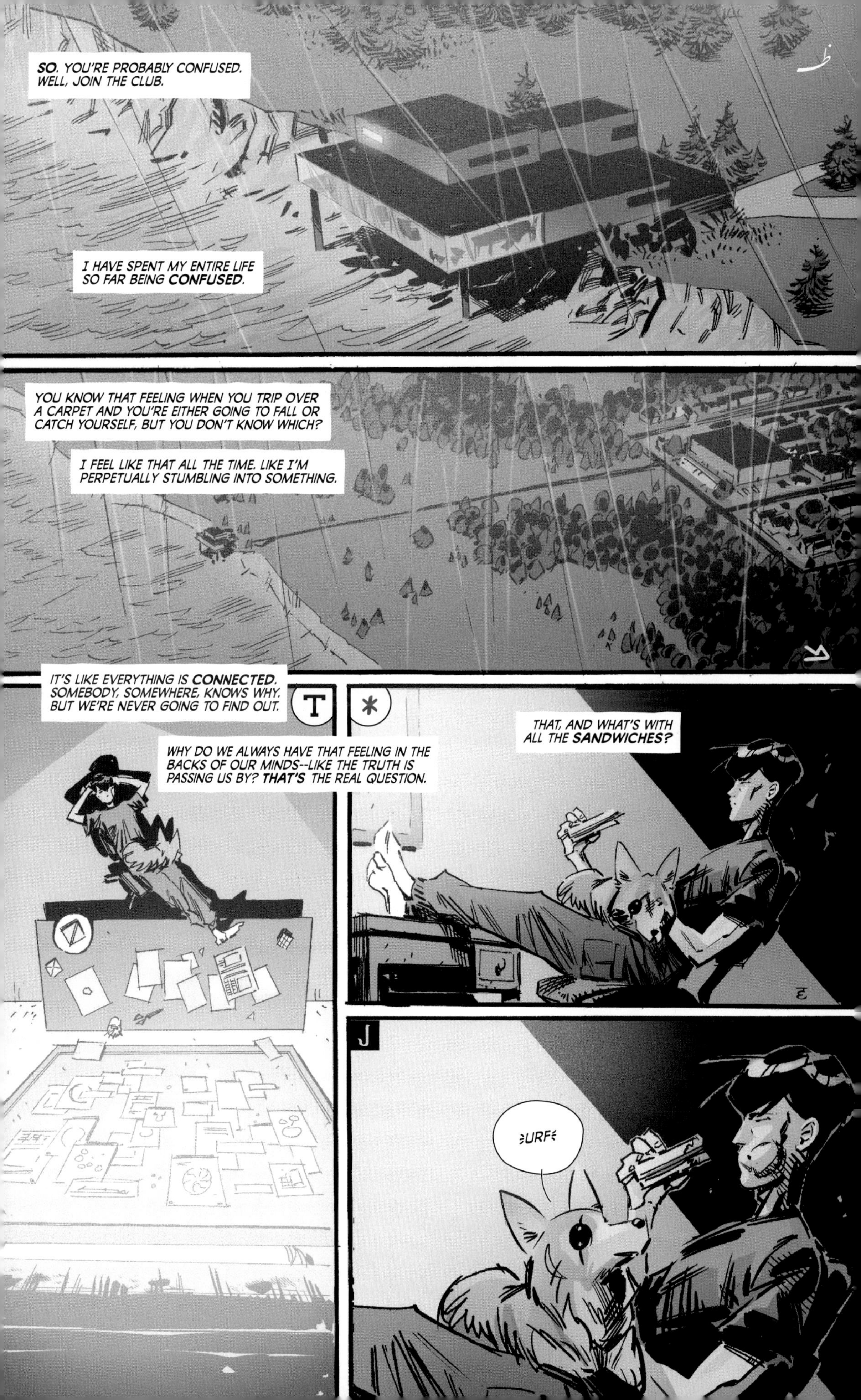
SO. YOU'RE PROBABLY CONFUSED. WELL, JOIN THE CLUB.
I HAVE SPENT MY ENTIRE LIFE SO FAR BEING CONFUSED.
YOU KNOW THAT FEELING WHEN YOU TRIP OVER A CARPET AND YOU'RE EITHER GOING TO FALL OR CATCH YOURSELF, BUT YOU DON'T KNOW WHICH?
I FEEL LIKE THAT ALL THE TIME. LIKE I'M PERPETUALLY STUMBLING INTO SOMETHING.
IT'S LIKE EVERYTHING IS CONNECTED. SOMEBODY, SOMEWHERE, KNOWS WHY. BUT WE'RE NEVER GOING TO FIND OUT.
WHY DO WE ALWAYS HAVE THAT FEELING IN THE BACKS OF OUR MINDS--LIKE THE TRUTH IS PASSING US BY? THAT'S THE REAL QUESTION.
THAT, AND WHAT'S WITH ALL THE SANDWICHES?
URF

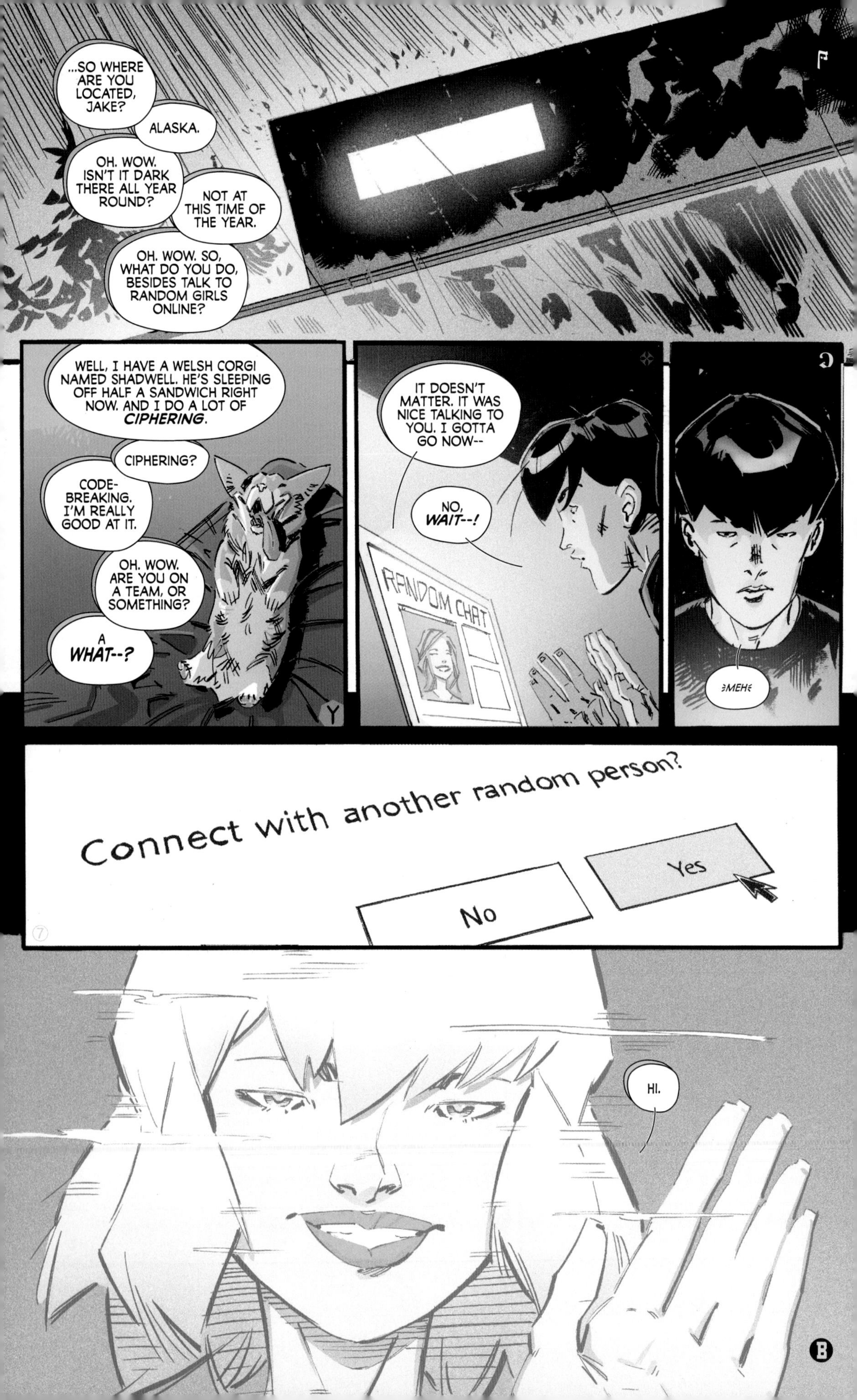
...SO WHERE ARE YOU LOCATED, JAKE?
ALASKA.
OH. WOW. ISN'T IT DARK THERE ALL YEAR ROUND?
NOT AT THIS TIME OF THE YEAR.
OH. WOW. SO, WHAT DO YOU DO, BESIDES TALK TO RANDOM GIRLS ONLINE?
WELL, I HAVE A WELSH CORGI NAMED SHADWELL. HE'S SLEEPING OFF HALF A SANDWICH RIGHT NOW. AND I DO A LOT OF ***CIPHERING***.
CIPHERING?
CODE-BREAKING. I'M REALLY GOOD AT IT.
OH. WOW. ARE YOU ON A TEAM, OR SOMETHING?
A ***WHAT--?***
IT DOESN'T MATTER. IT WAS NICE TALKING TO YOU. I GOTTA GO NOW--
NO, ***WAIT--!***
RANDOM CHAT
MEH
Connect with another random person?
No
Yes
HI.

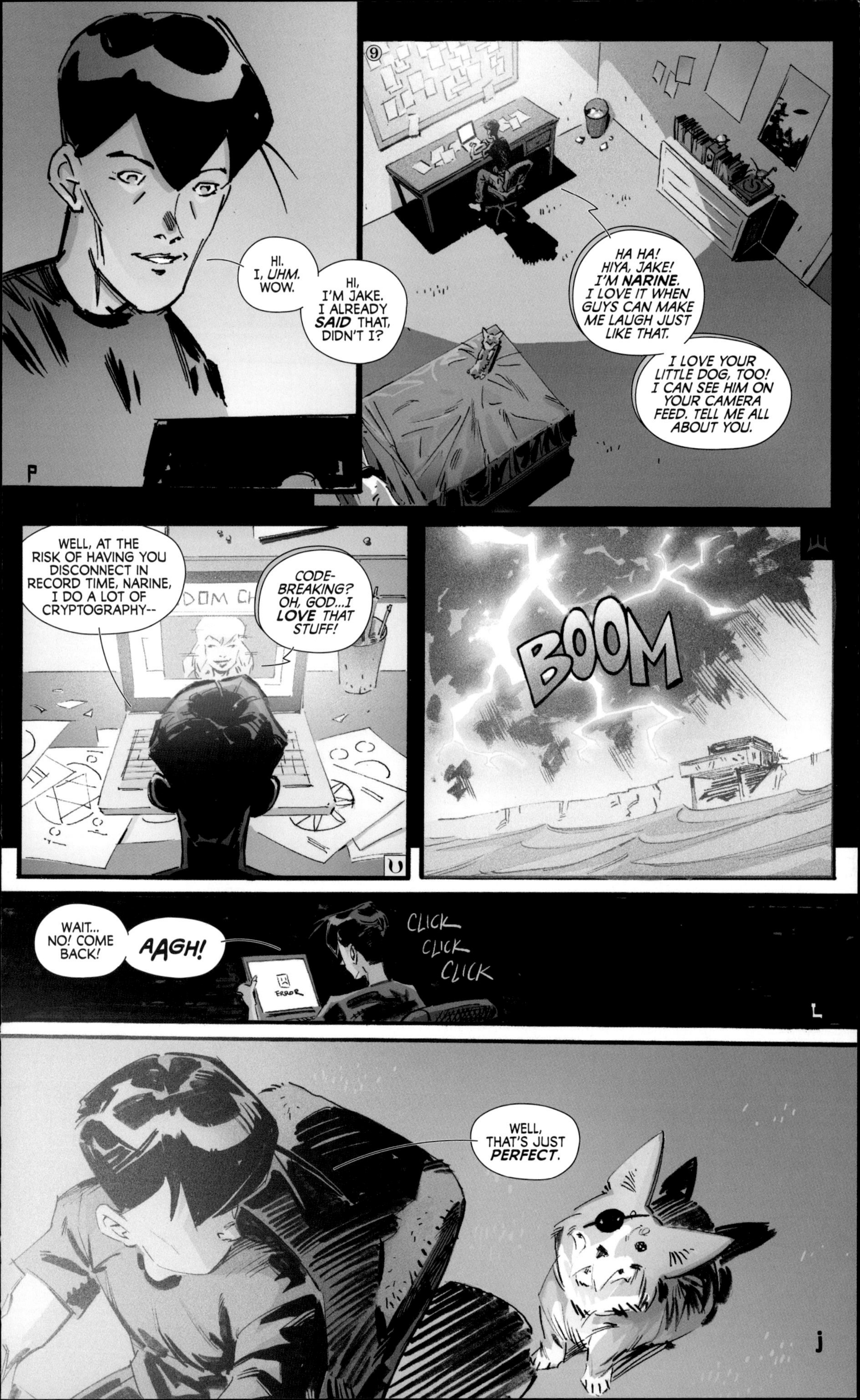
HI. I, UHM. WOW.
HI, I'M JAKE. I ALREADY SAID THAT, DIDN'T I?
HA HA! HIYA, JAKE! I'M NARINE. I LOVE IT WHEN GUYS CAN MAKE ME LAUGH JUST LIKE THAT.
I LOVE YOUR LITTLE DOG, TOO! I CAN SEE HIM ON YOUR CAMERA FEED. TELL ME ALL ABOUT YOU.
WELL, AT THE RISK OF HAVING YOU DISCONNECT IN RECORD TIME, NARINE, I DO A LOT OF CRYPTOGRAPHY--
CODE-BREAKING? OH, GOD...I LOVE THAT STUFF!
BOOM
WAIT... NO! COME BACK!
AAGH!
CLICK
CLICK
CLICK
ERROR
WELL, THAT'S JUST PERFECT.

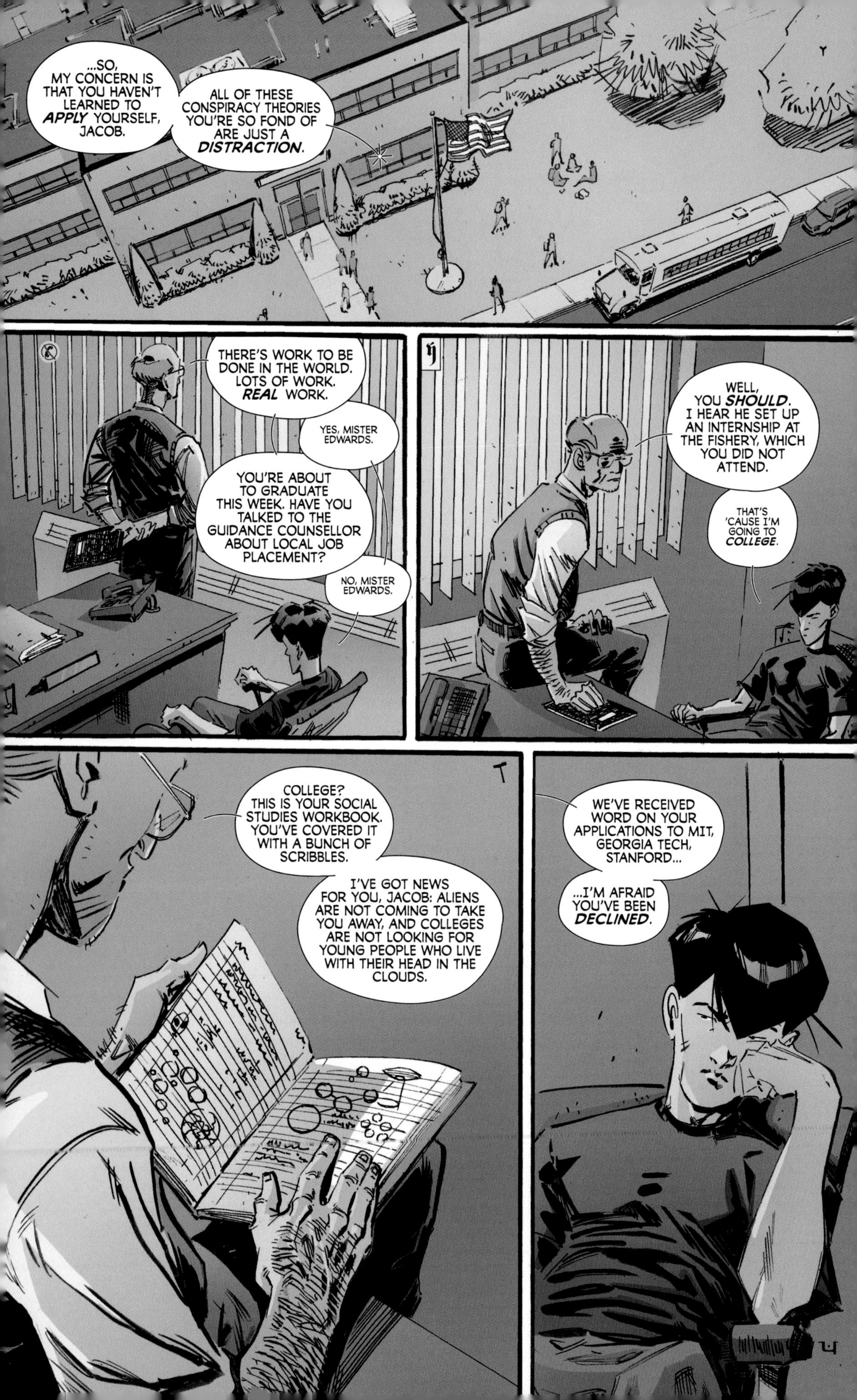
...SO, MY CONCERN IS THAT YOU HAVEN'T LEARNED TO *APPLY* YOURSELF, JACOB.
ALL OF THESE CONSPIRACY THEORIES YOU'RE SO FOND OF ARE JUST A *DISTRACTION*.
THERE'S WORK TO BE DONE IN THE WORLD. LOTS OF WORK. *REAL* WORK.
YES, MISTER EDWARDS.
YOU'RE ABOUT TO GRADUATE THIS WEEK. HAVE YOU TALKED TO THE GUIDANCE COUNSELLOR ABOUT LOCAL JOB PLACEMENT?
NO, MISTER EDWARDS.
WELL, YOU *SHOULD*. I HEAR HE SET UP AN INTERNSHIP AT THE FISHERY, WHICH YOU DID NOT ATTEND.
THAT'S 'CAUSE I'M GOING TO *COLLEGE*.
COLLEGE? THIS IS YOUR SOCIAL STUDIES WORKBOOK. YOU'VE COVERED IT WITH A BUNCH OF SCRIBBLES.
I'VE GOT NEWS FOR YOU, JACOB: ALIENS ARE NOT COMING TO TAKE YOU AWAY, AND COLLEGES ARE NOT LOOKING FOR YOUNG PEOPLE WHO LIVE WITH THEIR HEAD IN THE CLOUDS.
WE'VE RECEIVED WORD ON YOUR APPLICATIONS TO MIT, GEORGIA TECH, STANFORD...
...I'M AFRAID YOU'VE BEEN *DECLINED*.

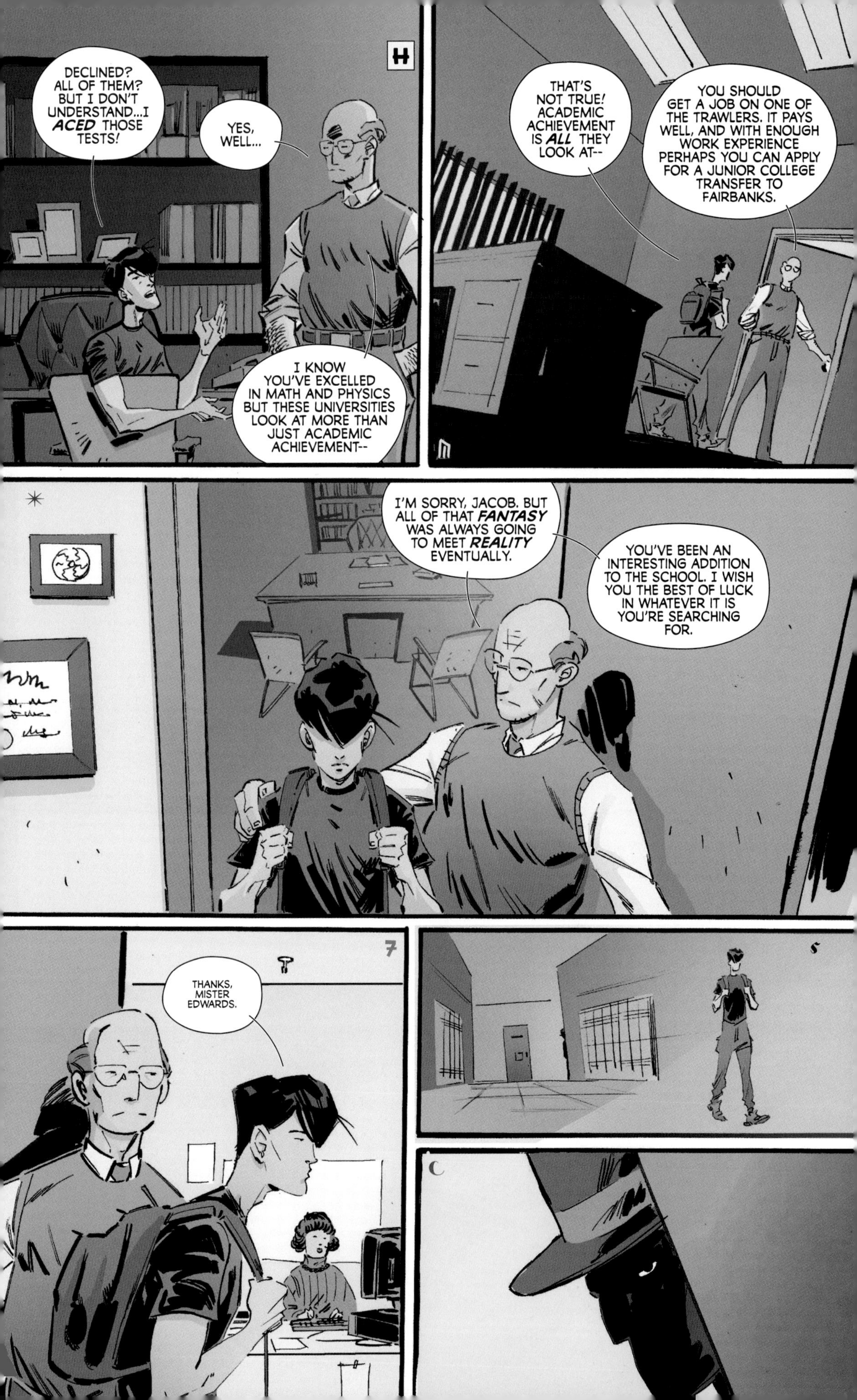
DECLINED? ALL OF THEM? BUT I DON'T UNDERSTAND...I ACED THOSE TESTS!
YES, WELL...
I KNOW YOU'VE EXCELLED IN MATH AND PHYSICS BUT THESE UNIVERSITIES LOOK AT MORE THAN JUST ACADEMIC ACHIEVEMENT--
THAT'S NOT TRUE! ACADEMIC ACHIEVEMENT IS ALL THEY LOOK AT--
YOU SHOULD GET A JOB ON ONE OF THE TRAWLERS. IT PAYS WELL, AND WITH ENOUGH WORK EXPERIENCE PERHAPS YOU CAN APPLY FOR A JUNIOR COLLEGE TRANSFER TO FAIRBANKS.
I'M SORRY, JACOB. BUT ALL OF THAT FANTASY WAS ALWAYS GOING TO MEET REALITY EVENTUALLY.
YOU'VE BEEN AN INTERESTING ADDITION TO THE SCHOOL. I WISH YOU THE BEST OF LUCK IN WHATEVER IT IS YOU'RE SEARCHING FOR.
THANKS, MISTER EDWARDS.

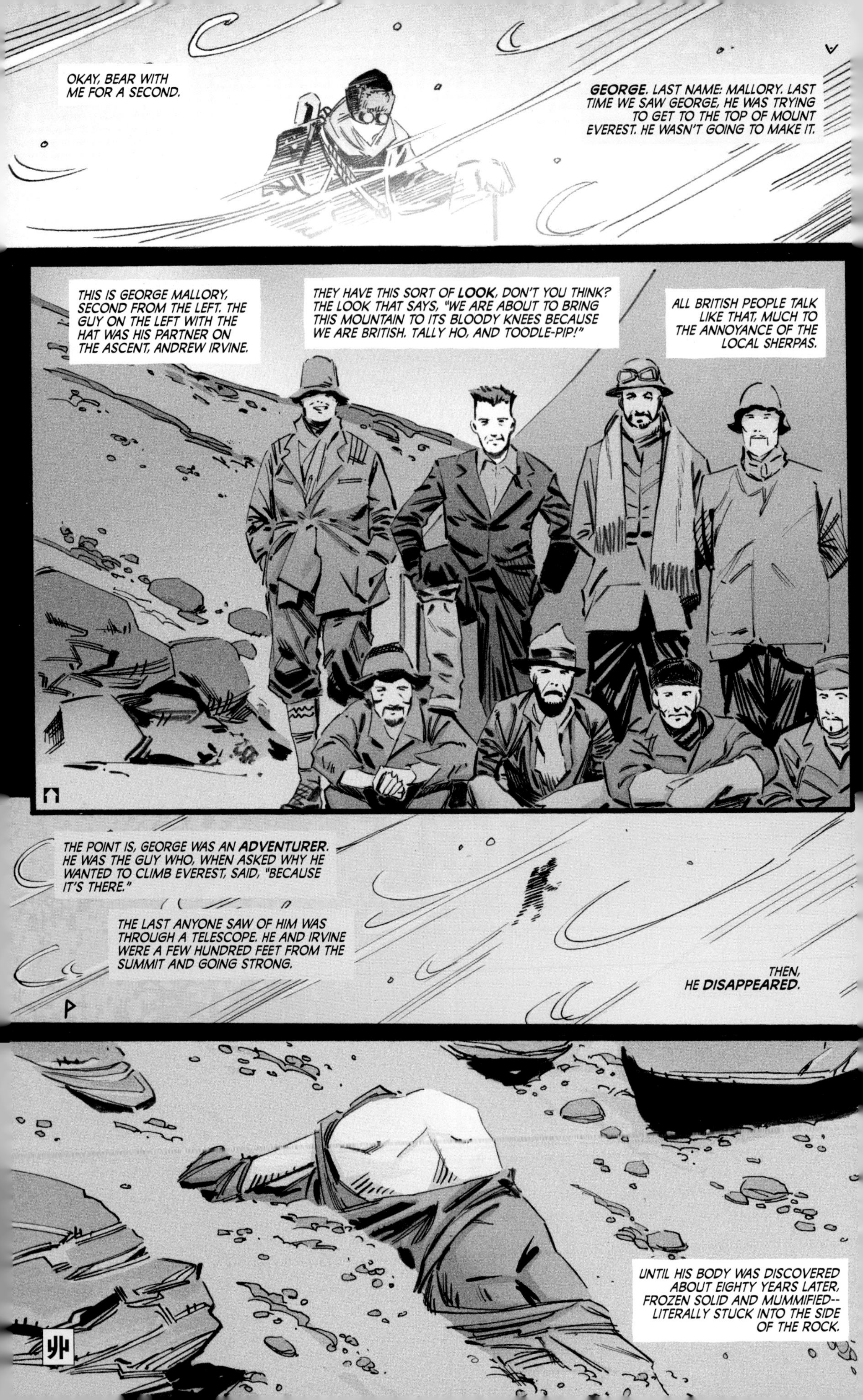
OKAY, BEAR WITH ME FOR A SECOND.
GEORGE. LAST NAME: MALLORY. LAST TIME WE SAW GEORGE, HE WAS TRYING TO GET TO THE TOP OF MOUNT EVEREST. HE WASN'T GOING TO MAKE IT.
THIS IS GEORGE MALLORY, SECOND FROM THE LEFT. THE GUY ON THE LEFT WITH THE HAT WAS HIS PARTNER ON THE ASCENT, ANDREW IRVINE.
THEY HAVE THIS SORT OF LOOK, DON'T YOU THINK? THE LOOK THAT SAYS, "WE ARE ABOUT TO BRING THIS MOUNTAIN TO ITS BLOODY KNEES BECAUSE WE ARE BRITISH. TALLY HO, AND TOODLE-PIP!"
ALL BRITISH PEOPLE TALK LIKE THAT, MUCH TO THE ANNOYANCE OF THE LOCAL SHERPAS.
THE POINT IS, GEORGE WAS AN ADVENTURER. HE WAS THE GUY WHO, WHEN ASKED WHY HE WANTED TO CLIMB EVEREST, SAID, "BECAUSE IT'S THERE."
THE LAST ANYONE SAW OF HIM WAS THROUGH A TELESCOPE. HE AND IRVINE WERE A FEW HUNDRED FEET FROM THE SUMMIT AND GOING STRONG.
THEN, HE DISAPPEARED.
UNTIL HIS BODY WAS DISCOVERED ABOUT EIGHTY YEARS LATER, FROZEN SOLID AND MUMMIFIED-- LITERALLY STUCK INTO THE SIDE OF THE ROCK.

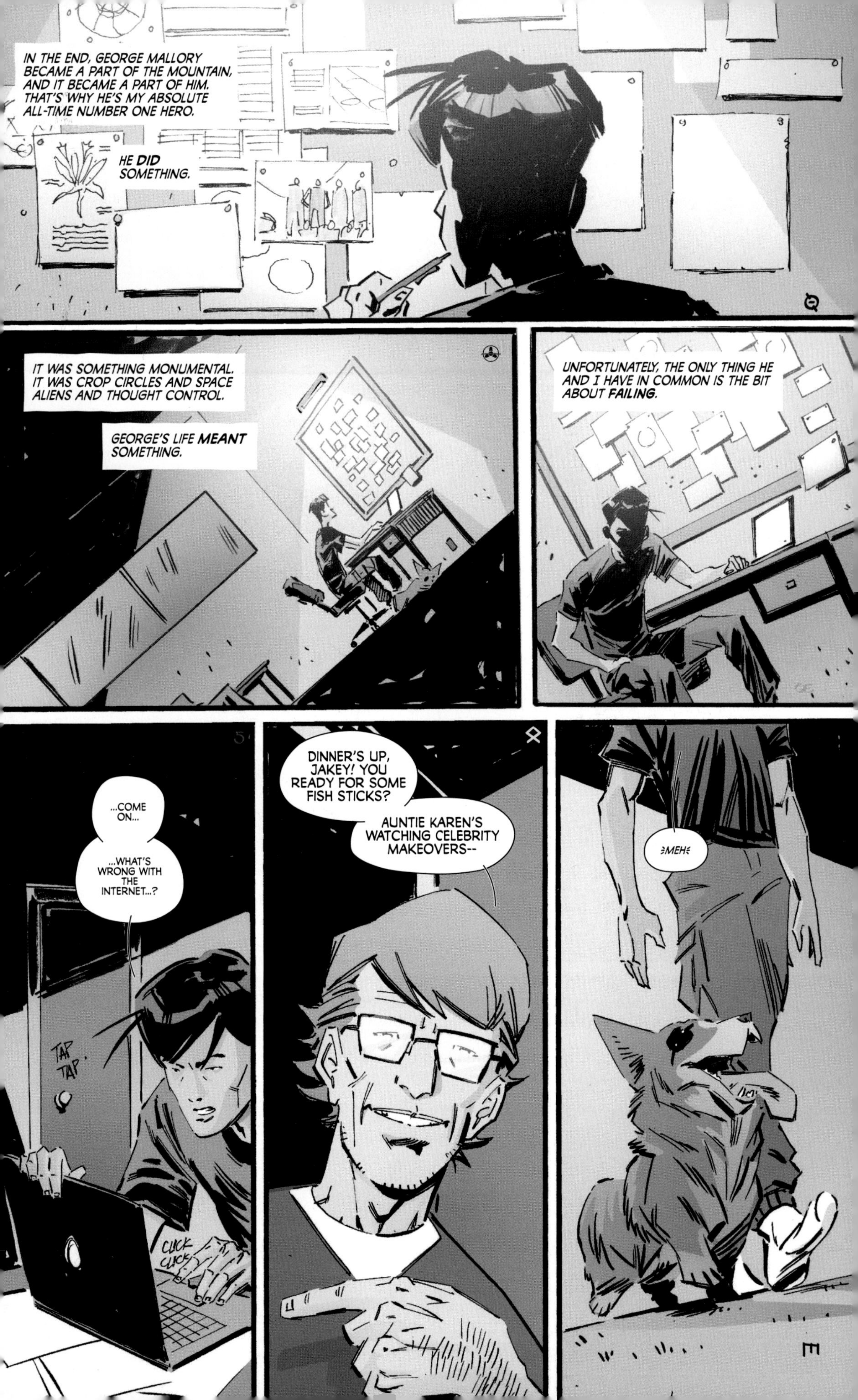

IN THE END, GEORGE MALLORY BECAME A PART OF THE MOUNTAIN, AND IT BECAME A PART OF HIM. THAT'S WHY HE'S MY ABSOLUTE ALL-TIME NUMBER ONE HERO.
HE DID SOMETHING.
IT WAS SOMETHING MONUMENTAL. IT WAS CROP CIRCLES AND SPACE ALIENS AND THOUGHT CONTROL.
GEORGE'S LIFE MEANT SOMETHING.
UNFORTUNATELY, THE ONLY THING HE AND I HAVE IN COMMON IS THE BIT ABOUT FAILING.
...COME ON...
...WHAT'S WRONG WITH THE INTERNET...?
TAP TAP
CLICK CLICK
DINNER'S UP, JAKEY! YOU READY FOR SOME FISH STICKS?
AUNTIE KAREN'S WATCHING CELEBRITY MAKEOVERS--
MEH

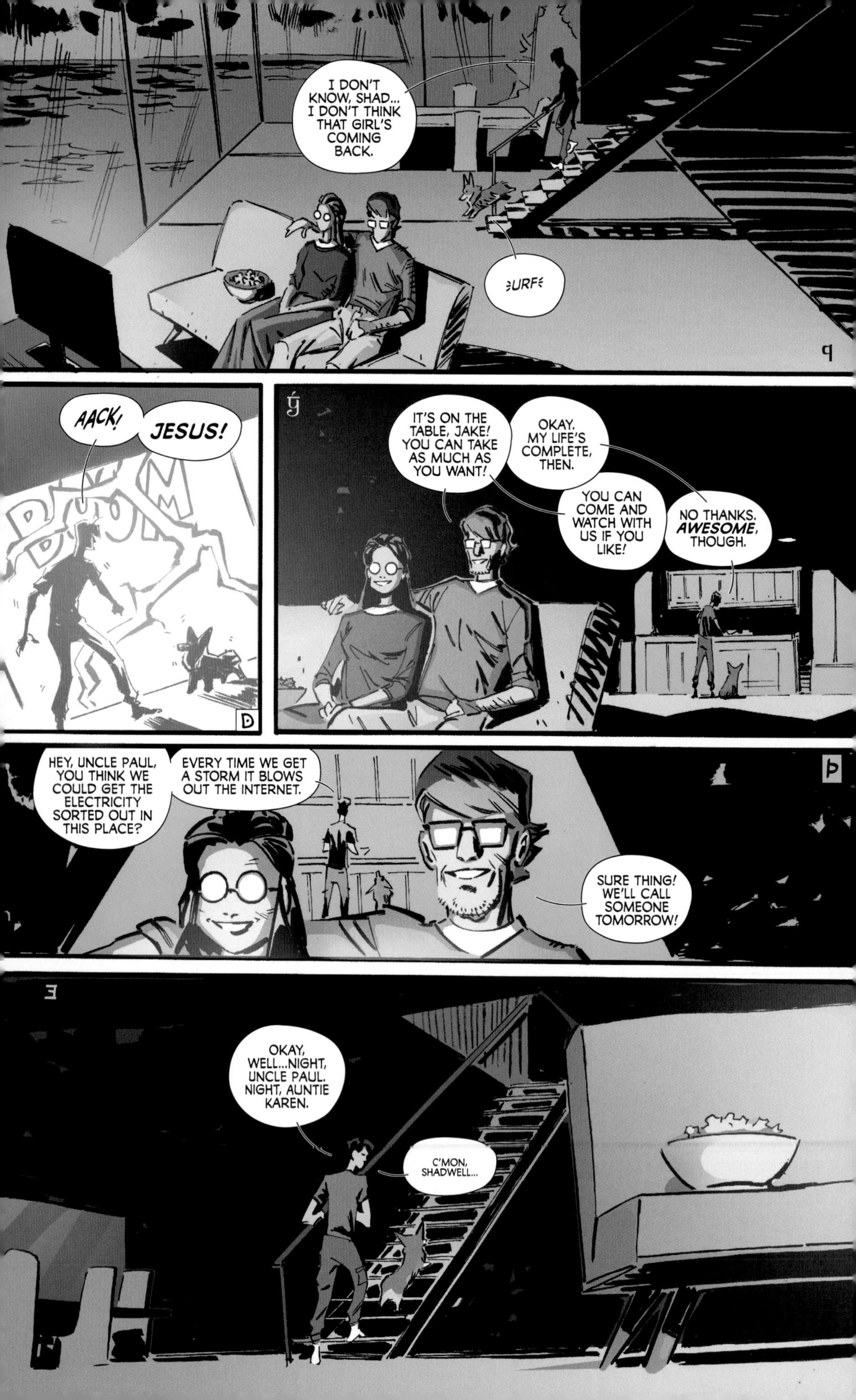

I DON'T KNOW, SHAD... I DON'T THINK THAT GIRL'S COMING BACK.
URF
AACK!
JESUS!
IT'S ON THE TABLE, JAKE! YOU CAN TAKE AS MUCH AS YOU WANT!
OKAY. MY LIFE'S COMPLETE, THEN.
YOU CAN COME AND WATCH WITH US IF YOU LIKE!
NO THANKS. AWESOME, THOUGH.
HEY, UNCLE PAUL, YOU THINK WE COULD GET THE ELECTRICITY SORTED OUT IN THIS PLACE?
EVERY TIME WE GET A STORM IT BLOWS OUT THE INTERNET.
SURE THING! WE'LL CALL SOMEONE TOMORROW!
OKAY, WELL...NIGHT, UNCLE PAUL. NIGHT, AUNTIE KAREN.
C'MON, SHADWELL...

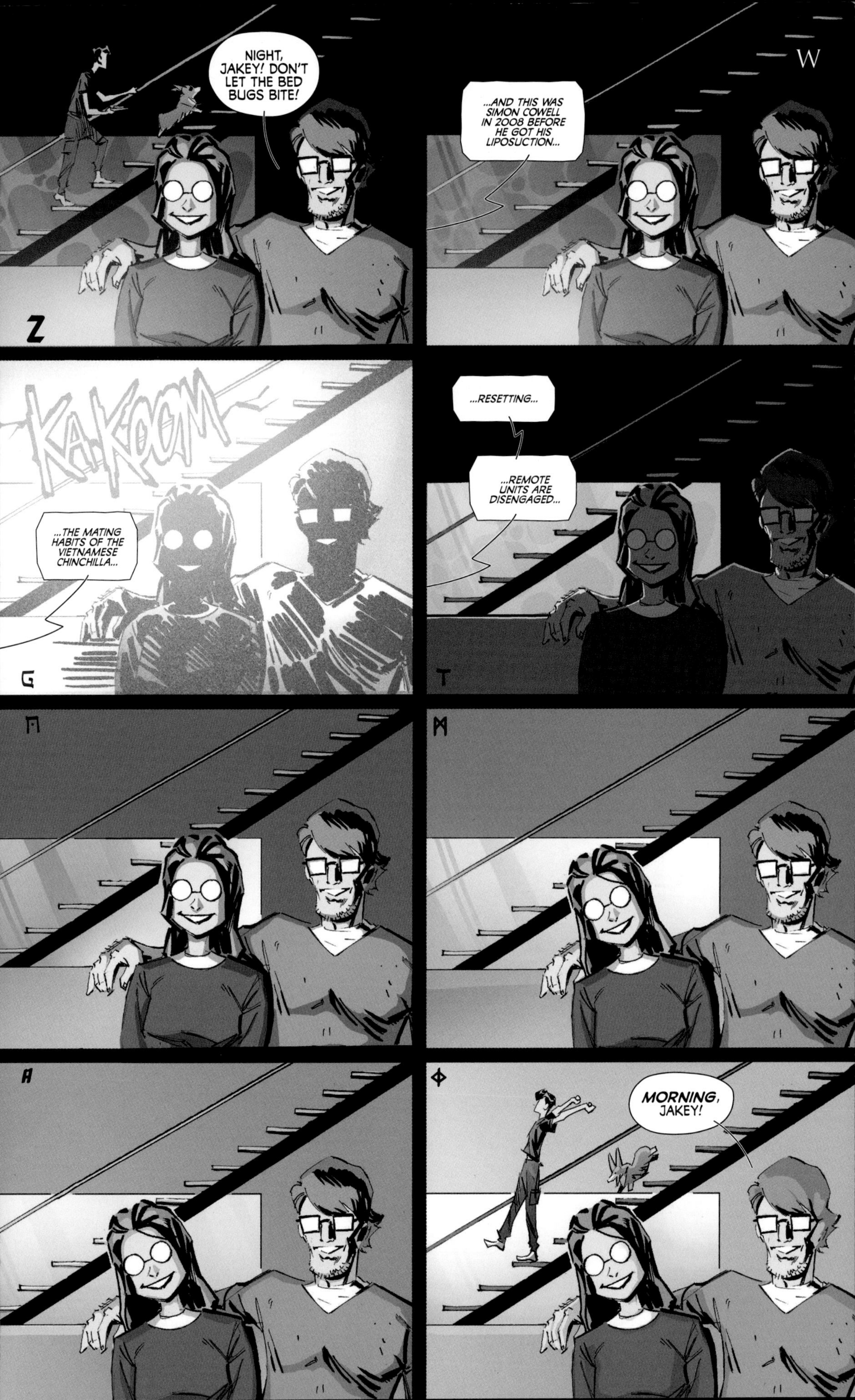
W
NIGHT, JAKEY! DON'T LET THE BED BUGS BITE!
Z
...AND THIS WAS SIMON COWELL IN 2008 BEFORE HE GOT HIS LIPOSUCTION...
KA-KOOM
...THE MATING HABITS OF THE VIETNAMESE CHINCHILLA...
G
...RESETTING...
...REMOTE UNITS ARE DISENGAGED...
T
MORNING, JAKEY!

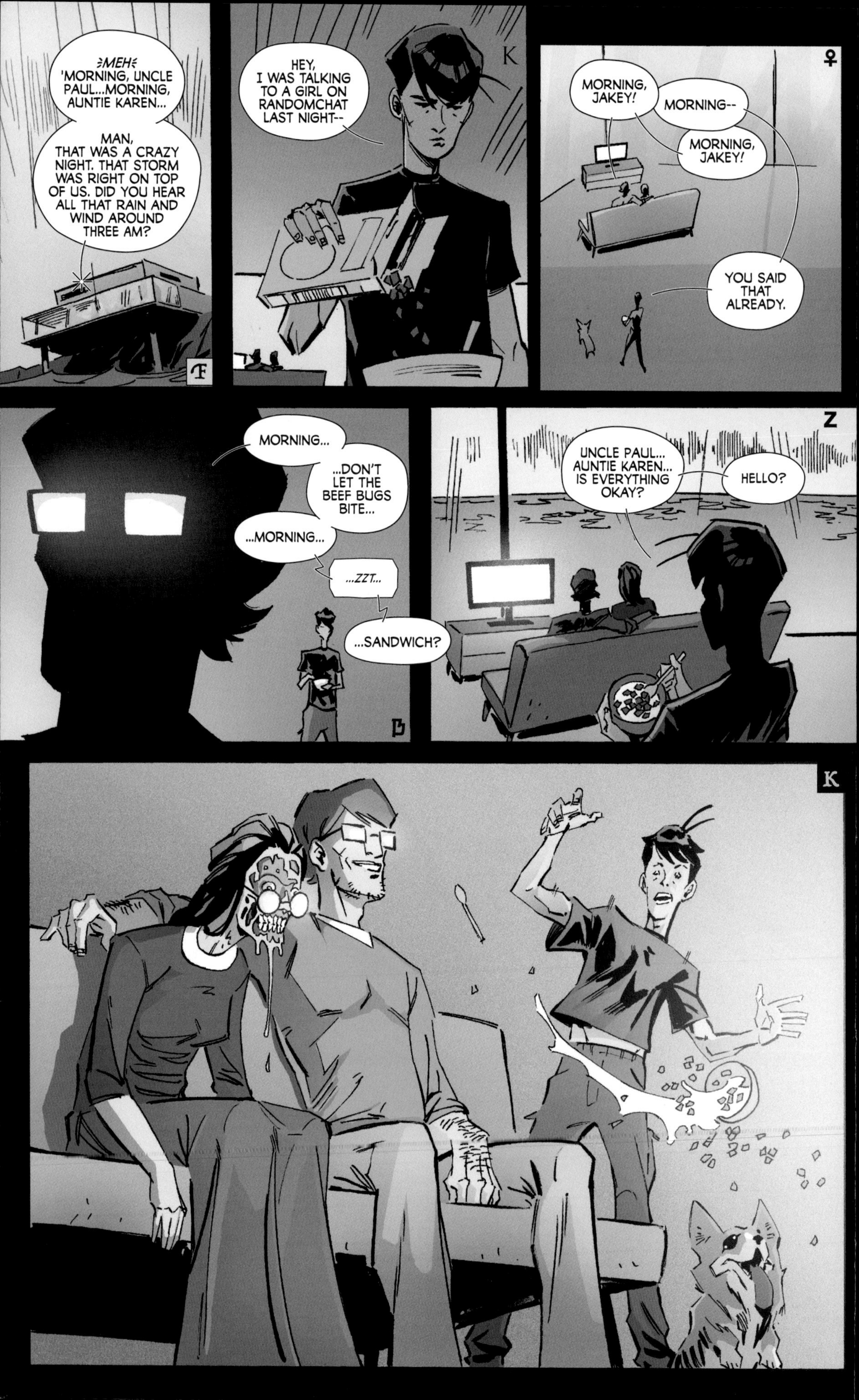

MEH
'MORNING, UNCLE PAUL...MORNING, AUNTIE KAREN...
MAN, THAT WAS A CRAZY NIGHT. THAT STORM WAS RIGHT ON TOP OF US. DID YOU HEAR ALL THAT RAIN AND WIND AROUND THREE AM?
HEY, I WAS TALKING TO A GIRL ON RANDOMCHAT LAST NIGHT--
MORNING, JAKEY!
MORNING--
MORNING, JAKEY!
YOU SAID THAT ALREADY.
MORNING...
...DON'T LET THE BEEF BUGS BITE...
...MORNING...
...ZZT...
...SANDWICH?
UNCLE PAUL... AUNTIE KAREN... IS EVERYTHING OKAY?
HELLO?

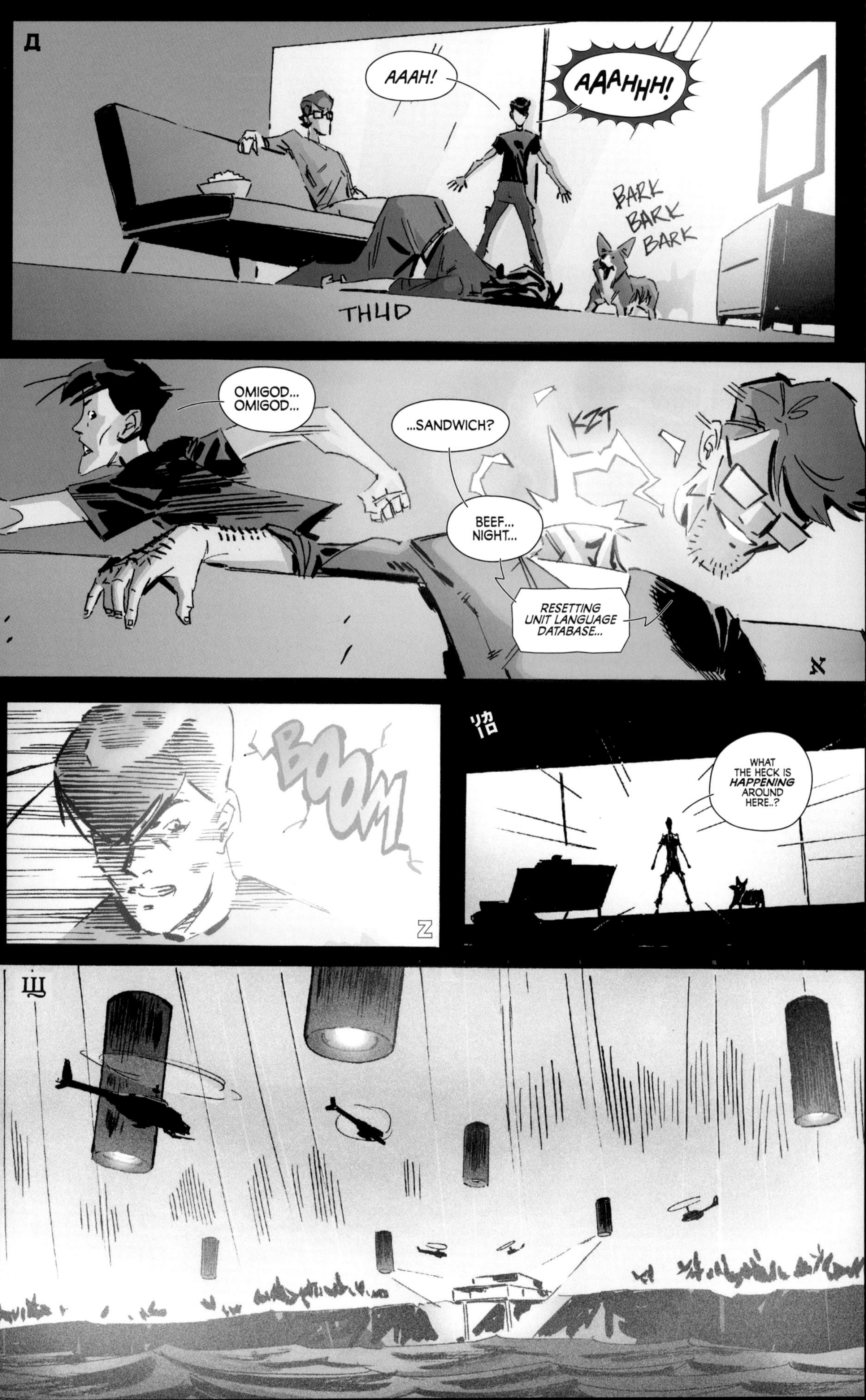

Д
AAAH!
AAAHHH!
BARK BARK BARK
THUD
OMIGOD... OMIGOD...
...SANDWICH?
KZT
BEEF... NIGHT...
RESETTING UNIT LANGUAGE DATABASE...
BOOM
WHAT THE HECK IS HAPPENING AROUND HERE..?

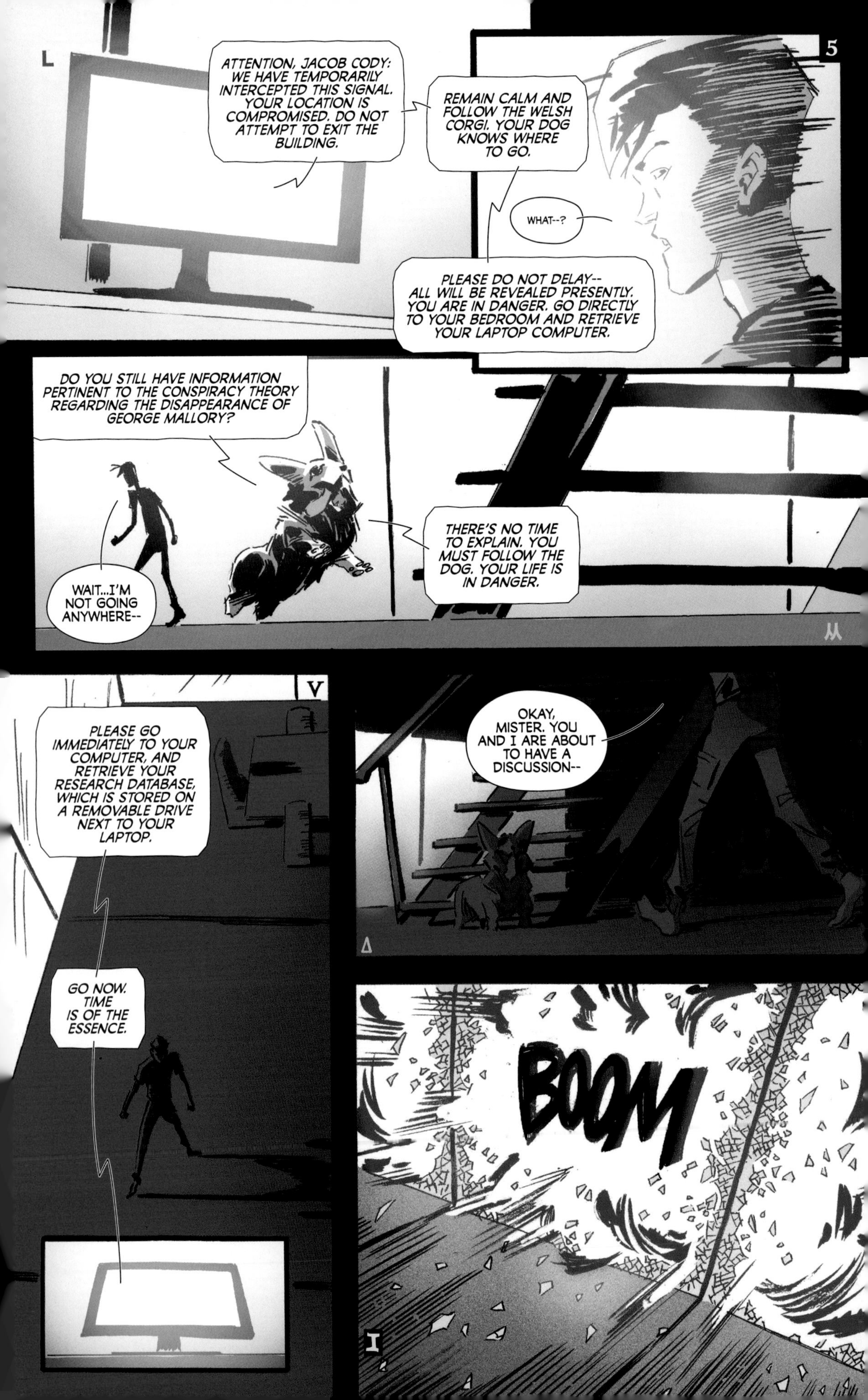
5
ATTENTION, JACOB CODY: WE HAVE TEMPORARILY INTERCEPTED THIS SIGNAL. YOUR LOCATION IS COMPROMISED. DO NOT ATTEMPT TO EXIT THE BUILDING.
REMAIN CALM AND FOLLOW THE WELSH CORGI. YOUR DOG KNOWS WHERE TO GO.
WHAT--?
PLEASE DO NOT DELAY-- ALL WILL BE REVEALED PRESENTLY. YOU ARE IN DANGER. GO DIRECTLY TO YOUR BEDROOM AND RETRIEVE YOUR LAPTOP COMPUTER.
DO YOU STILL HAVE INFORMATION PERTINENT TO THE CONSPIRACY THEORY REGARDING THE DISAPPEARANCE OF GEORGE MALLORY?
WAIT...I'M NOT GOING ANYWHERE--
THERE'S NO TIME TO EXPLAIN. YOU MUST FOLLOW THE DOG. YOUR LIFE IS IN DANGER.
PLEASE GO IMMEDIATELY TO YOUR COMPUTER, AND RETRIEVE YOUR RESEARCH DATABASE, WHICH IS STORED ON A REMOVABLE DRIVE NEXT TO YOUR LAPTOP.
GO NOW. TIME IS OF THE ESSENCE.
OKAY, MISTER. YOU AND I ARE ABOUT TO HAVE A DISCUSSION--
BOOM

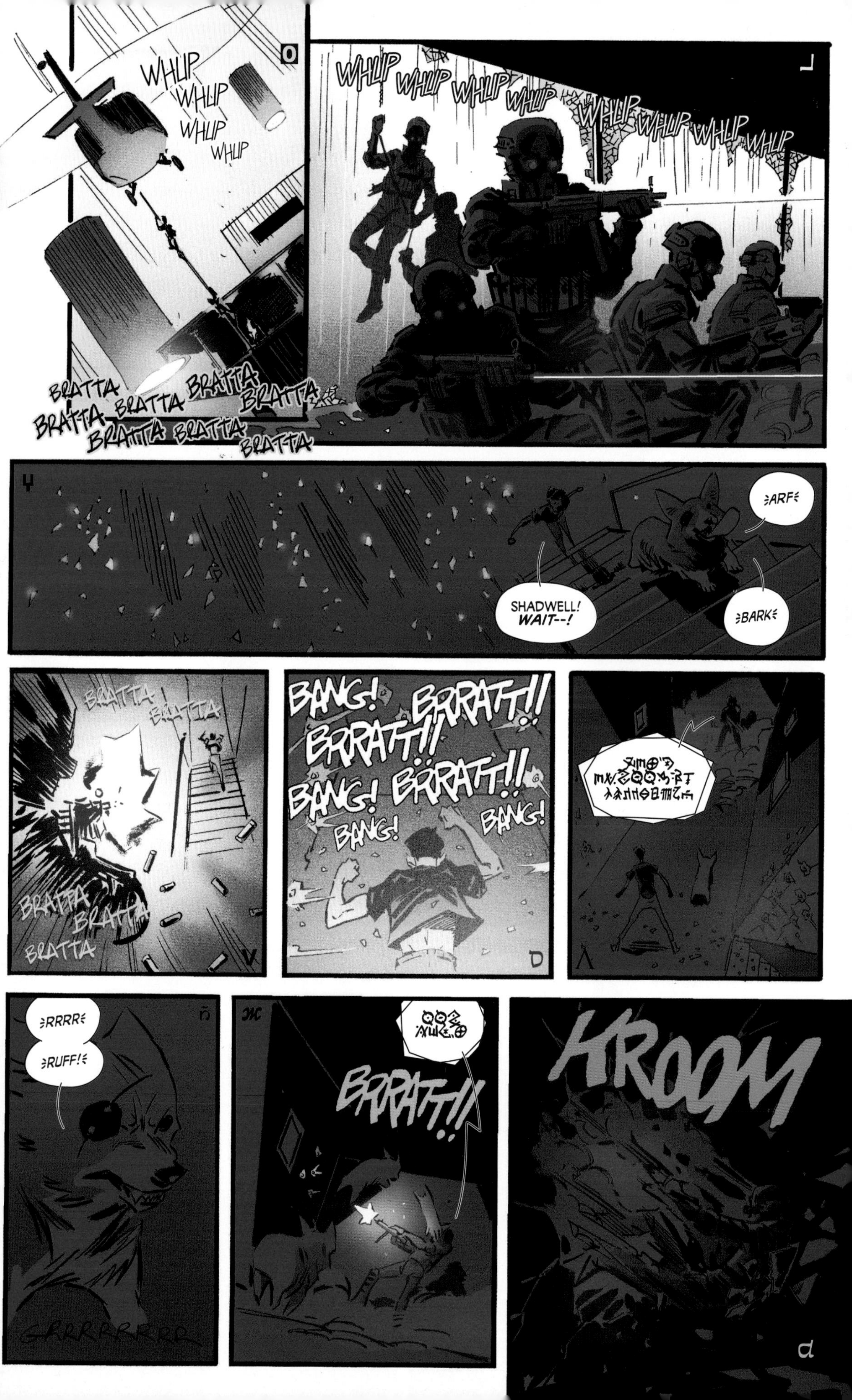

WHUP WHUP WHUP WHUP
BRATTA BRATTA BRATTA BRATTA BRATTA BRATTA BRATTA BRATTA
WHUP WHUP WHUP WHUP WHUP WHUP WHUP WHUP
ARF
SHADWELL! WAIT--!
BARK
BRATTA BRATTA
BRATTA BRATTA BRATTA
BANG! BRRATT!! BRRATT!!
BANG! BRRATT!!
BANG! BANG!
RRRR
RUFF!
GRRRRRRRR
BRRATT!!
KROOM

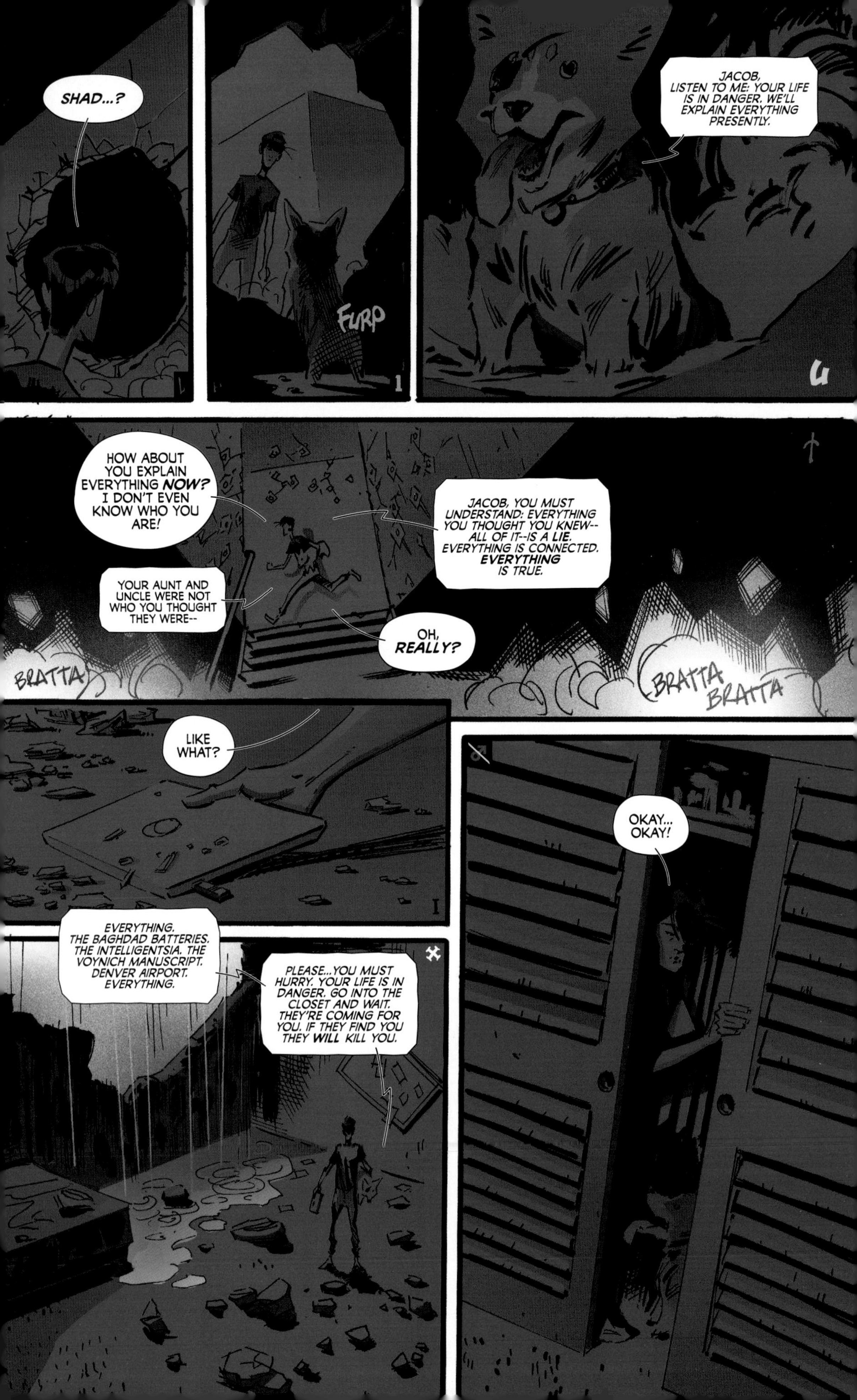

SHAD...?
FURP
JACOB, LISTEN TO ME: YOUR LIFE IS IN DANGER. WE'LL EXPLAIN EVERYTHING PRESENTLY.
HOW ABOUT YOU EXPLAIN EVERYTHING NOW? I DON'T EVEN KNOW WHO YOU ARE!
JACOB, YOU MUST UNDERSTAND: EVERYTHING YOU THOUGHT YOU KNEW--ALL OF IT--IS A LIE. EVERYTHING IS CONNECTED. EVERYTHING IS TRUE.
YOUR AUNT AND UNCLE WERE NOT WHO YOU THOUGHT THEY WERE--
OH, REALLY?
BRATTA
BRATTA BRATTA
LIKE WHAT?
EVERYTHING. THE BAGHDAD BATTERIES. THE INTELLIGENTSIA. THE VOYNICH MANUSCRIPT. DENVER AIRPORT. EVERYTHING.
PLEASE...YOU MUST HURRY. YOUR LIFE IS IN DANGER. GO INTO THE CLOSET AND WAIT. THEY'RE COMING FOR YOU. IF THEY FIND YOU THEY WILL KILL YOU.
OKAY... OKAY!

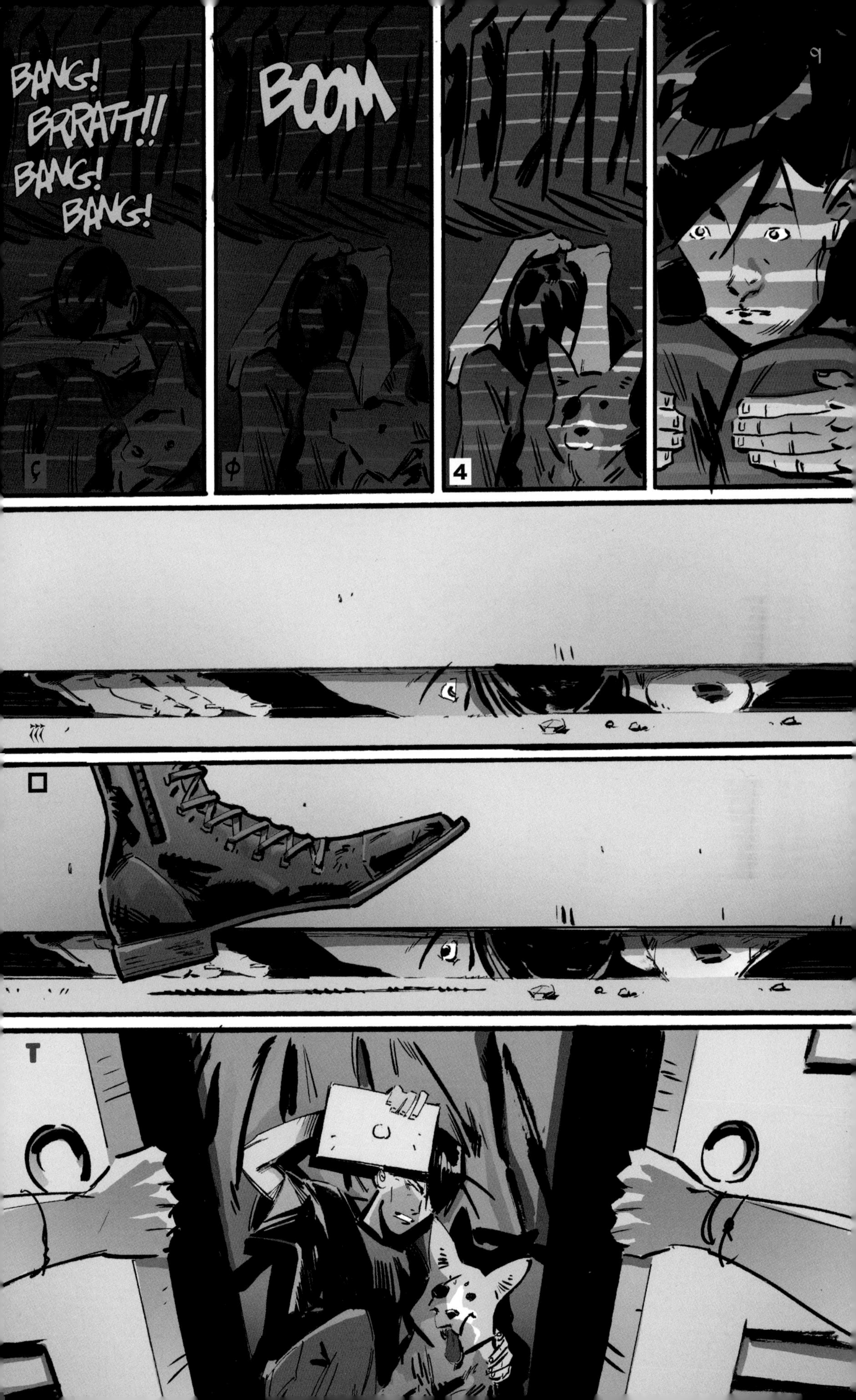
BANG!
BRRATT!!
BANG!
BANG!
BOOM

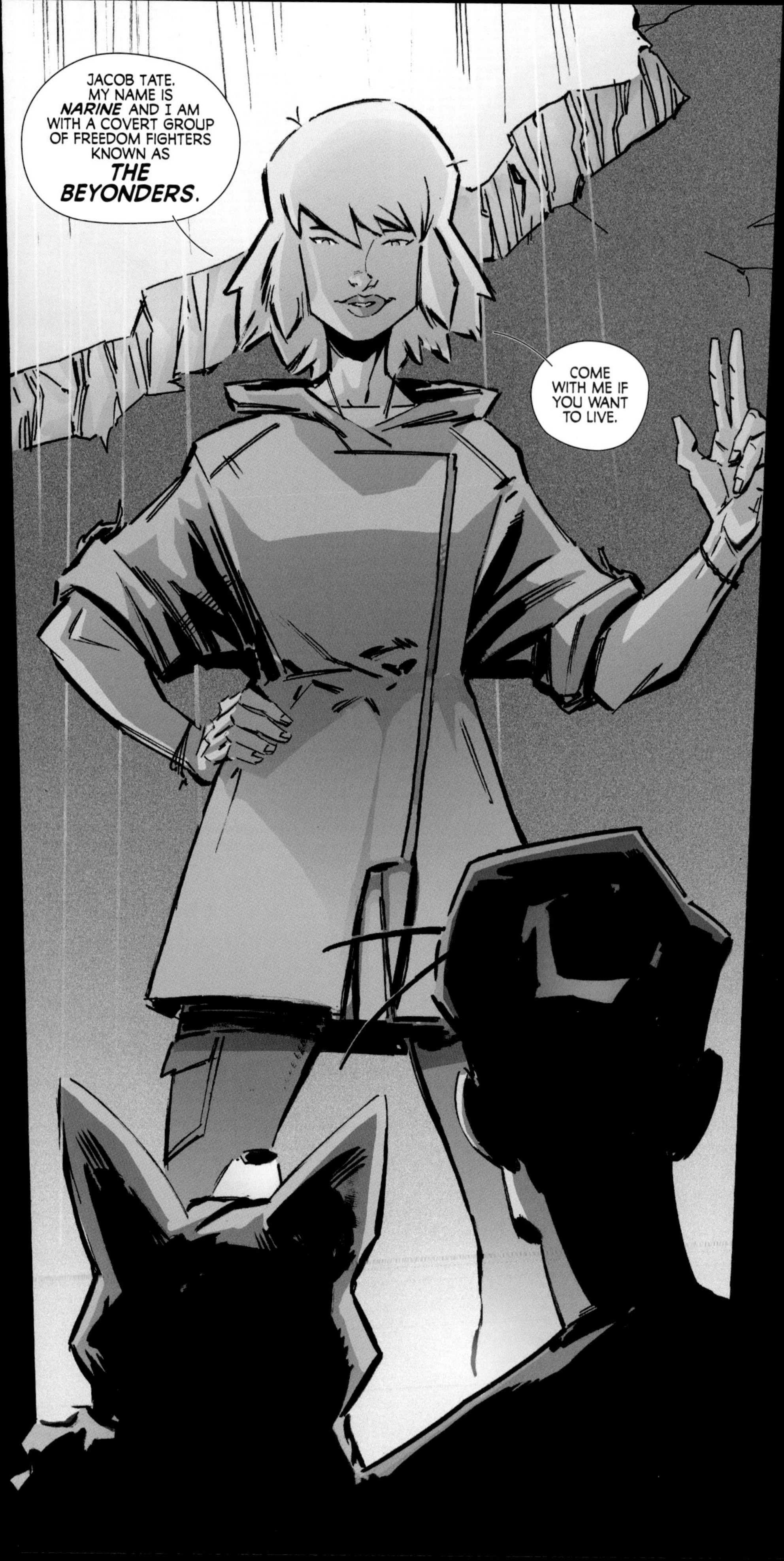
JACOB TATE. MY NAME IS NARINE AND I AM WITH A COVERT GROUP OF FREEDOM FIGHTERS KNOWN AS THE BEYONDERS.
COME WITH ME IF YOU WANT TO LIVE.

2

EVERYTHING GETS WEIRD

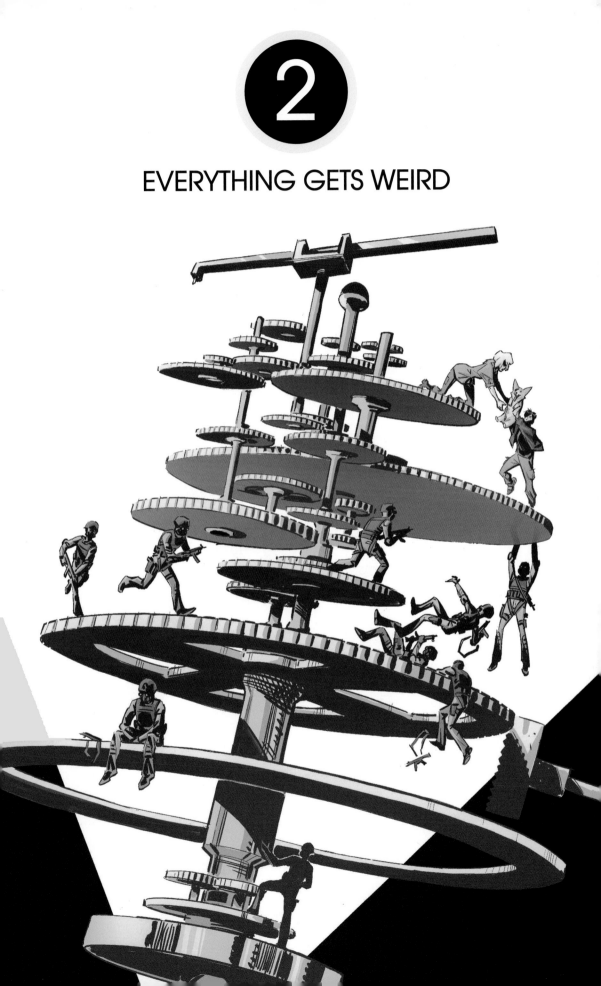

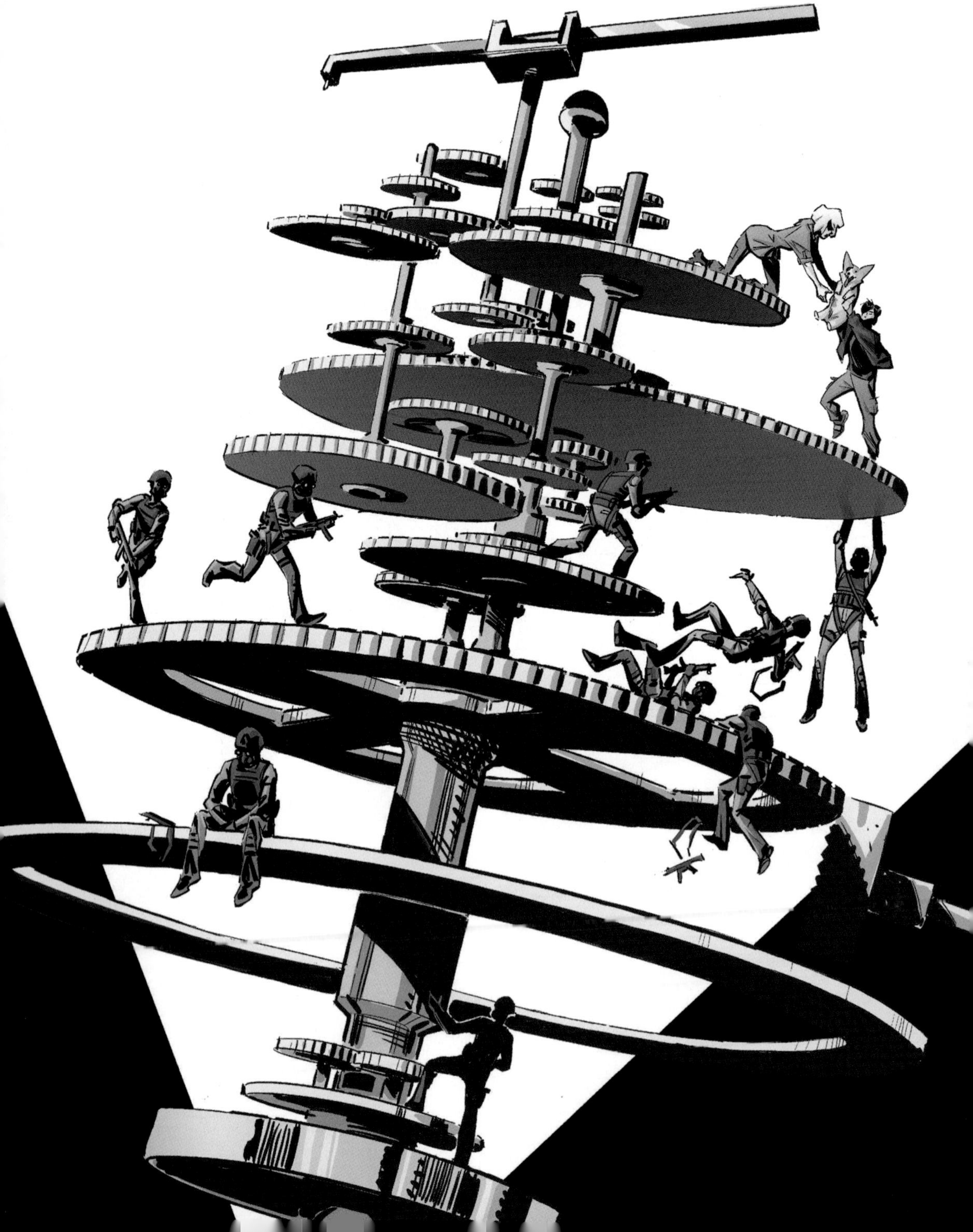

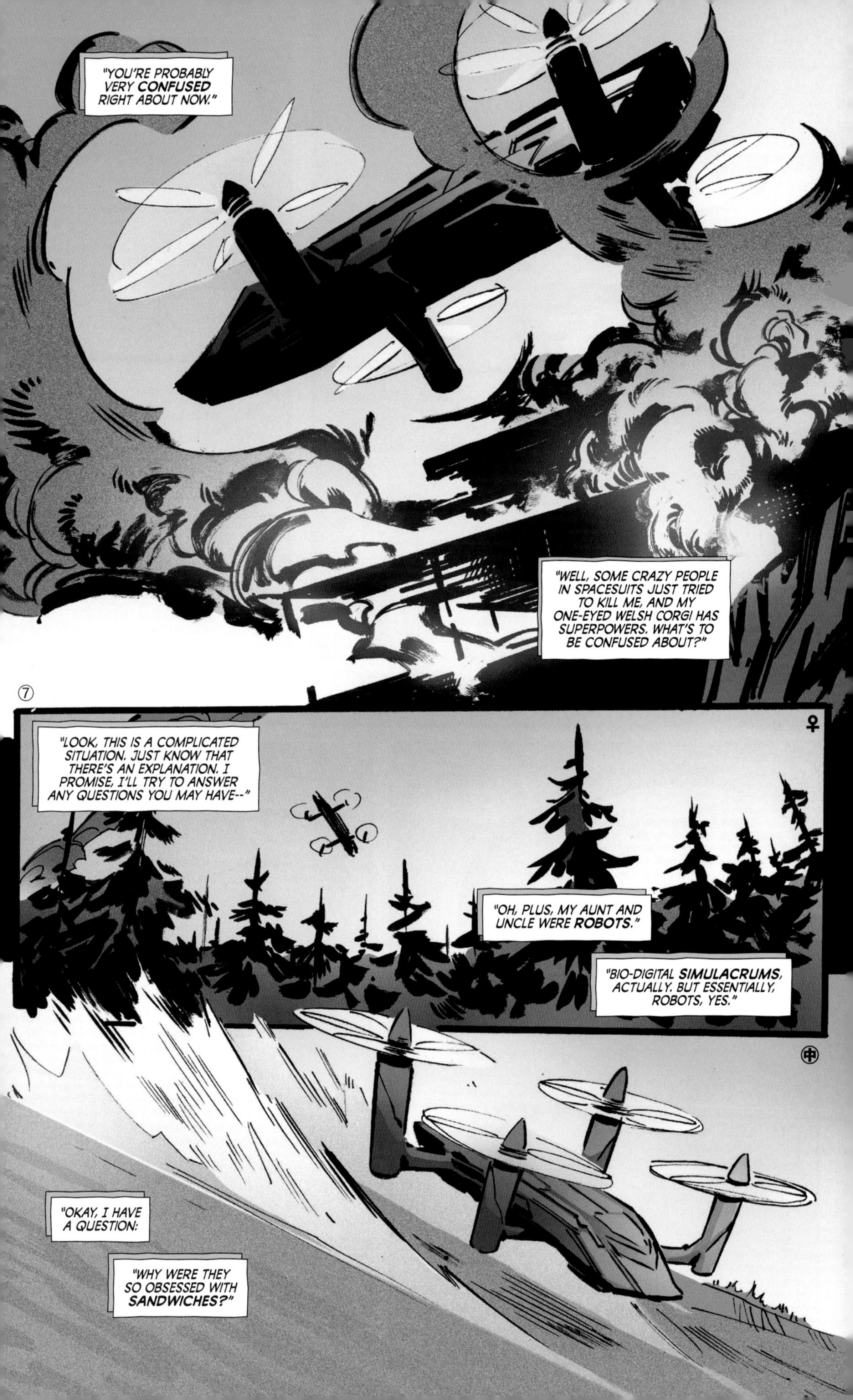
"YOU'RE PROBABLY VERY CONFUSED RIGHT ABOUT NOW."
"WELL, SOME CRAZY PEOPLE IN SPACESUITS JUST TRIED TO KILL ME, AND MY ONE-EYED WELSH CORGI HAS SUPERPOWERS. WHAT'S TO BE CONFUSED ABOUT?"
7
"LOOK, THIS IS A COMPLICATED SITUATION. JUST KNOW THAT THERE'S AN EXPLANATION. I PROMISE, I'LL TRY TO ANSWER ANY QUESTIONS YOU MAY HAVE--"
"OH, PLUS, MY AUNT AND UNCLE WERE ROBOTS."
"BIO-DIGITAL SIMULACRUMS, ACTUALLY. BUT ESSENTIALLY, ROBOTS, YES."
"OKAY, I HAVE A QUESTION:
"WHY WERE THEY SO OBSESSED WITH SANDWICHES?"

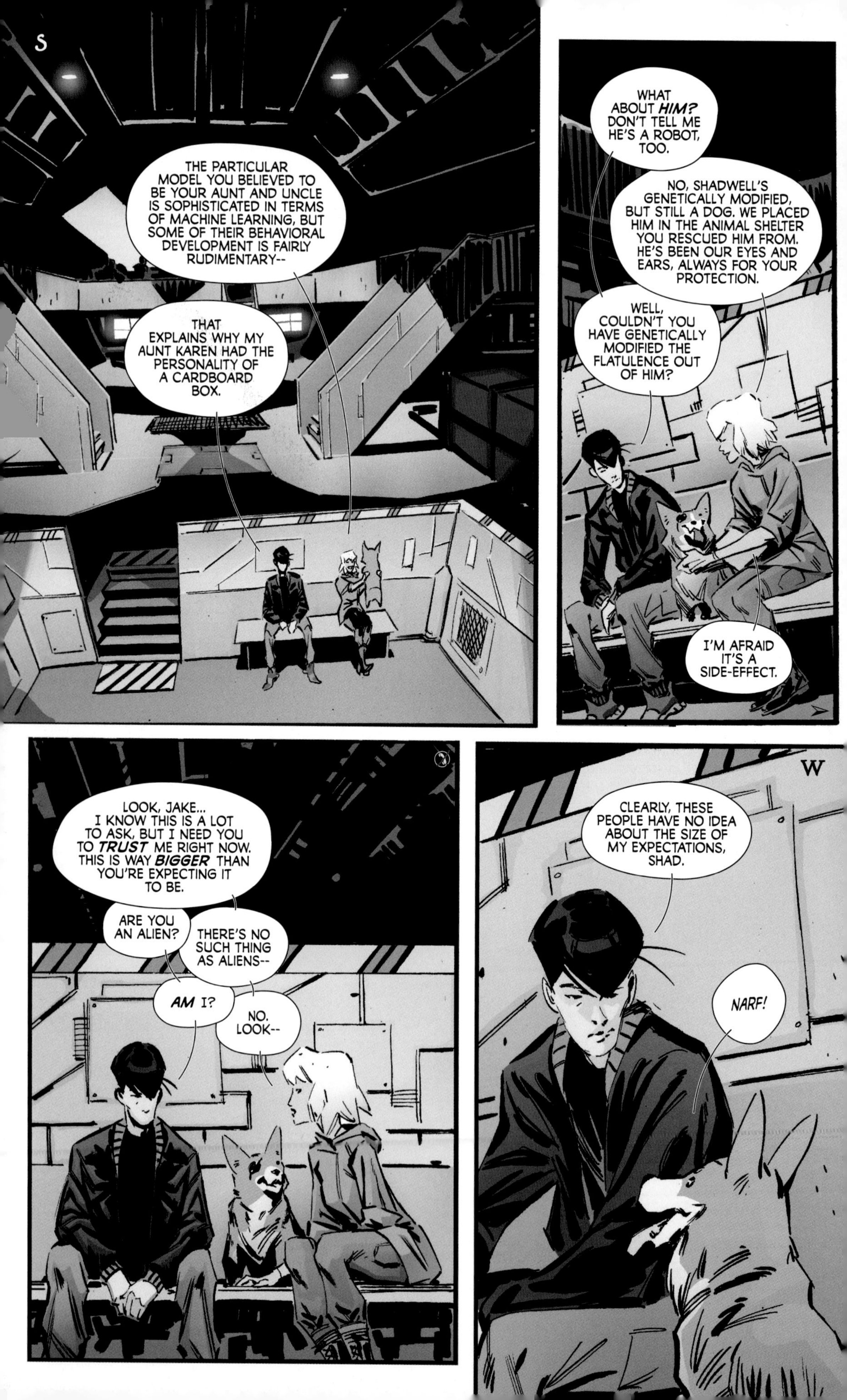
S
THE PARTICULAR MODEL YOU BELIEVED TO BE YOUR AUNT AND UNCLE IS SOPHISTICATED IN TERMS OF MACHINE LEARNING, BUT SOME OF THEIR BEHAVIORAL DEVELOPMENT IS FAIRLY RUDIMENTARY--
THAT EXPLAINS WHY MY AUNT KAREN HAD THE PERSONALITY OF A CARDBOARD BOX.
WHAT ABOUT *HIM?* DON'T TELL ME HE'S A ROBOT, TOO.
NO, SHADWELL'S GENETICALLY MODIFIED, BUT STILL A DOG. WE PLACED HIM IN THE ANIMAL SHELTER YOU RESCUED HIM FROM. HE'S BEEN OUR EYES AND EARS, ALWAYS FOR YOUR PROTECTION.
WELL, COULDN'T YOU HAVE GENETICALLY MODIFIED THE FLATULENCE OUT OF HIM?
I'M AFRAID IT'S A SIDE-EFFECT.
LOOK, JAKE... I KNOW THIS IS A LOT TO ASK, BUT I NEED YOU TO *TRUST* ME RIGHT NOW. THIS IS WAY *BIGGER* THAN YOU'RE EXPECTING IT TO BE.
ARE YOU AN ALIEN?
THERE'S NO SUCH THING AS ALIENS--
AM I?
NO. LOOK--
W
CLEARLY, THESE PEOPLE HAVE NO IDEA ABOUT THE SIZE OF MY EXPECTATIONS, SHAD.
NARF!

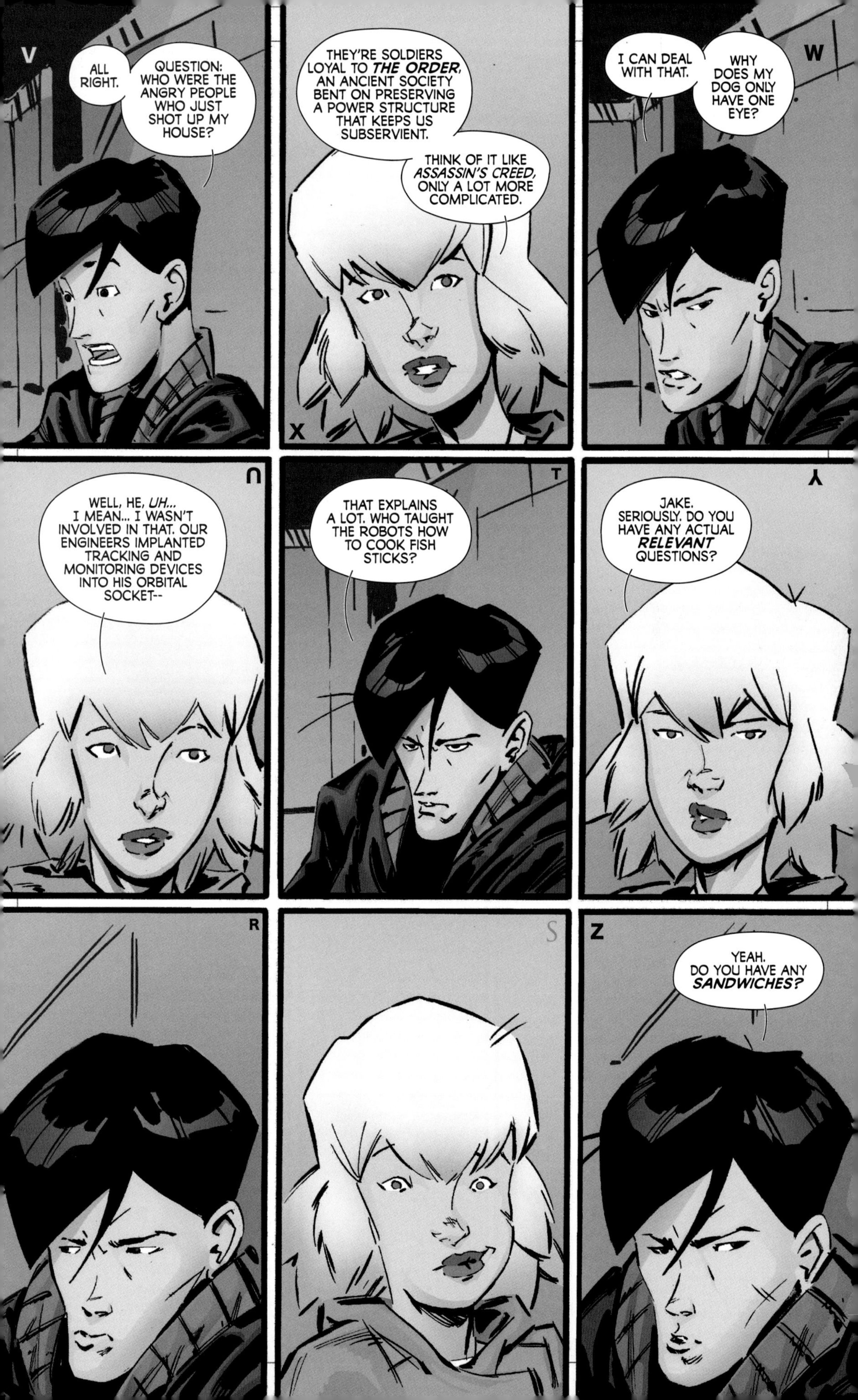
ALL RIGHT.
QUESTION: WHO WERE THE ANGRY PEOPLE WHO JUST SHOT UP MY HOUSE?
THEY'RE SOLDIERS LOYAL TO *THE ORDER*, AN ANCIENT SOCIETY BENT ON PRESERVING A POWER STRUCTURE THAT KEEPS US SUBSERVIENT.
THINK OF IT LIKE *ASSASSIN'S CREED*, ONLY A LOT MORE COMPLICATED.
I CAN DEAL WITH THAT.
WHY DOES MY DOG ONLY HAVE ONE EYE?
WELL, HE, *UH*... I MEAN... I WASN'T INVOLVED IN THAT. OUR ENGINEERS IMPLANTED TRACKING AND MONITORING DEVICES INTO HIS ORBITAL SOCKET--
THAT EXPLAINS A LOT. WHO TAUGHT THE ROBOTS HOW TO COOK FISH STICKS?
JAKE. SERIOUSLY. DO YOU HAVE ANY ACTUAL *RELEVANT* QUESTIONS?
YEAH. DO YOU HAVE ANY *SANDWICHES?*

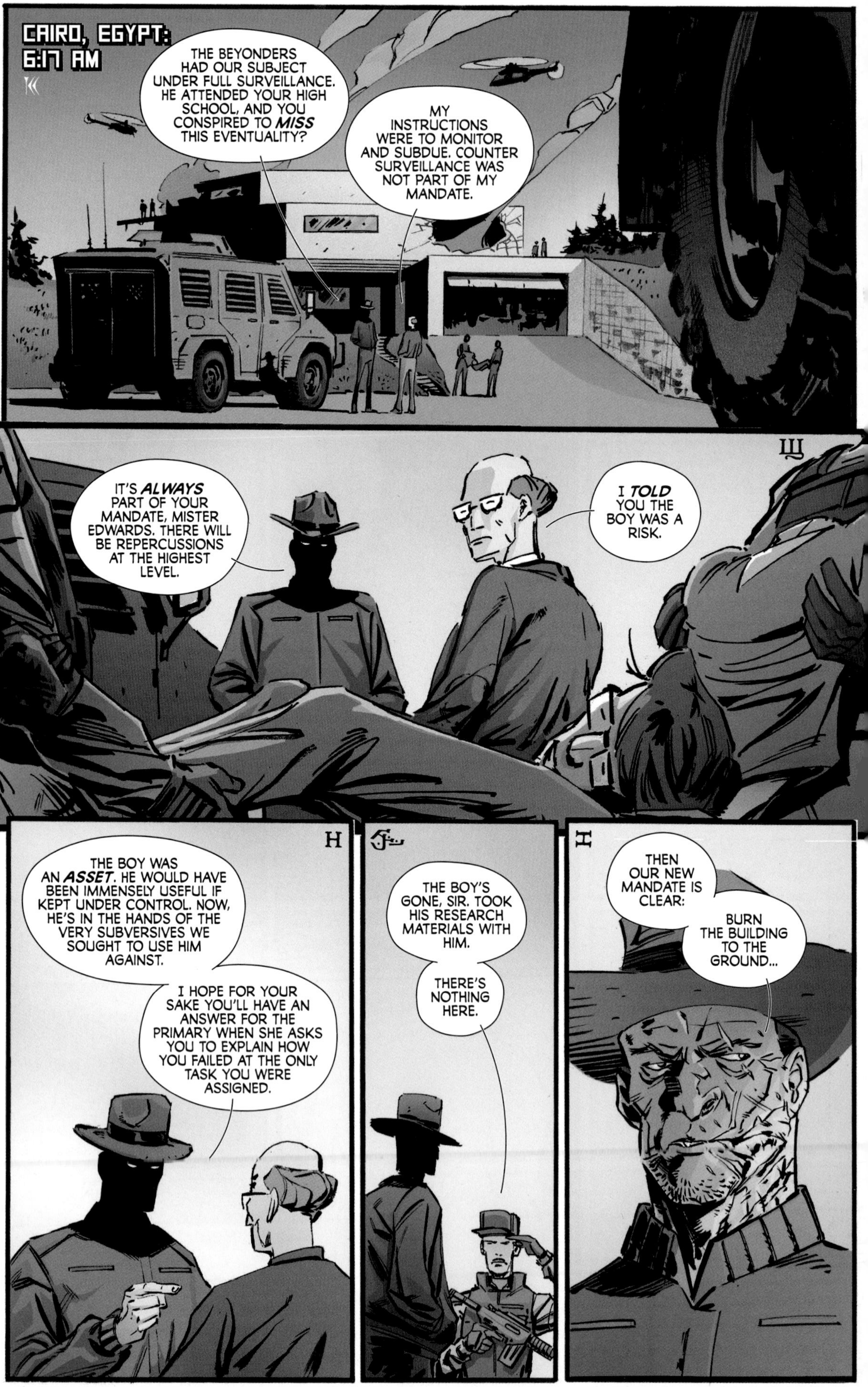
CAIRO, EGYPT:
6:17 AM
THE BEYONDERS HAD OUR SUBJECT UNDER FULL SURVEILLANCE. HE ATTENDED YOUR HIGH SCHOOL, AND YOU CONSPIRED TO MISS THIS EVENTUALITY?
MY INSTRUCTIONS WERE TO MONITOR AND SUBDUE. COUNTER SURVEILLANCE WAS NOT PART OF MY MANDATE.
IT'S ALWAYS PART OF YOUR MANDATE, MISTER EDWARDS. THERE WILL BE REPERCUSSIONS AT THE HIGHEST LEVEL.
I TOLD YOU THE BOY WAS A RISK.
THE BOY WAS AN ASSET. HE WOULD HAVE BEEN IMMENSELY USEFUL IF KEPT UNDER CONTROL. NOW, HE'S IN THE HANDS OF THE VERY SUBVERSIVES WE SOUGHT TO USE HIM AGAINST.
I HOPE FOR YOUR SAKE YOU'LL HAVE AN ANSWER FOR THE PRIMARY WHEN SHE ASKS YOU TO EXPLAIN HOW YOU FAILED AT THE ONLY TASK YOU WERE ASSIGNED.
THE BOY'S GONE, SIR. TOOK HIS RESEARCH MATERIALS WITH HIM.
THERE'S NOTHING HERE.
THEN OUR NEW MANDATE IS CLEAR:
BURN THE BUILDING TO THE GROUND...

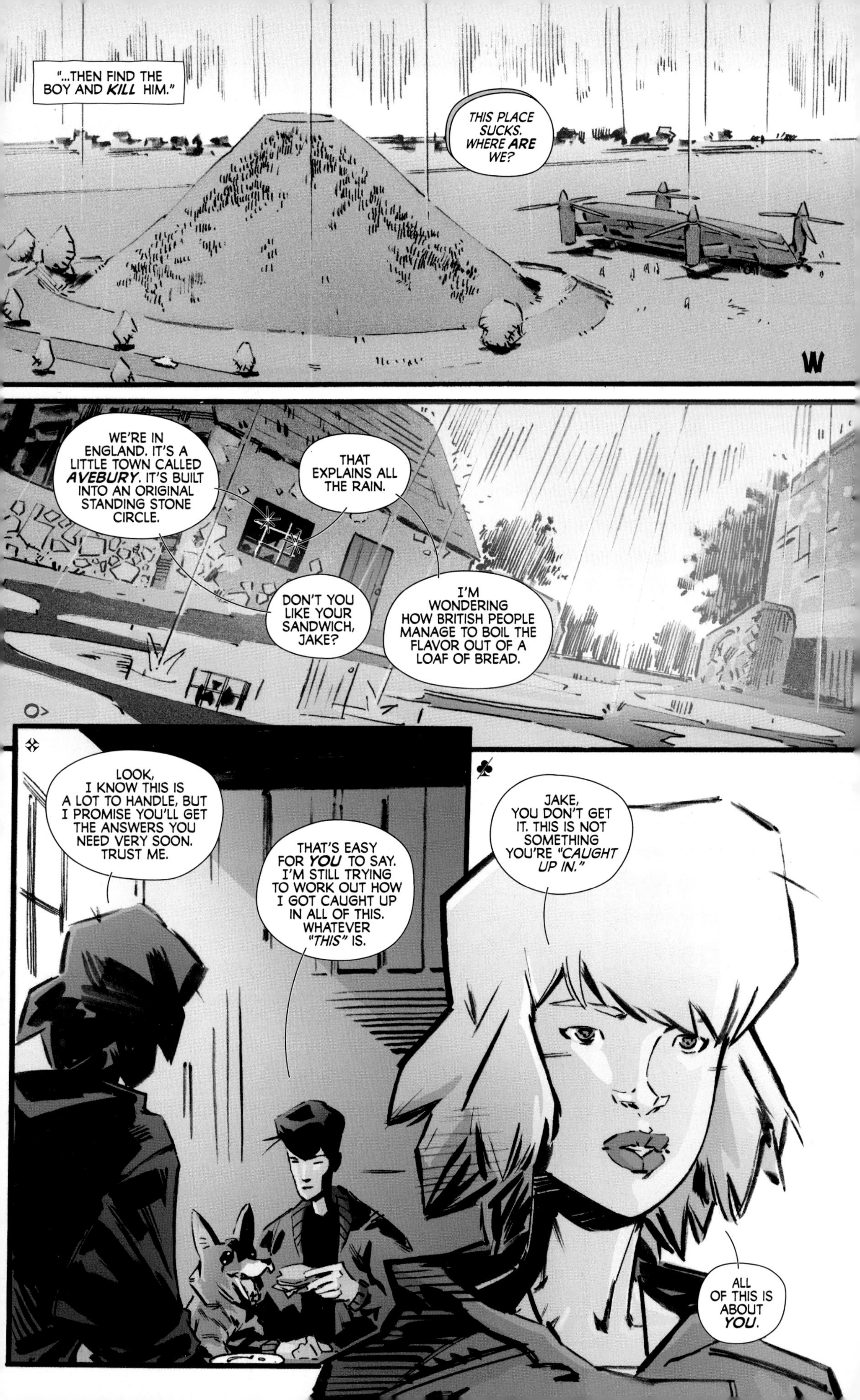

"...THEN FIND THE BOY AND *KILL* HIM."
*THIS PLACE SUCKS. WHERE **ARE** WE?*
WE'RE IN ENGLAND. IT'S A LITTLE TOWN CALLED ***AVEBURY***. IT'S BUILT INTO AN ORIGINAL STANDING STONE CIRCLE.
THAT EXPLAINS ALL THE RAIN.
DON'T YOU LIKE YOUR SANDWICH, JAKE?
I'M WONDERING HOW BRITISH PEOPLE MANAGE TO BOIL THE FLAVOR OUT OF A LOAF OF BREAD.
LOOK, I KNOW THIS IS A LOT TO HANDLE, BUT I PROMISE YOU'LL GET THE ANSWERS YOU NEED VERY SOON. TRUST ME.
THAT'S EASY FOR ***YOU*** TO SAY. I'M STILL TRYING TO WORK OUT HOW I GOT CAUGHT UP IN ALL OF THIS. WHATEVER *"THIS"* IS.
JAKE, YOU DON'T GET IT. THIS IS NOT SOMETHING YOU'RE *"CAUGHT UP IN."*
ALL OF THIS IS ABOUT ***YOU***.

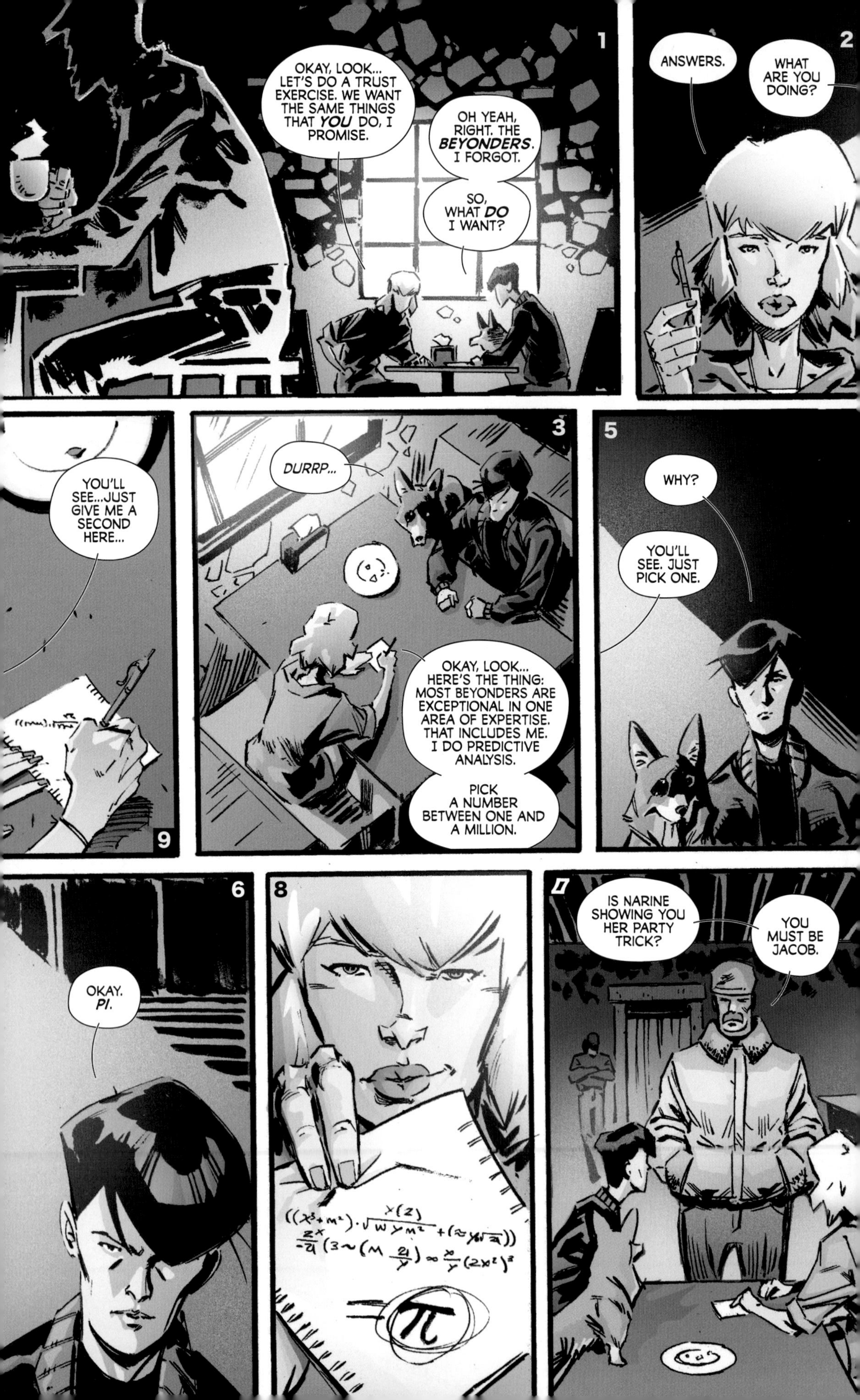
1
OKAY, LOOK... LET'S DO A TRUST EXERCISE. WE WANT THE SAME THINGS THAT *YOU* DO, I PROMISE.
OH YEAH, RIGHT. THE *BEYONDERS*. I FORGOT.
SO, WHAT *DO* I WANT?
2
ANSWERS.
WHAT ARE YOU DOING?
9
YOU'LL SEE...JUST GIVE ME A SECOND HERE...
3
DURRP...
OKAY, LOOK... HERE'S THE THING: MOST BEYONDERS ARE EXCEPTIONAL IN ONE AREA OF EXPERTISE. THAT INCLUDES ME. I DO PREDICTIVE ANALYSIS.
PICK A NUMBER BETWEEN ONE AND A MILLION.
5
WHY?
YOU'LL SEE. JUST PICK ONE.
6
OKAY. *PI*.
8
π
IS NARINE SHOWING YOU HER PARTY TRICK?
YOU MUST BE JACOB.

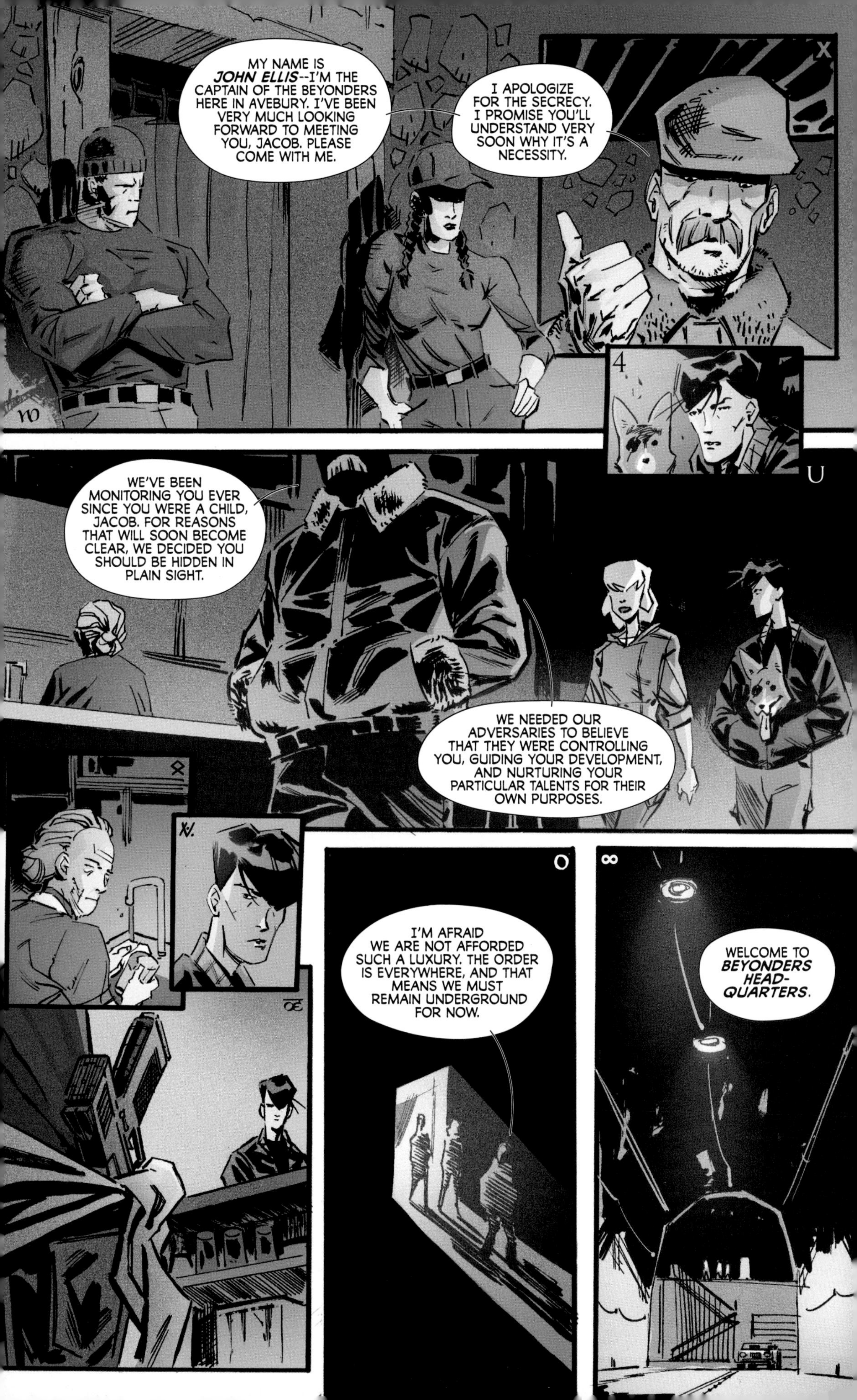

MY NAME IS JOHN ELLIS--I'M THE CAPTAIN OF THE BEYONDERS HERE IN AVEBURY. I'VE BEEN VERY MUCH LOOKING FORWARD TO MEETING YOU, JACOB. PLEASE COME WITH ME.
I APOLOGIZE FOR THE SECRECY. I PROMISE YOU'LL UNDERSTAND VERY SOON WHY IT'S A NECESSITY.
WE'VE BEEN MONITORING YOU EVER SINCE YOU WERE A CHILD, JACOB. FOR REASONS THAT WILL SOON BECOME CLEAR, WE DECIDED YOU SHOULD BE HIDDEN IN PLAIN SIGHT.
WE NEEDED OUR ADVERSARIES TO BELIEVE THAT THEY WERE CONTROLLING YOU, GUIDING YOUR DEVELOPMENT, AND NURTURING YOUR PARTICULAR TALENTS FOR THEIR OWN PURPOSES.
I'M AFRAID WE ARE NOT AFFORDED SUCH A LUXURY. THE ORDER IS EVERYWHERE, AND THAT MEANS WE MUST REMAIN UNDERGROUND FOR NOW.
WELCOME TO BEYONDERS HEAD-QUARTERS.

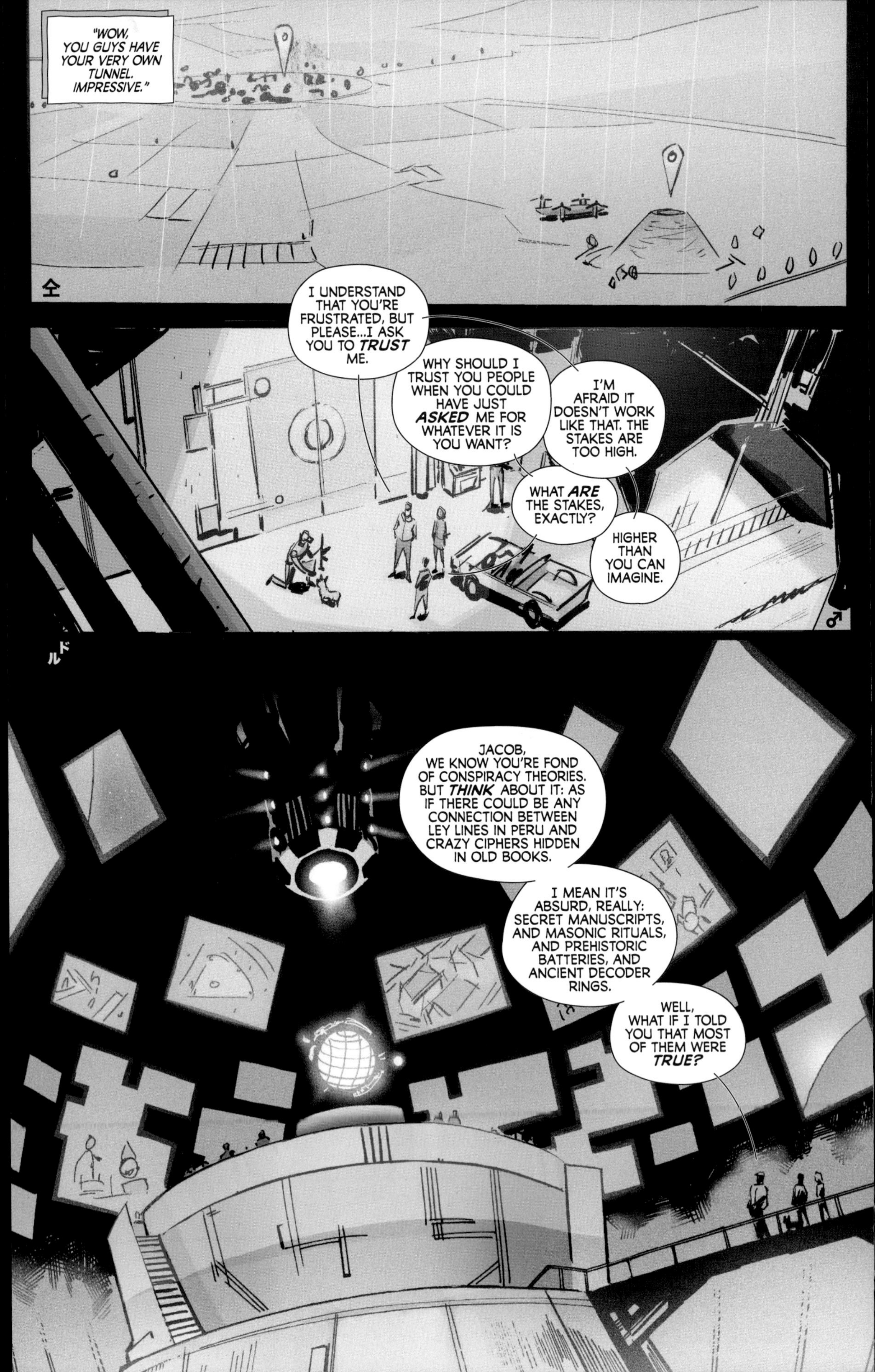
"WOW, YOU GUYS HAVE YOUR VERY OWN TUNNEL. IMPRESSIVE."
I UNDERSTAND THAT YOU'RE FRUSTRATED, BUT PLEASE...I ASK YOU TO *TRUST* ME.
WHY SHOULD I TRUST YOU PEOPLE WHEN YOU COULD HAVE JUST *ASKED* ME FOR WHATEVER IT IS YOU WANT?
I'M AFRAID IT DOESN'T WORK LIKE THAT. THE STAKES ARE TOO HIGH.
WHAT *ARE* THE STAKES, EXACTLY?
HIGHER THAN YOU CAN IMAGINE.
JACOB, WE KNOW YOU'RE FOND OF CONSPIRACY THEORIES. BUT *THINK* ABOUT IT: AS IF THERE COULD BE ANY CONNECTION BETWEEN LEY LINES IN PERU AND CRAZY CIPHERS HIDDEN IN OLD BOOKS.
I MEAN IT'S ABSURD, REALLY: SECRET MANUSCRIPTS, AND MASONIC RITUALS, AND PREHISTORIC BATTERIES, AND ANCIENT DECODER RINGS.
WELL, WHAT IF I TOLD YOU THAT MOST OF THEM WERE *TRUE?*

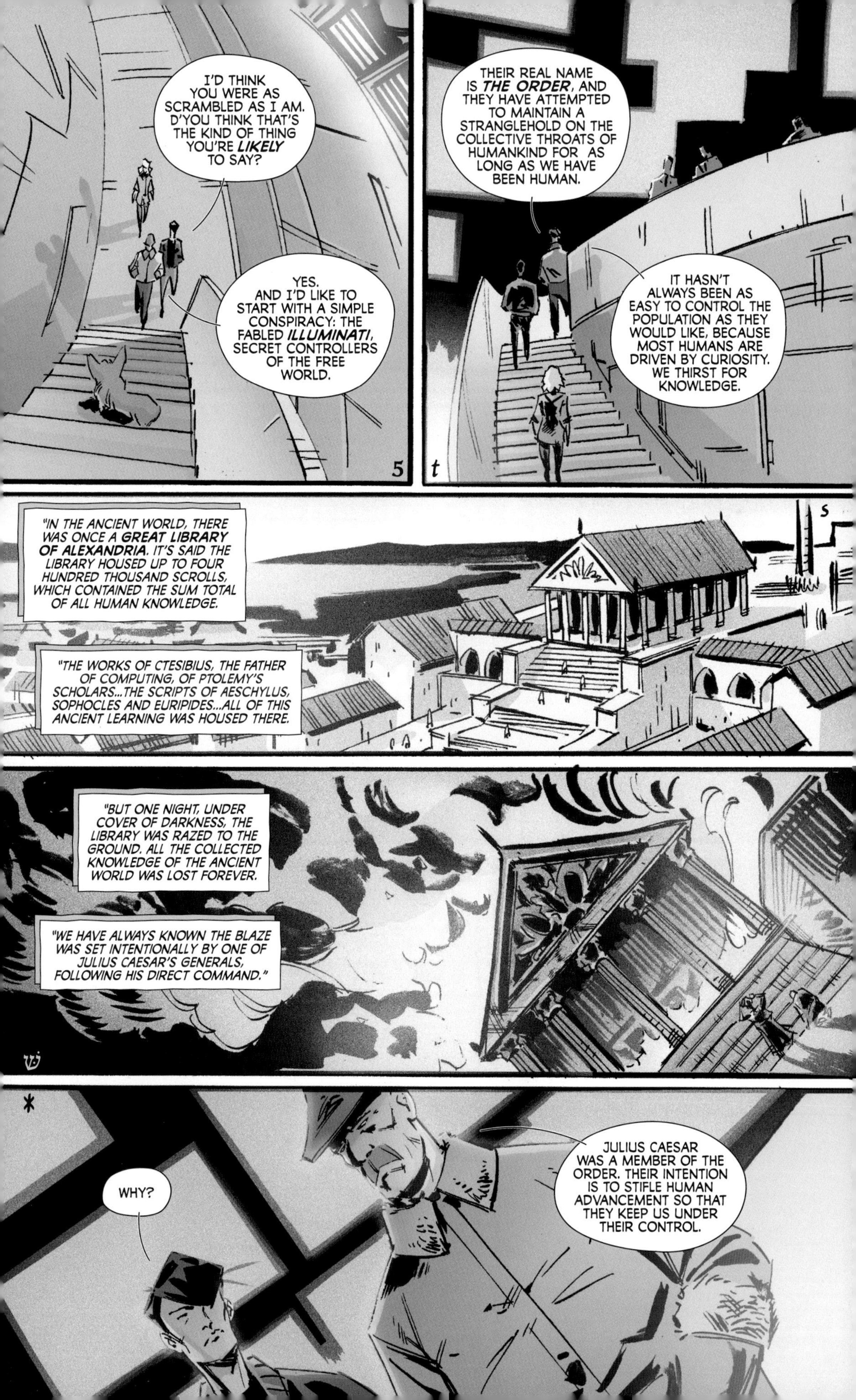
I'D THINK YOU WERE AS SCRAMBLED AS I AM. D'YOU THINK THAT'S THE KIND OF THING YOU'RE *LIKELY* TO SAY?
YES. AND I'D LIKE TO START WITH A SIMPLE CONSPIRACY: THE FABLED *ILLUMINATI*, SECRET CONTROLLERS OF THE FREE WORLD.
THEIR REAL NAME IS ***THE ORDER***, AND THEY HAVE ATTEMPTED TO MAINTAIN A STRANGLEHOLD ON THE COLLECTIVE THROATS OF HUMANKIND FOR AS LONG AS WE HAVE BEEN HUMAN.
IT HASN'T ALWAYS BEEN AS EASY TO CONTROL THE POPULATION AS THEY WOULD LIKE, BECAUSE MOST HUMANS ARE DRIVEN BY CURIOSITY. WE THIRST FOR KNOWLEDGE.
"IN THE ANCIENT WORLD, THERE WAS ONCE A **GREAT LIBRARY OF ALEXANDRIA**. IT'S SAID THE LIBRARY HOUSED UP TO FOUR HUNDRED THOUSAND SCROLLS, WHICH CONTAINED THE SUM TOTAL OF ALL HUMAN KNOWLEDGE.
"THE WORKS OF CTESIBIUS, THE FATHER OF COMPUTING, OF PTOLEMY'S SCHOLARS...THE SCRIPTS OF AESCHYLUS, SOPHOCLES AND EURIPIDES...ALL OF THIS ANCIENT LEARNING WAS HOUSED THERE.
"BUT ONE NIGHT, UNDER COVER OF DARKNESS, THE LIBRARY WAS RAZED TO THE GROUND. ALL THE COLLECTED KNOWLEDGE OF THE ANCIENT WORLD WAS LOST FOREVER.
"WE HAVE ALWAYS KNOWN THE BLAZE WAS SET INTENTIONALLY BY ONE OF JULIUS CAESAR'S GENERALS, FOLLOWING HIS DIRECT COMMAND."
JULIUS CAESAR WAS A MEMBER OF THE ORDER. THEIR INTENTION IS TO STIFLE HUMAN ADVANCEMENT SO THAT THEY KEEP US UNDER THEIR CONTROL.
WHY?

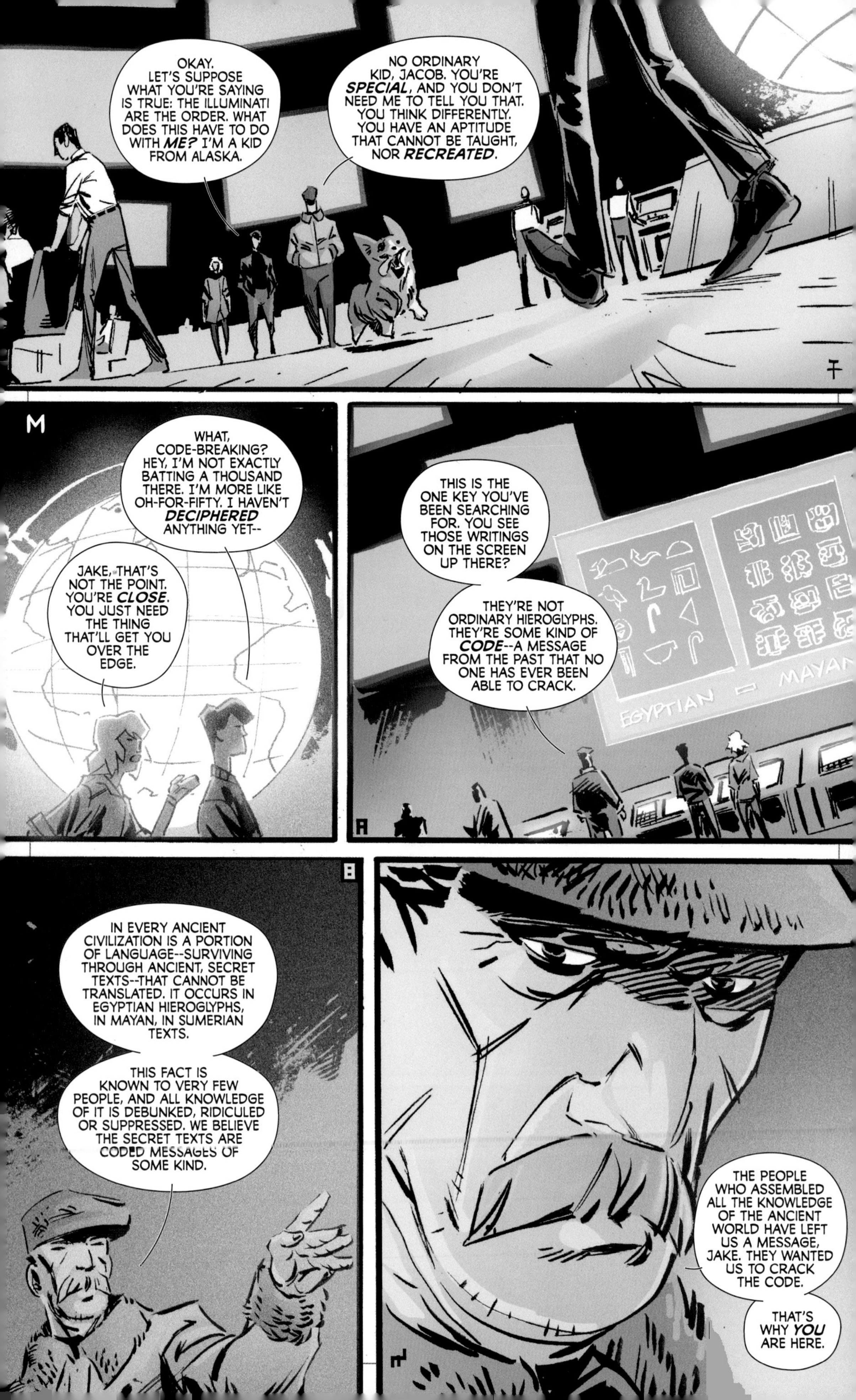
OKAY. LET'S SUPPOSE WHAT YOU'RE SAYING IS TRUE: THE ILLUMINATI ARE THE ORDER. WHAT DOES THIS HAVE TO DO WITH ME? I'M A KID FROM ALASKA.
NO ORDINARY KID, JACOB. YOU'RE SPECIAL, AND YOU DON'T NEED ME TO TELL YOU THAT. YOU THINK DIFFERENTLY. YOU HAVE AN APTITUDE THAT CANNOT BE TAUGHT, NOR RECREATED.
M
WHAT, CODE-BREAKING? HEY, I'M NOT EXACTLY BATTING A THOUSAND THERE. I'M MORE LIKE OH-FOR-FIFTY. I HAVEN'T DECIPHERED ANYTHING YET--
JAKE, THAT'S NOT THE POINT. YOU'RE CLOSE. YOU JUST NEED THE THING THAT'LL GET YOU OVER THE EDGE.
THIS IS THE ONE KEY YOU'VE BEEN SEARCHING FOR. YOU SEE THOSE WRITINGS ON THE SCREEN UP THERE?
THEY'RE NOT ORDINARY HIEROGLYPHS. THEY'RE SOME KIND OF CODE--A MESSAGE FROM THE PAST THAT NO ONE HAS EVER BEEN ABLE TO CRACK.
EGYPTIAN — MAYAN
IN EVERY ANCIENT CIVILIZATION IS A PORTION OF LANGUAGE--SURVIVING THROUGH ANCIENT, SECRET TEXTS--THAT CANNOT BE TRANSLATED. IT OCCURS IN EGYPTIAN HIEROGLYPHS, IN MAYAN, IN SUMERIAN TEXTS.
THIS FACT IS KNOWN TO VERY FEW PEOPLE, AND ALL KNOWLEDGE OF IT IS DEBUNKED, RIDICULED OR SUPPRESSED. WE BELIEVE THE SECRET TEXTS ARE CODED MESSAGES OF SOME KIND.
THE PEOPLE WHO ASSEMBLED ALL THE KNOWLEDGE OF THE ANCIENT WORLD HAVE LEFT US A MESSAGE, JAKE. THEY WANTED US TO CRACK THE CODE.
THAT'S WHY YOU ARE HERE.

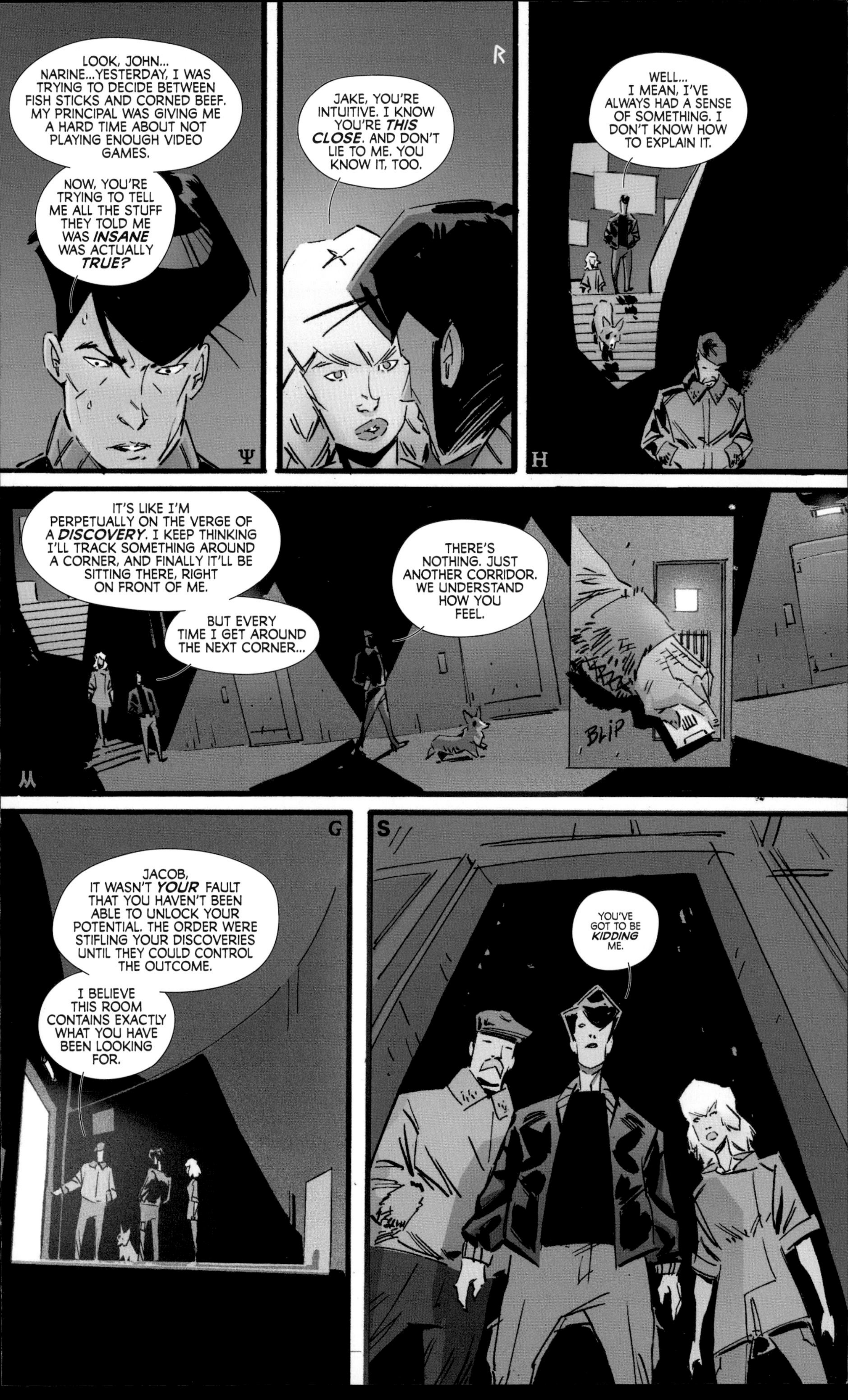
LOOK, JOHN... NARINE...YESTERDAY, I WAS TRYING TO DECIDE BETWEEN FISH STICKS AND CORNED BEEF. MY PRINCIPAL WAS GIVING ME A HARD TIME ABOUT NOT PLAYING ENOUGH VIDEO GAMES.
NOW, YOU'RE TRYING TO TELL ME ALL THE STUFF THEY TOLD ME WAS *INSANE* WAS ACTUALLY *TRUE?*
JAKE, YOU'RE INTUITIVE. I KNOW YOU'RE *THIS CLOSE*. AND DON'T LIE TO ME. YOU KNOW IT, TOO.
WELL... I MEAN, I'VE ALWAYS HAD A SENSE OF SOMETHING. I DON'T KNOW HOW TO EXPLAIN IT.
IT'S LIKE I'M PERPETUALLY ON THE VERGE OF A *DISCOVERY*. I KEEP THINKING I'LL TRACK SOMETHING AROUND A CORNER, AND FINALLY IT'LL BE SITTING THERE, RIGHT ON FRONT OF ME.
BUT EVERY TIME I GET AROUND THE NEXT CORNER...
THERE'S NOTHING. JUST ANOTHER CORRIDOR. WE UNDERSTAND HOW YOU FEEL.
BLIP
JACOB, IT WASN'T *YOUR* FAULT THAT YOU HAVEN'T BEEN ABLE TO UNLOCK YOUR POTENTIAL. THE ORDER WERE STIFLING YOUR DISCOVERIES UNTIL THEY COULD CONTROL THE OUTCOME.
I BELIEVE THIS ROOM CONTAINS EXACTLY WHAT YOU HAVE BEEN LOOKING FOR.
YOU'VE GOT TO BE *KIDDING* ME.

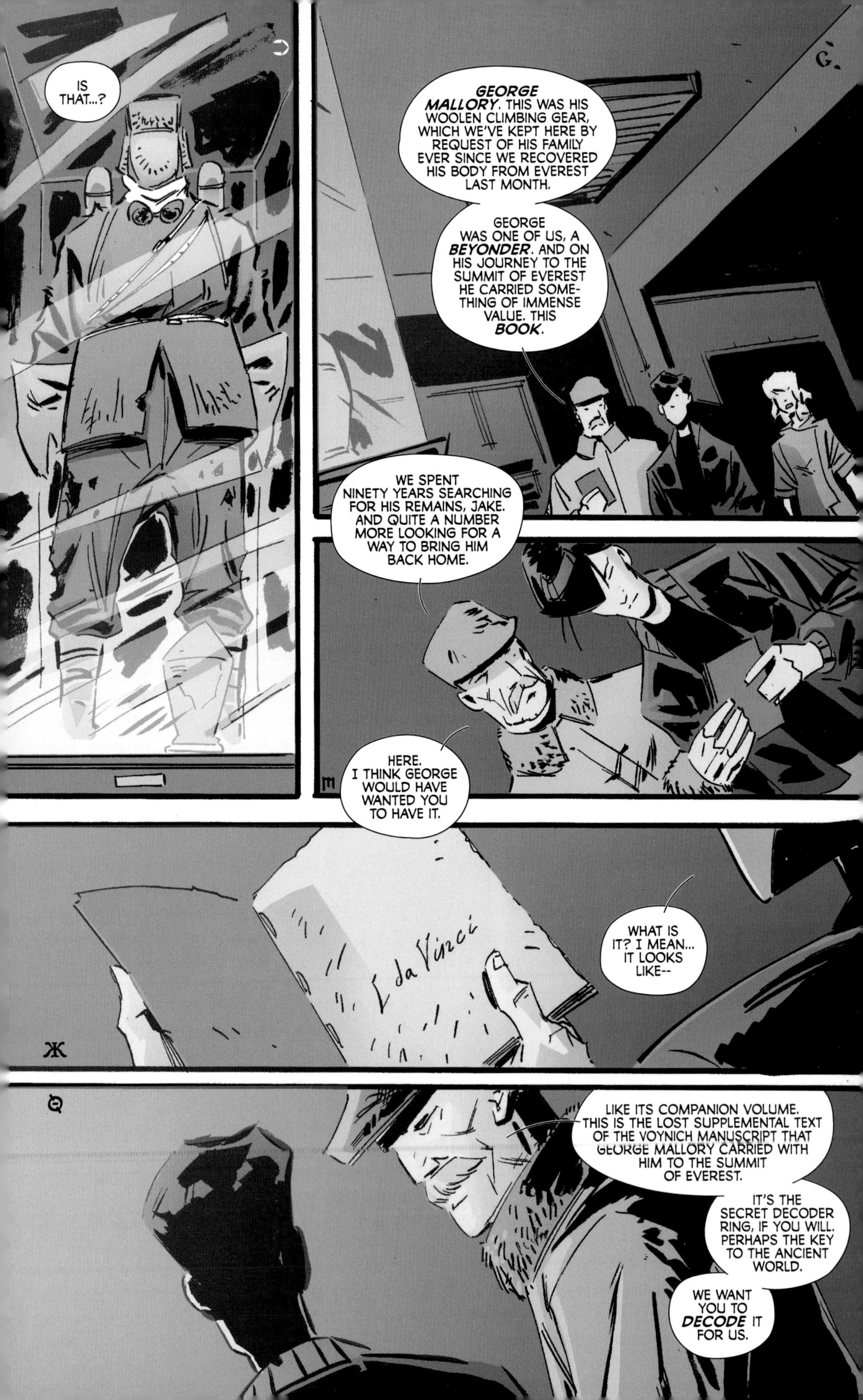
IS THAT...?
GEORGE MALLORY. THIS WAS HIS WOOLEN CLIMBING GEAR, WHICH WE'VE KEPT HERE BY REQUEST OF HIS FAMILY EVER SINCE WE RECOVERED HIS BODY FROM EVEREST LAST MONTH.
GEORGE WAS ONE OF US, A BEYONDER. AND ON HIS JOURNEY TO THE SUMMIT OF EVEREST HE CARRIED SOME-THING OF IMMENSE VALUE. THIS BOOK.
WE SPENT NINETY YEARS SEARCHING FOR HIS REMAINS, JAKE. AND QUITE A NUMBER MORE LOOKING FOR A WAY TO BRING HIM BACK HOME.
HERE. I THINK GEORGE WOULD HAVE WANTED YOU TO HAVE IT.
L da Vinci
WHAT IS IT? I MEAN... IT LOOKS LIKE--
LIKE ITS COMPANION VOLUME. THIS IS THE LOST SUPPLEMENTAL TEXT OF THE VOYNICH MANUSCRIPT THAT GEORGE MALLORY CARRIED WITH HIM TO THE SUMMIT OF EVEREST.
IT'S THE SECRET DECODER RING, IF YOU WILL. PERHAPS THE KEY TO THE ANCIENT WORLD.
WE WANT YOU TO DECODE IT FOR US.

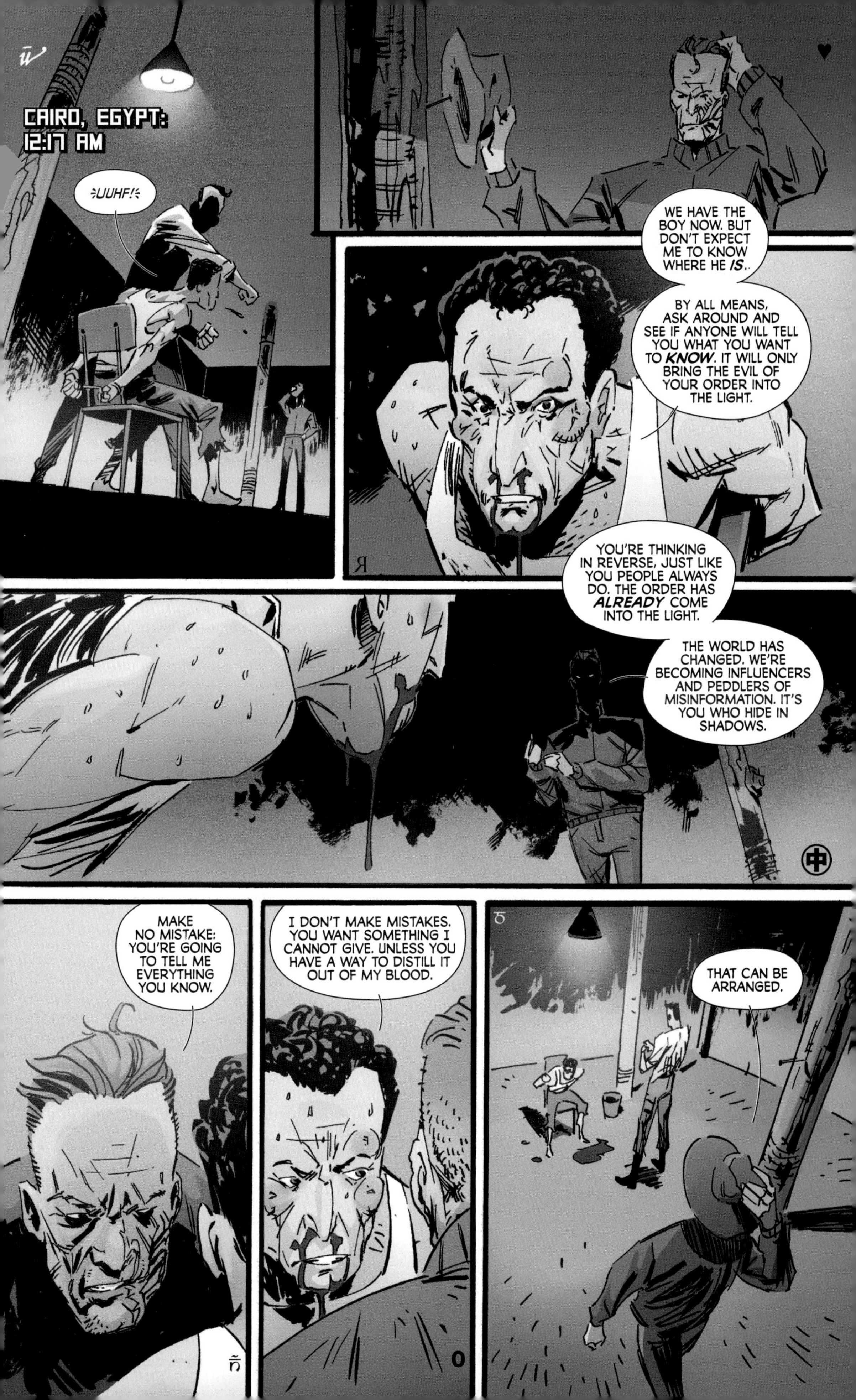
CAIRO, EGYPT:
12:17 AM
UUHF!
WE HAVE THE BOY NOW. BUT DON'T EXPECT ME TO KNOW WHERE HE *IS*..
BY ALL MEANS, ASK AROUND AND SEE IF ANYONE WILL TELL YOU WHAT YOU WANT TO ***KNOW***. IT WILL ONLY BRING THE EVIL OF YOUR ORDER INTO THE LIGHT.
YOU'RE THINKING IN REVERSE, JUST LIKE YOU PEOPLE ALWAYS DO. THE ORDER HAS ***ALREADY*** COME INTO THE LIGHT.
THE WORLD HAS CHANGED. WE'RE BECOMING INFLUENCERS AND PEDDLERS OF MISINFORMATION. IT'S YOU WHO HIDE IN SHADOWS.
MAKE NO MISTAKE: YOU'RE GOING TO TELL ME EVERYTHING YOU KNOW.
I DON'T MAKE MISTAKES. YOU WANT SOMETHING I CANNOT GIVE. UNLESS YOU HAVE A WAY TO DISTILL IT OUT OF MY BLOOD.
THAT CAN BE ARRANGED.

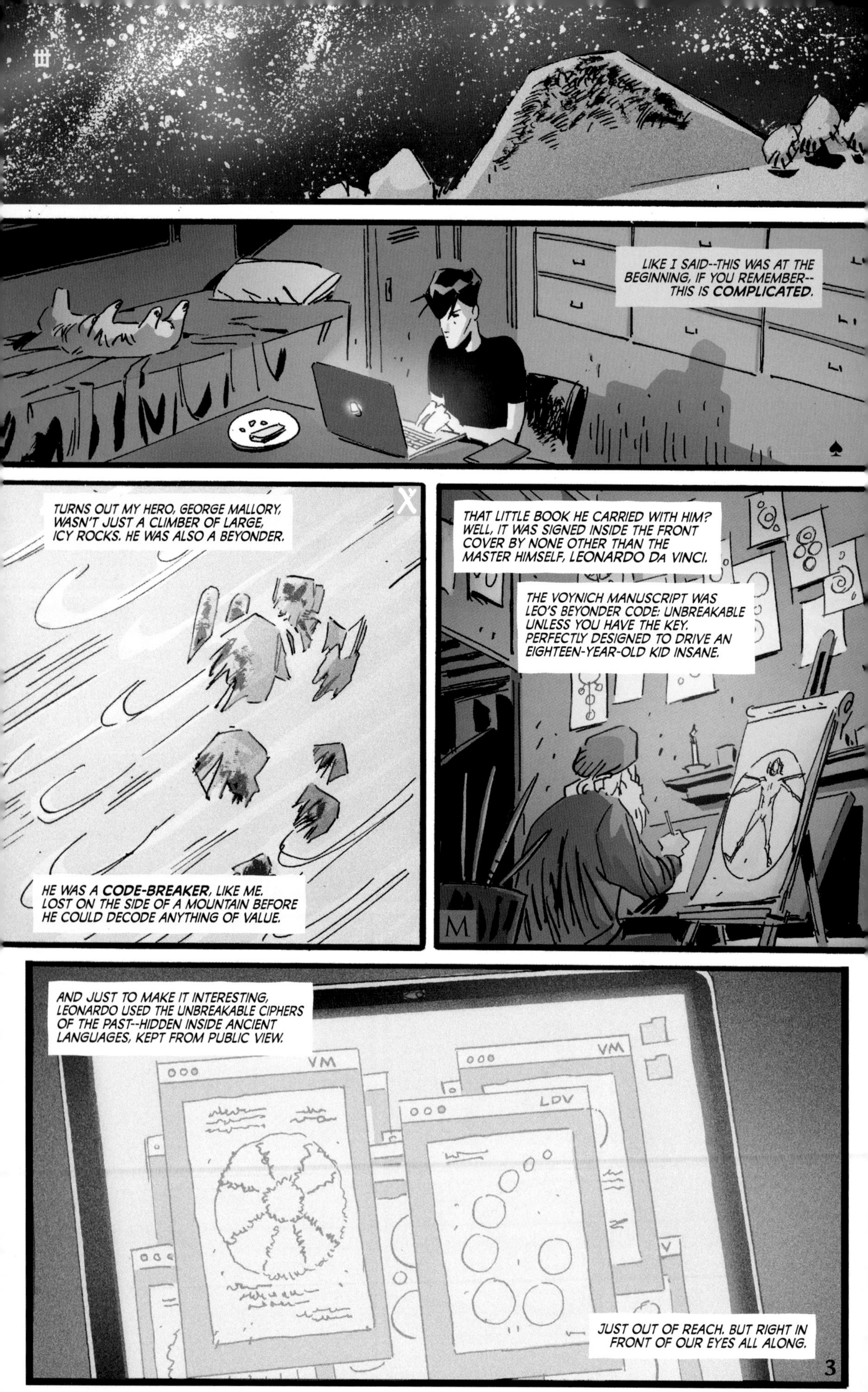
LIKE I SAID--THIS WAS AT THE BEGINNING, IF YOU REMEMBER--THIS IS COMPLICATED.
TURNS OUT MY HERO, GEORGE MALLORY, WASN'T JUST A CLIMBER OF LARGE, ICY ROCKS. HE WAS ALSO A BEYONDER.
HE WAS A CODE-BREAKER, LIKE ME. LOST ON THE SIDE OF A MOUNTAIN BEFORE HE COULD DECODE ANYTHING OF VALUE.
THAT LITTLE BOOK HE CARRIED WITH HIM? WELL, IT WAS SIGNED INSIDE THE FRONT COVER BY NONE OTHER THAN THE MASTER HIMSELF, LEONARDO DA VINCI.
THE VOYNICH MANUSCRIPT WAS LEO'S BEYONDER CODE: UNBREAKABLE UNLESS YOU HAVE THE KEY. PERFECTLY DESIGNED TO DRIVE AN EIGHTEEN-YEAR-OLD KID INSANE.
M
AND JUST TO MAKE IT INTERESTING, LEONARDO USED THE UNBREAKABLE CIPHERS OF THE PAST--HIDDEN INSIDE ANCIENT LANGUAGES, KEPT FROM PUBLIC VIEW.
VM
VM
LDV
JUST OUT OF REACH. BUT RIGHT IN FRONT OF OUR EYES ALL ALONG.

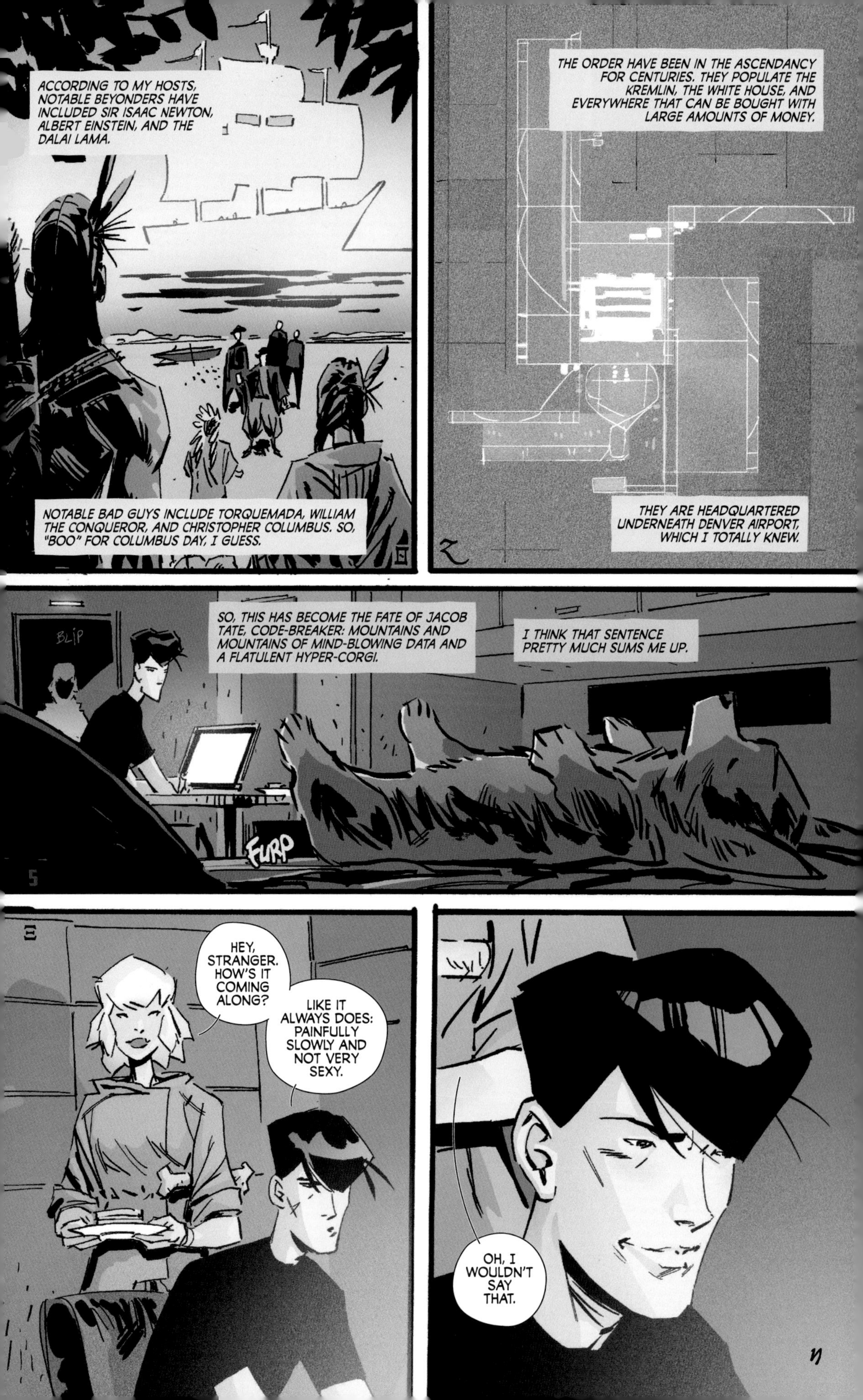
ACCORDING TO MY HOSTS, NOTABLE BEYONDERS HAVE INCLUDED SIR ISAAC NEWTON, ALBERT EINSTEIN, AND THE DALAI LAMA.
NOTABLE BAD GUYS INCLUDE TORQUEMADA, WILLIAM THE CONQUEROR, AND CHRISTOPHER COLUMBUS. SO, "BOO" FOR COLUMBUS DAY, I GUESS.
THE ORDER HAVE BEEN IN THE ASCENDANCY FOR CENTURIES. THEY POPULATE THE KREMLIN, THE WHITE HOUSE, AND EVERYWHERE THAT CAN BE BOUGHT WITH LARGE AMOUNTS OF MONEY.
THEY ARE HEADQUARTERED UNDERNEATH DENVER AIRPORT, WHICH I TOTALLY KNEW.
SO, THIS HAS BECOME THE FATE OF JACOB TATE, CODE-BREAKER: MOUNTAINS AND MOUNTAINS OF MIND-BLOWING DATA AND A FLATULENT HYPER-CORGI.
I THINK THAT SENTENCE PRETTY MUCH SUMS ME UP.
BLIP
FURP
HEY, STRANGER. HOW'S IT COMING ALONG?
LIKE IT ALWAYS DOES: PAINFULLY SLOWLY AND NOT VERY SEXY.
OH, I WOULDN'T SAY THAT.

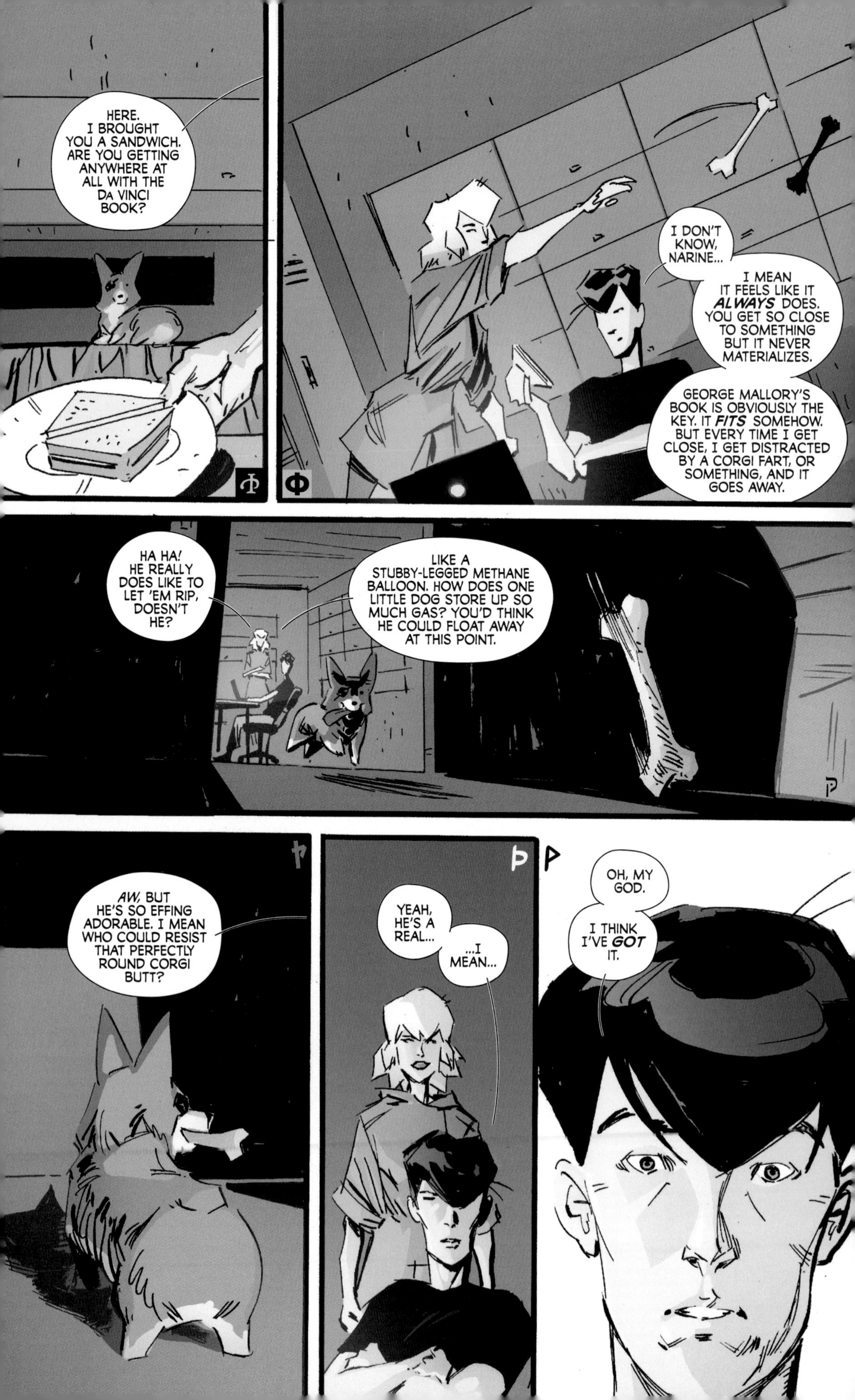
HERE. I BROUGHT YOU A SANDWICH. ARE YOU GETTING ANYWHERE AT ALL WITH THE DA VINCI BOOK?
I DON'T KNOW, NARINE...
I MEAN IT FEELS LIKE IT ALWAYS DOES. YOU GET SO CLOSE TO SOMETHING BUT IT NEVER MATERIALIZES.
GEORGE MALLORY'S BOOK IS OBVIOUSLY THE KEY. IT FITS SOMEHOW. BUT EVERY TIME I GET CLOSE, I GET DISTRACTED BY A CORGI FART, OR SOMETHING, AND IT GOES AWAY.
HA HA! HE REALLY DOES LIKE TO LET 'EM RIP, DOESN'T HE?
LIKE A STUBBY-LEGGED METHANE BALLOON. HOW DOES ONE LITTLE DOG STORE UP SO MUCH GAS? YOU'D THINK HE COULD FLOAT AWAY AT THIS POINT.
AW, BUT HE'S SO EFFING ADORABLE. I MEAN WHO COULD RESIST THAT PERFECTLY ROUND CORGI BUTT?
YEAH, HE'S A REAL...
...I MEAN...
OH, MY GOD.
I THINK I'VE GOT IT.

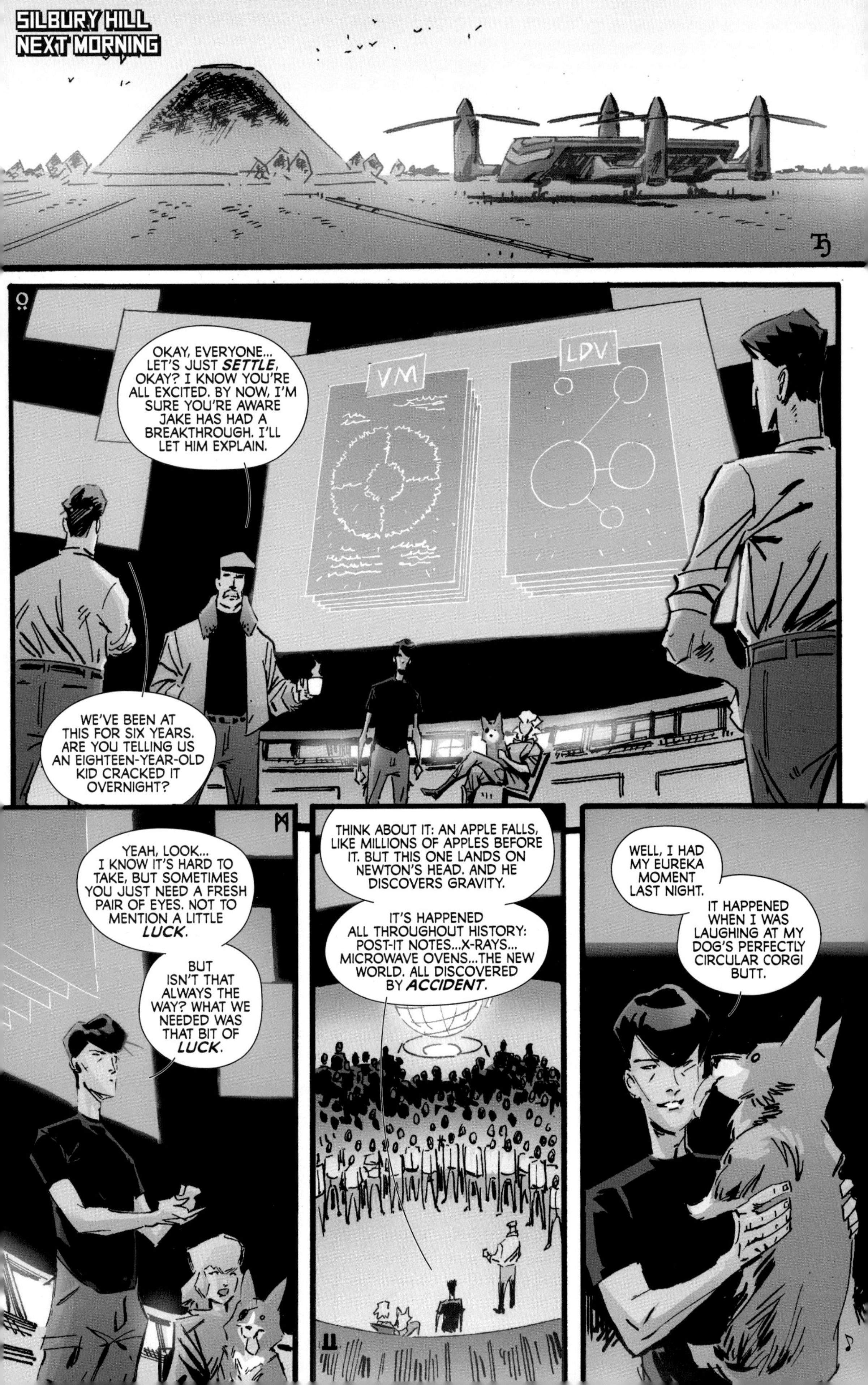
SILBURY HILL
NEXT MORNING
VM
LDV
OKAY, EVERYONE... LET'S JUST SETTLE, OKAY? I KNOW YOU'RE ALL EXCITED. BY NOW, I'M SURE YOU'RE AWARE JAKE HAS HAD A BREAKTHROUGH. I'LL LET HIM EXPLAIN.
WE'VE BEEN AT THIS FOR SIX YEARS. ARE YOU TELLING US AN EIGHTEEN-YEAR-OLD KID CRACKED IT OVERNIGHT?
YEAH, LOOK... I KNOW IT'S HARD TO TAKE, BUT SOMETIMES YOU JUST NEED A FRESH PAIR OF EYES. NOT TO MENTION A LITTLE LUCK.
BUT ISN'T THAT ALWAYS THE WAY? WHAT WE NEEDED WAS THAT BIT OF LUCK.
THINK ABOUT IT: AN APPLE FALLS, LIKE MILLIONS OF APPLES BEFORE IT. BUT THIS ONE LANDS ON NEWTON'S HEAD. AND HE DISCOVERS GRAVITY.
IT'S HAPPENED ALL THROUGHOUT HISTORY: POST-IT NOTES...X-RAYS... MICROWAVE OVENS...THE NEW WORLD. ALL DISCOVERED BY ACCIDENT.
WELL, I HAD MY EUREKA MOMENT LAST NIGHT.
IT HAPPENED WHEN I WAS LAUGHING AT MY DOG'S PERFECTLY CIRCULAR CORGI BUTT.

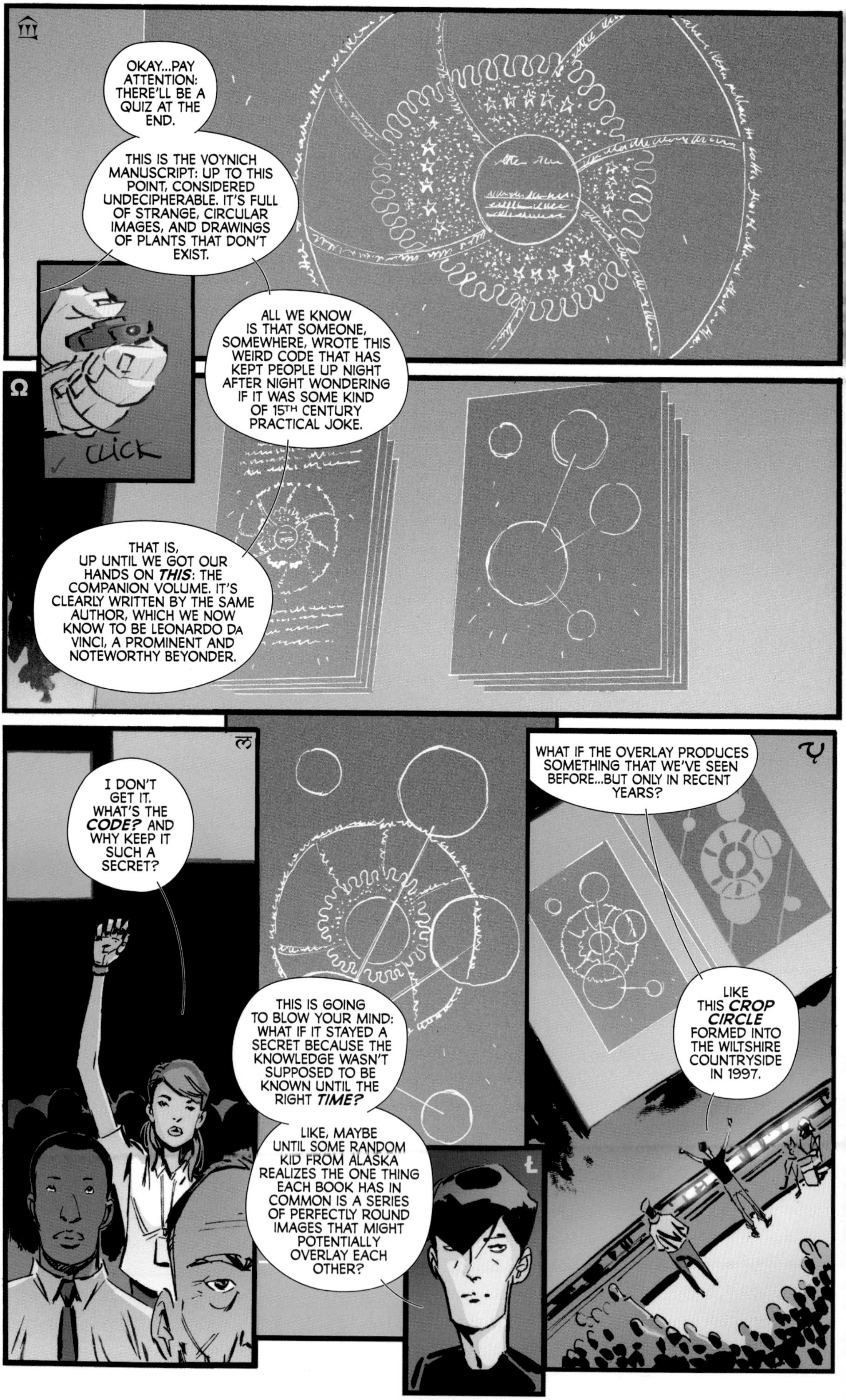
OKAY...PAY ATTENTION: THERE'LL BE A QUIZ AT THE END.
THIS IS THE VOYNICH MANUSCRIPT: UP TO THIS POINT, CONSIDERED UNDECIPHERABLE. IT'S FULL OF STRANGE, CIRCULAR IMAGES, AND DRAWINGS OF PLANTS THAT DON'T EXIST.
CLICK
ALL WE KNOW IS THAT SOMEONE, SOMEWHERE, WROTE THIS WEIRD CODE THAT HAS KEPT PEOPLE UP NIGHT AFTER NIGHT WONDERING IF IT WAS SOME KIND OF 15TH CENTURY PRACTICAL JOKE.
THAT IS, UP UNTIL WE GOT OUR HANDS ON *THIS*: THE COMPANION VOLUME. IT'S CLEARLY WRITTEN BY THE SAME AUTHOR, WHICH WE NOW KNOW TO BE LEONARDO DA VINCI, A PROMINENT AND NOTEWORTHY BEYONDER.
I DON'T GET IT. WHAT'S THE *CODE?* AND WHY KEEP IT SUCH A SECRET?
THIS IS GOING TO BLOW YOUR MIND: WHAT IF IT STAYED A SECRET BECAUSE THE KNOWLEDGE WASN'T SUPPOSED TO BE KNOWN UNTIL THE RIGHT *TIME?*
LIKE, MAYBE UNTIL SOME RANDOM KID FROM ALASKA REALIZES THE ONE THING EACH BOOK HAS IN COMMON IS A SERIES OF PERFECTLY ROUND IMAGES THAT MIGHT POTENTIALLY OVERLAY EACH OTHER?
WHAT IF THE OVERLAY PRODUCES SOMETHING THAT WE'VE SEEN BEFORE...BUT ONLY IN RECENT YEARS?
LIKE THIS *CROP CIRCLE* FORMED INTO THE WILTSHIRE COUNTRYSIDE IN 1997.

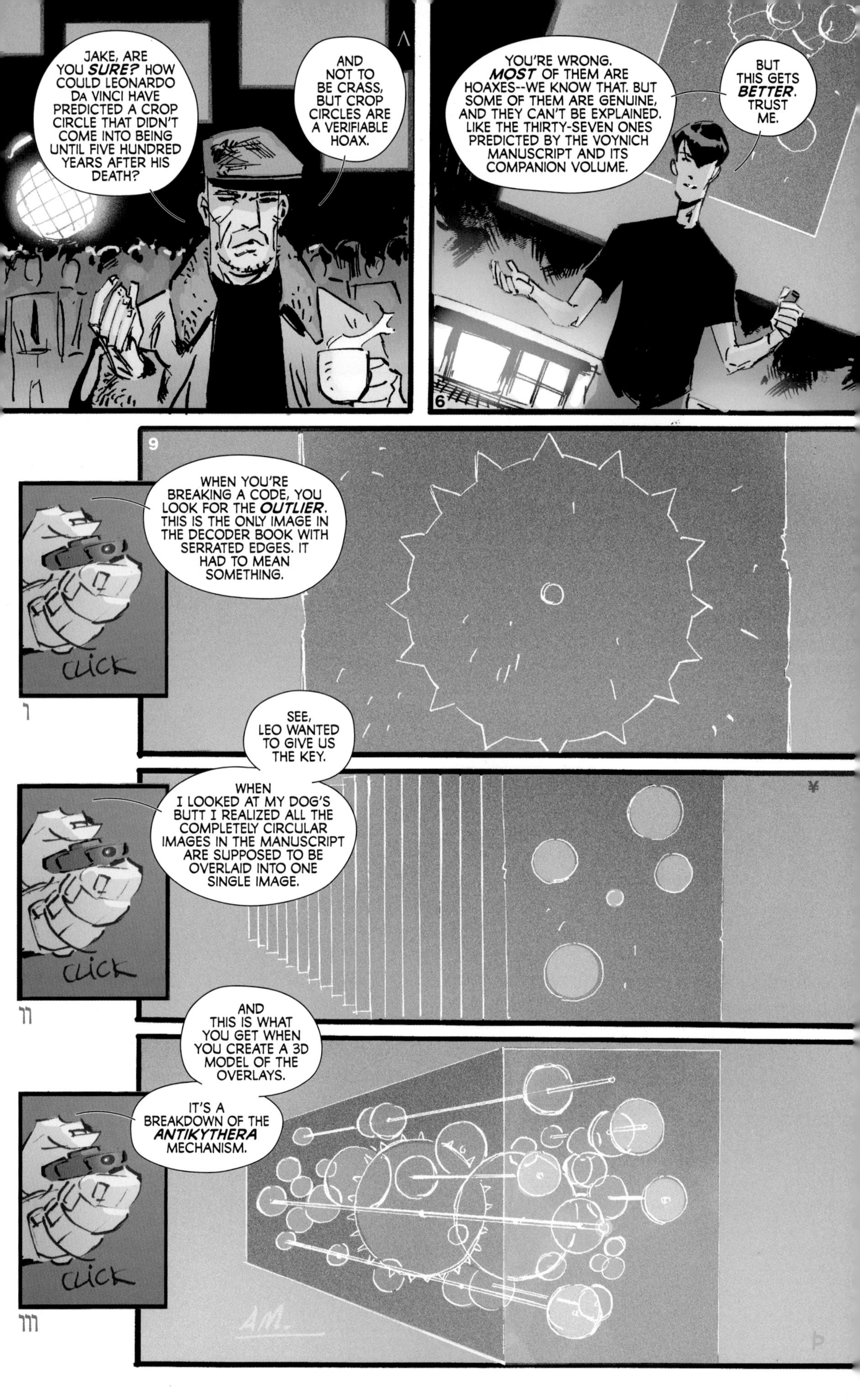
JAKE, ARE YOU SURE? HOW COULD LEONARDO DA VINCI HAVE PREDICTED A CROP CIRCLE THAT DIDN'T COME INTO BEING UNTIL FIVE HUNDRED YEARS AFTER HIS DEATH?
AND NOT TO BE CRASS, BUT CROP CIRCLES ARE A VERIFIABLE HOAX.
YOU'RE WRONG. MOST OF THEM ARE HOAXES--WE KNOW THAT. BUT SOME OF THEM ARE GENUINE, AND THEY CAN'T BE EXPLAINED. LIKE THE THIRTY-SEVEN ONES PREDICTED BY THE VOYNICH MANUSCRIPT AND ITS COMPANION VOLUME.
BUT THIS GETS BETTER. TRUST ME.
6
9
WHEN YOU'RE BREAKING A CODE, YOU LOOK FOR THE OUTLIER. THIS IS THE ONLY IMAGE IN THE DECODER BOOK WITH SERRATED EDGES. IT HAD TO MEAN SOMETHING.
CLICK
SEE, LEO WANTED TO GIVE US THE KEY.
WHEN I LOOKED AT MY DOG'S BUTT I REALIZED ALL THE COMPLETELY CIRCULAR IMAGES IN THE MANUSCRIPT ARE SUPPOSED TO BE OVERLAID INTO ONE SINGLE IMAGE.
CLICK
AND THIS IS WHAT YOU GET WHEN YOU CREATE A 3D MODEL OF THE OVERLAYS.
IT'S A BREAKDOWN OF THE ANTIKYTHERA MECHANISM.
CLICK
AM.

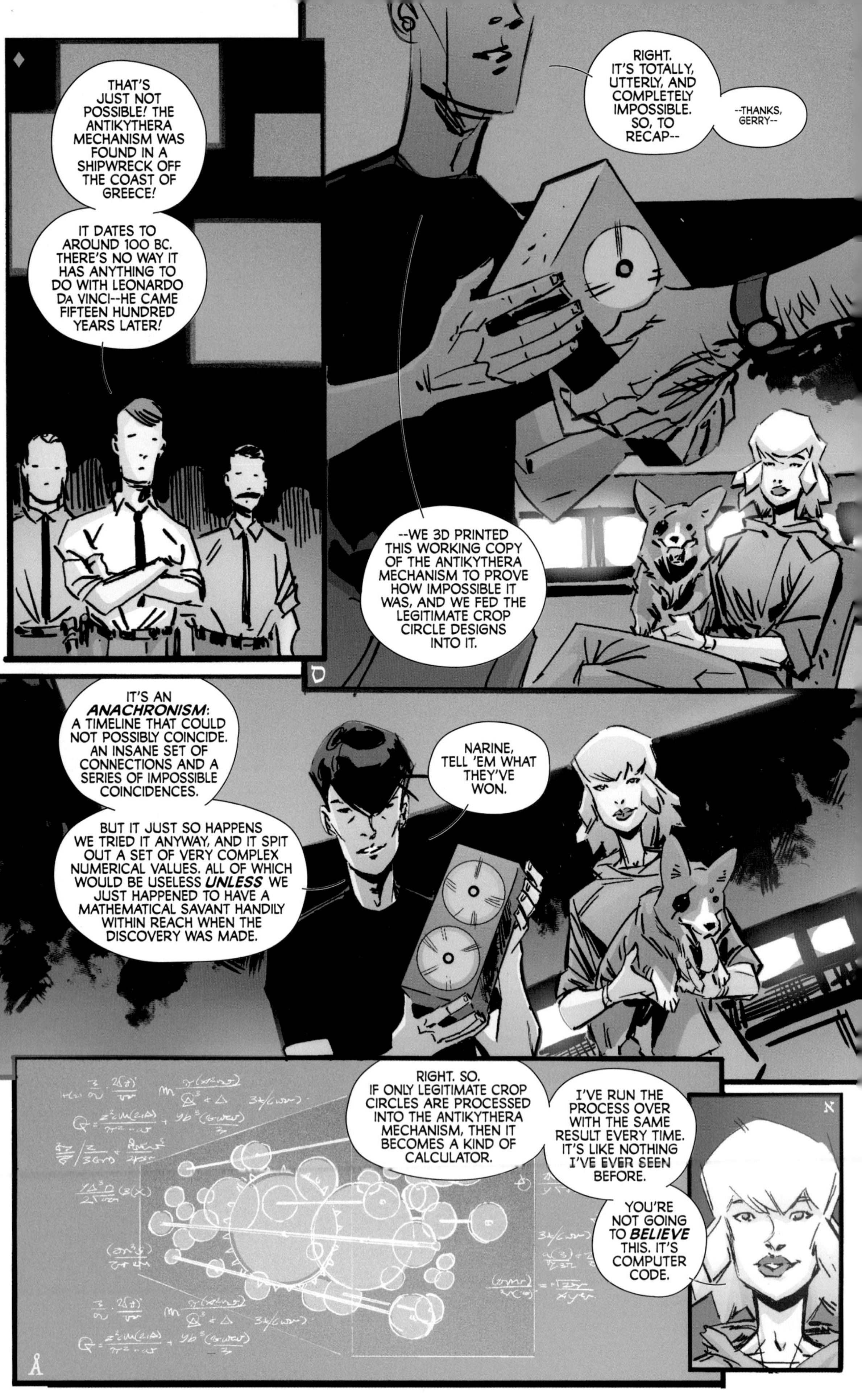
THAT'S JUST NOT POSSIBLE! THE ANTIKYTHERA MECHANISM WAS FOUND IN A SHIPWRECK OFF THE COAST OF GREECE!
IT DATES TO AROUND 100 BC. THERE'S NO WAY IT HAS ANYTHING TO DO WITH LEONARDO DA VINCI--HE CAME FIFTEEN HUNDRED YEARS LATER!
RIGHT. IT'S TOTALLY, UTTERLY, AND COMPLETELY IMPOSSIBLE. SO, TO RECAP--
--THANKS, GERRY--
--WE 3D PRINTED THIS WORKING COPY OF THE ANTIKYTHERA MECHANISM TO PROVE HOW IMPOSSIBLE IT WAS, AND WE FED THE LEGITIMATE CROP CIRCLE DESIGNS INTO IT.
IT'S AN ANACHRONISM: A TIMELINE THAT COULD NOT POSSIBLY COINCIDE. AN INSANE SET OF CONNECTIONS AND A SERIES OF IMPOSSIBLE COINCIDENCES.
BUT IT JUST SO HAPPENS WE TRIED IT ANYWAY, AND IT SPIT OUT A SET OF VERY COMPLEX NUMERICAL VALUES. ALL OF WHICH WOULD BE USELESS UNLESS WE JUST HAPPENED TO HAVE A MATHEMATICAL SAVANT HANDILY WITHIN REACH WHEN THE DISCOVERY WAS MADE.
NARINE, TELL 'EM WHAT THEY'VE WON.
RIGHT. SO. IF ONLY LEGITIMATE CROP CIRCLES ARE PROCESSED INTO THE ANTIKYTHERA MECHANISM, THEN IT BECOMES A KIND OF CALCULATOR.
I'VE RUN THE PROCESS OVER WITH THE SAME RESULT EVERY TIME. IT'S LIKE NOTHING I'VE EVER SEEN BEFORE.
YOU'RE NOT GOING TO BELIEVE THIS. IT'S COMPUTER CODE.

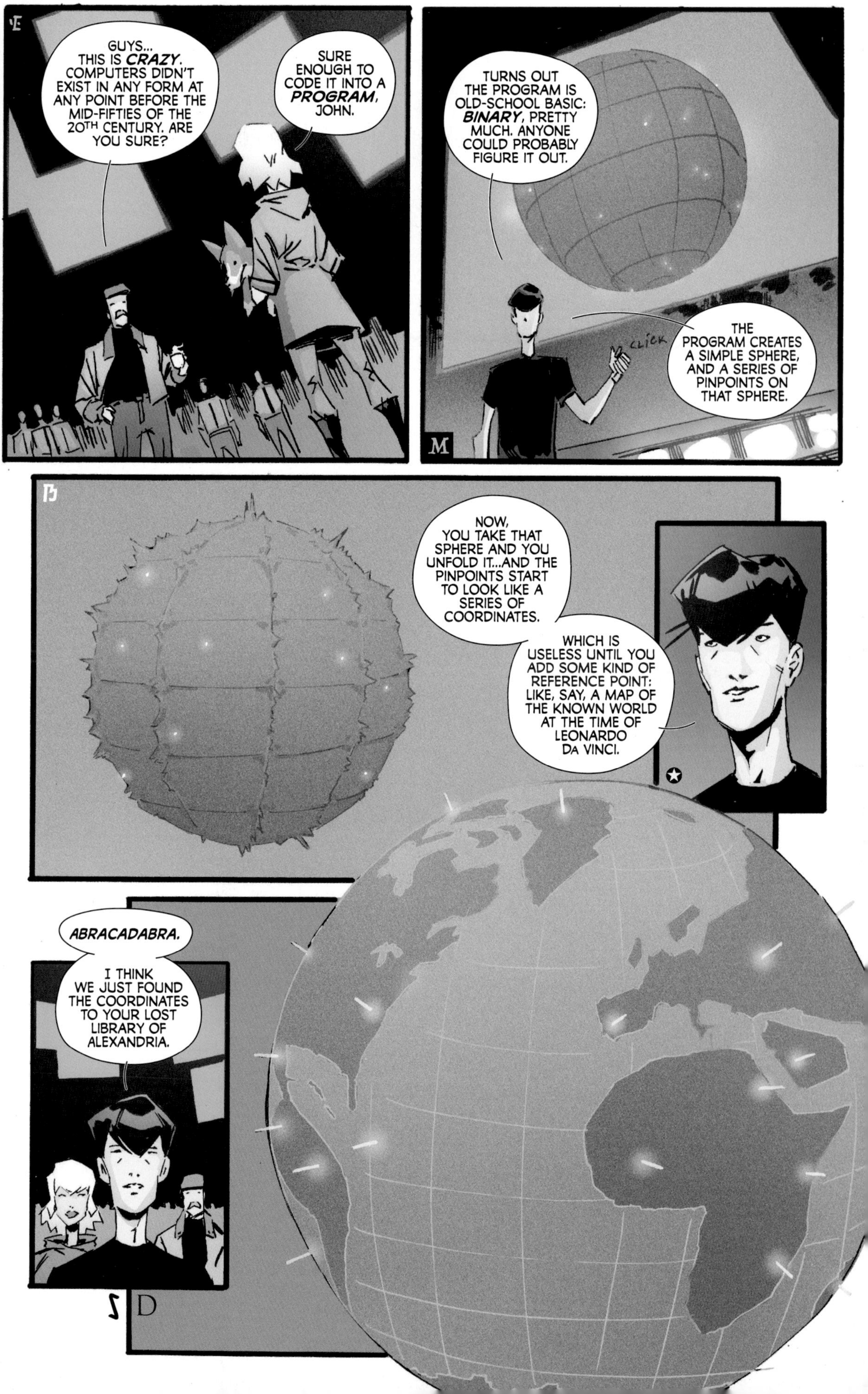
GUYS... THIS IS CRAZY. COMPUTERS DIDN'T EXIST IN ANY FORM AT ANY POINT BEFORE THE MID-FIFTIES OF THE 20TH CENTURY. ARE YOU SURE?
SURE ENOUGH TO CODE IT INTO A PROGRAM, JOHN.
TURNS OUT THE PROGRAM IS OLD-SCHOOL BASIC: BINARY, PRETTY MUCH. ANYONE COULD PROBABLY FIGURE IT OUT.
CLICK
THE PROGRAM CREATES A SIMPLE SPHERE, AND A SERIES OF PINPOINTS ON THAT SPHERE.
NOW, YOU TAKE THAT SPHERE AND YOU UNFOLD IT...AND THE PINPOINTS START TO LOOK LIKE A SERIES OF COORDINATES.
WHICH IS USELESS UNTIL YOU ADD SOME KIND OF REFERENCE POINT: LIKE, SAY, A MAP OF THE KNOWN WORLD AT THE TIME OF LEONARDO DA VINCI.
ABRACADABRA.
I THINK WE JUST FOUND THE COORDINATES TO YOUR LOST LIBRARY OF ALEXANDRIA.

3

EVERYTHING GOES BADLY

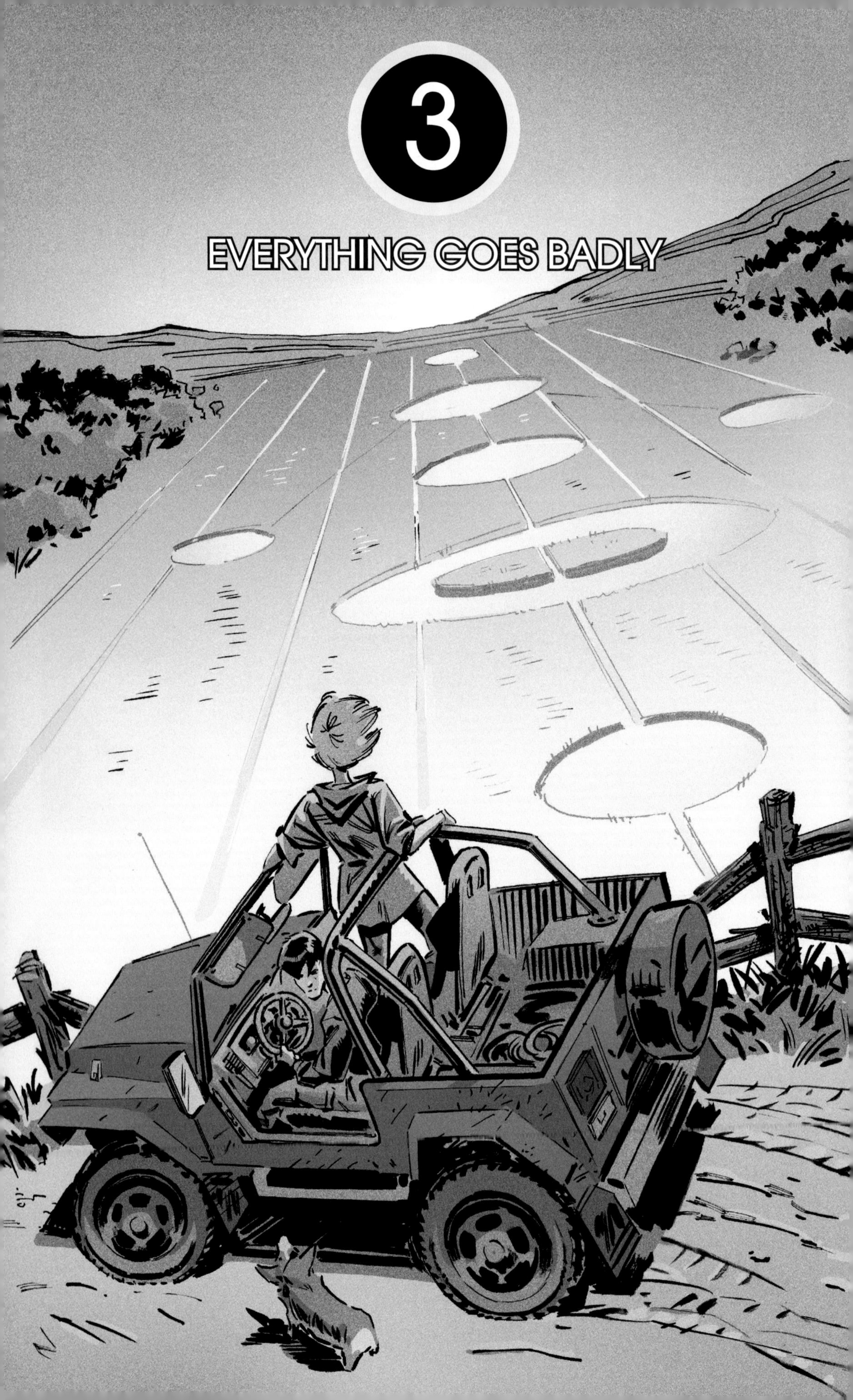

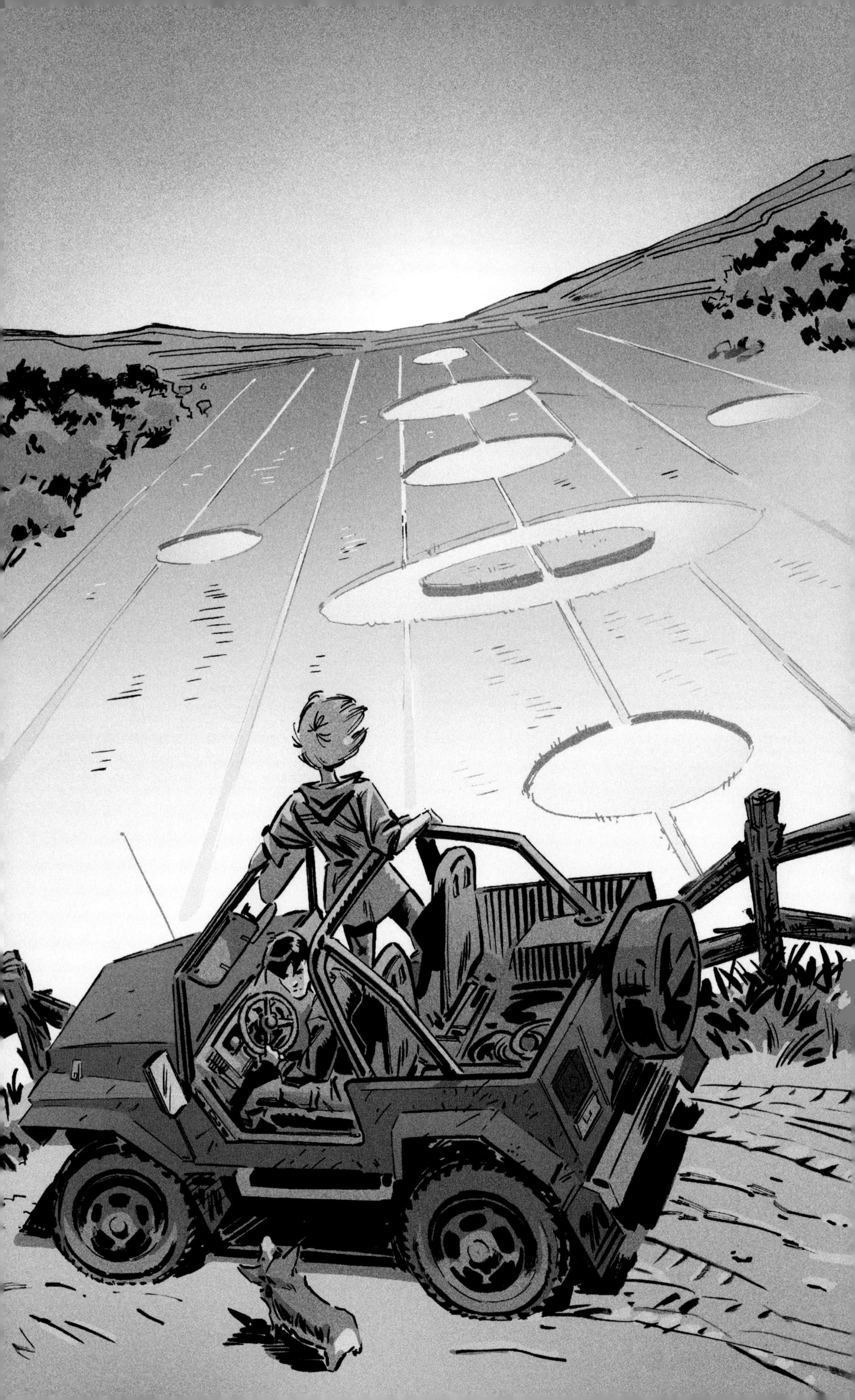

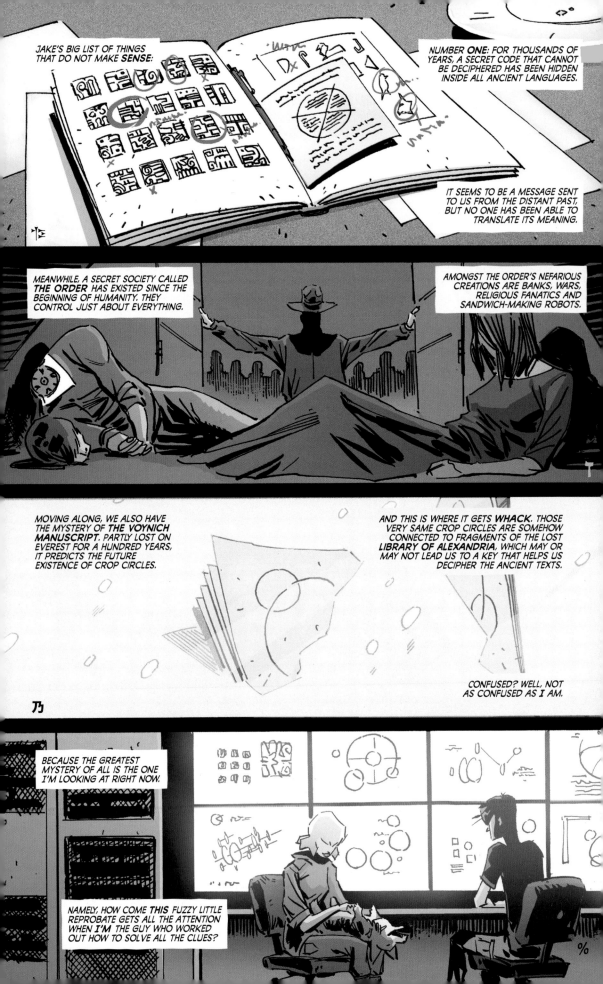

JAKE'S BIG LIST OF THINGS THAT DO NOT MAKE **SENSE**:

NUMBER **ONE**: FOR THOUSANDS OF YEARS, A SECRET CODE THAT CANNOT BE DECIPHERED HAS BEEN HIDDEN INSIDE ALL ANCIENT LANGUAGES.

IT SEEMS TO BE A MESSAGE SENT TO US FROM THE DISTANT PAST, BUT NO ONE HAS BEEN ABLE TO TRANSLATE ITS MEANING.

MEANWHILE, A SECRET SOCIETY CALLED **THE ORDER** HAS EXISTED SINCE THE BEGINNING OF HUMANITY. THEY CONTROL JUST ABOUT EVERYTHING.

AMONGST THE ORDER'S NEFARIOUS CREATIONS ARE BANKS, WARS, RELIGIOUS FANATICS AND SANDWICH-MAKING ROBOTS.

MOVING ALONG, WE ALSO HAVE THE MYSTERY OF **THE VOYNICH MANUSCRIPT**. PARTLY LOST ON EVEREST FOR A HUNDRED YEARS, IT PREDICTS THE FUTURE EXISTENCE OF CROP CIRCLES.

AND THIS IS WHERE IT GETS **WHACK**. THOSE VERY SAME CROP CIRCLES ARE SOMEHOW CONNECTED TO FRAGMENTS OF THE LOST **LIBRARY OF ALEXANDRIA**, WHICH MAY OR MAY NOT LEAD US TO A KEY THAT HELPS US DECIPHER THE ANCIENT TEXTS.

CONFUSED? WELL, NOT AS CONFUSED AS **I** AM.

BECAUSE THE GREATEST MYSTERY OF ALL IS THE ONE I'M LOOKING AT RIGHT NOW.

NAMELY, HOW COME **THIS** FUZZY LITTLE REPROBATE GETS ALL THE ATTENTION WHEN **I'M** THE GUY WHO WORKED OUT HOW TO SOLVE ALL THE CLUES?

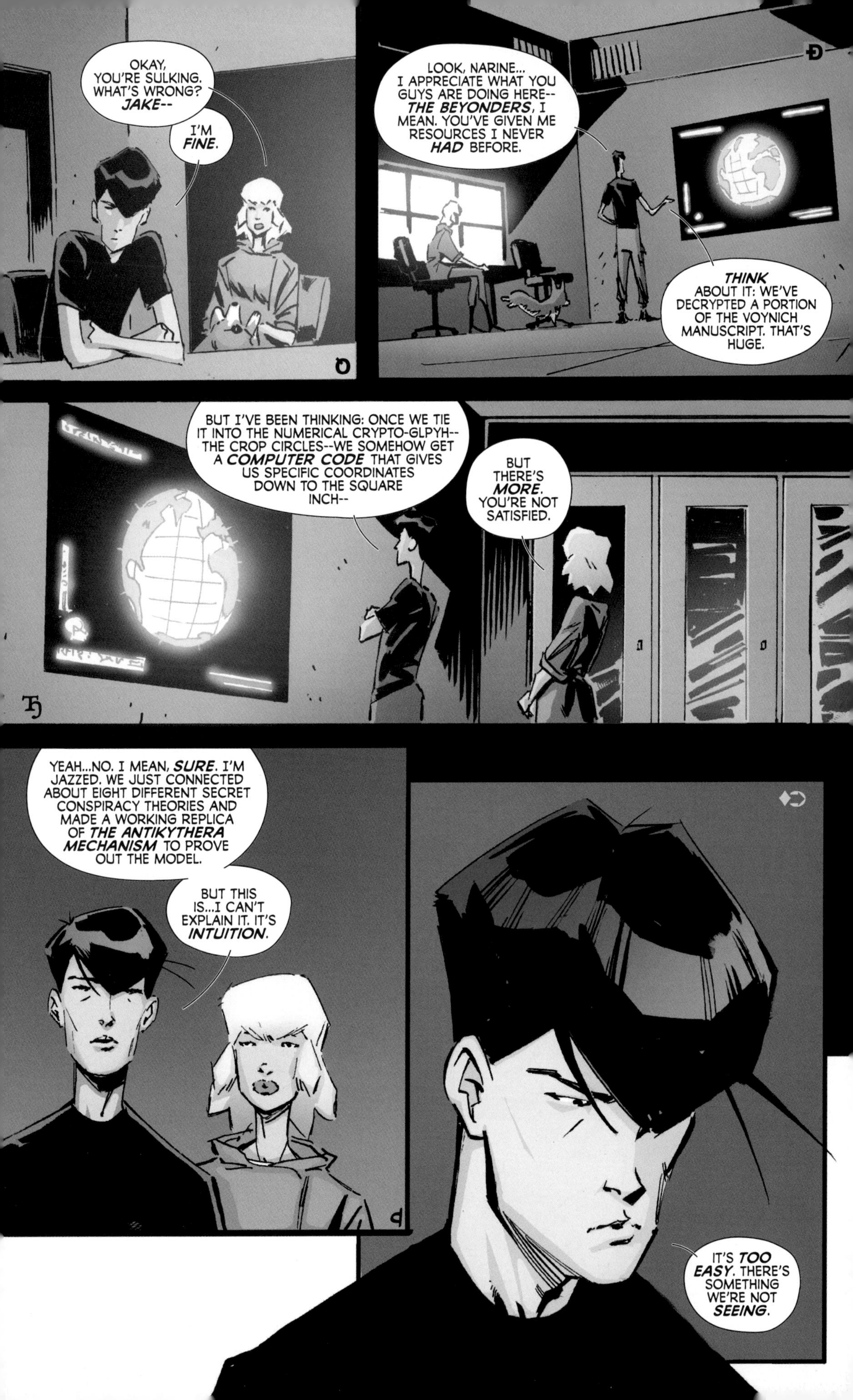
OKAY, YOU'RE SULKING. WHAT'S WRONG? JAKE--
I'M FINE.
LOOK, NARINE... I APPRECIATE WHAT YOU GUYS ARE DOING HERE-- THE BEYONDERS, I MEAN. YOU'VE GIVEN ME RESOURCES I NEVER HAD BEFORE.
THINK ABOUT IT: WE'VE DECRYPTED A PORTION OF THE VOYNICH MANUSCRIPT. THAT'S HUGE.
BUT I'VE BEEN THINKING: ONCE WE TIE IT INTO THE NUMERICAL CRYPTO-GLPYH-- THE CROP CIRCLES--WE SOMEHOW GET A COMPUTER CODE THAT GIVES US SPECIFIC COORDINATES DOWN TO THE SQUARE INCH--
BUT THERE'S MORE. YOU'RE NOT SATISFIED.
YEAH...NO. I MEAN, SURE. I'M JAZZED. WE JUST CONNECTED ABOUT EIGHT DIFFERENT SECRET CONSPIRACY THEORIES AND MADE A WORKING REPLICA OF THE ANTIKYTHERA MECHANISM TO PROVE OUT THE MODEL.
BUT THIS IS...I CAN'T EXPLAIN IT. IT'S INTUITION.
IT'S TOO EASY. THERE'S SOMETHING WE'RE NOT SEEING.

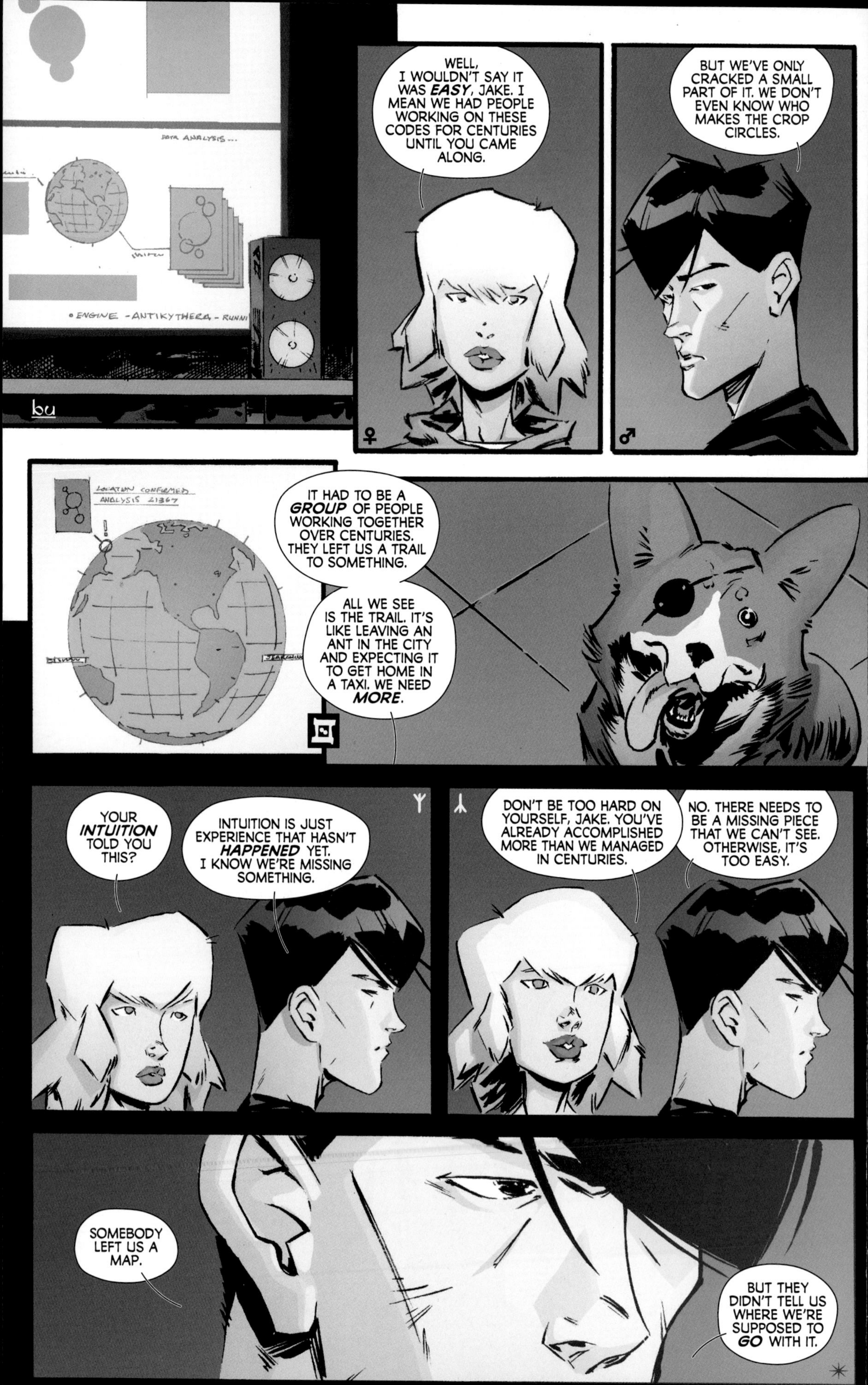
DATA ANALYSIS...
ENGINE -ANTIKYTHERA- RUNNI
WELL, I WOULDN'T SAY IT WAS EASY, JAKE. I MEAN WE HAD PEOPLE WORKING ON THESE CODES FOR CENTURIES UNTIL YOU CAME ALONG.
BUT WE'VE ONLY CRACKED A SMALL PART OF IT. WE DON'T EVEN KNOW WHO MAKES THE CROP CIRCLES.
LOCATION CONFIRMED
ANALYSIS 21367
IT HAD TO BE A GROUP OF PEOPLE WORKING TOGETHER OVER CENTURIES. THEY LEFT US A TRAIL TO SOMETHING.
ALL WE SEE IS THE TRAIL. IT'S LIKE LEAVING AN ANT IN THE CITY AND EXPECTING IT TO GET HOME IN A TAXI. WE NEED MORE.
YOUR INTUITION TOLD YOU THIS?
INTUITION IS JUST EXPERIENCE THAT HASN'T HAPPENED YET. I KNOW WE'RE MISSING SOMETHING.
DON'T BE TOO HARD ON YOURSELF, JAKE. YOU'VE ALREADY ACCOMPLISHED MORE THAN WE MANAGED IN CENTURIES.
NO. THERE NEEDS TO BE A MISSING PIECE THAT WE CAN'T SEE. OTHERWISE, IT'S TOO EASY.
SOMEBODY LEFT US A MAP.
BUT THEY DIDN'T TELL US WHERE WE'RE SUPPOSED TO GO WITH IT.

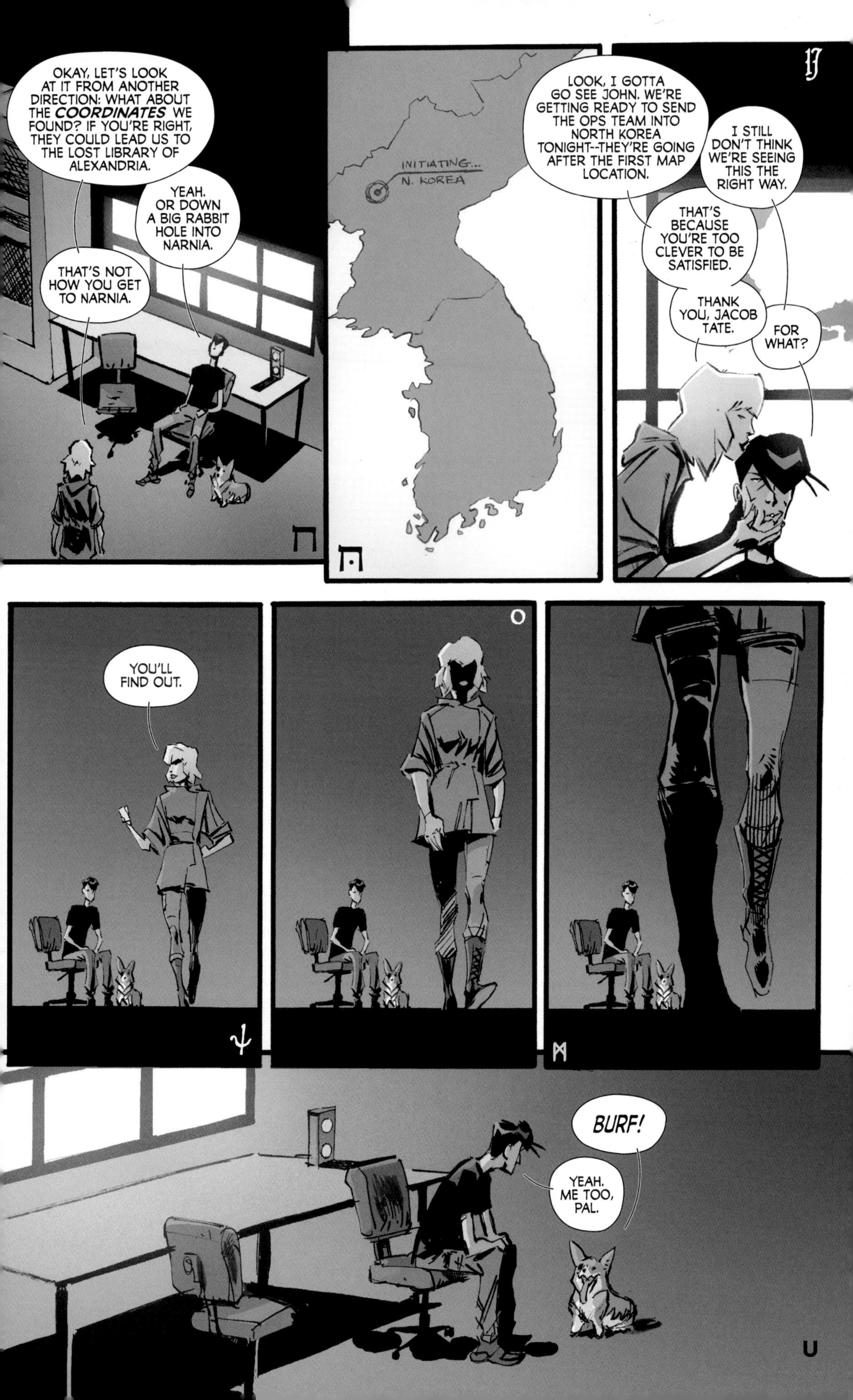
17
OKAY, LET'S LOOK AT IT FROM ANOTHER DIRECTION: WHAT ABOUT THE COORDINATES WE FOUND? IF YOU'RE RIGHT, THEY COULD LEAD US TO THE LOST LIBRARY OF ALEXANDRIA.
YEAH. OR DOWN A BIG RABBIT HOLE INTO NARNIA.
THAT'S NOT HOW YOU GET TO NARNIA.
INITIATING... N. KOREA
LOOK, I GOTTA GO SEE JOHN. WE'RE GETTING READY TO SEND THE OPS TEAM INTO NORTH KOREA TONIGHT--THEY'RE GOING AFTER THE FIRST MAP LOCATION.
I STILL DON'T THINK WE'RE SEEING THIS THE RIGHT WAY.
THAT'S BECAUSE YOU'RE TOO CLEVER TO BE SATISFIED.
THANK YOU, JACOB TATE.
FOR WHAT?
YOU'LL FIND OUT.
BURF!
YEAH. ME TOO, PAL.

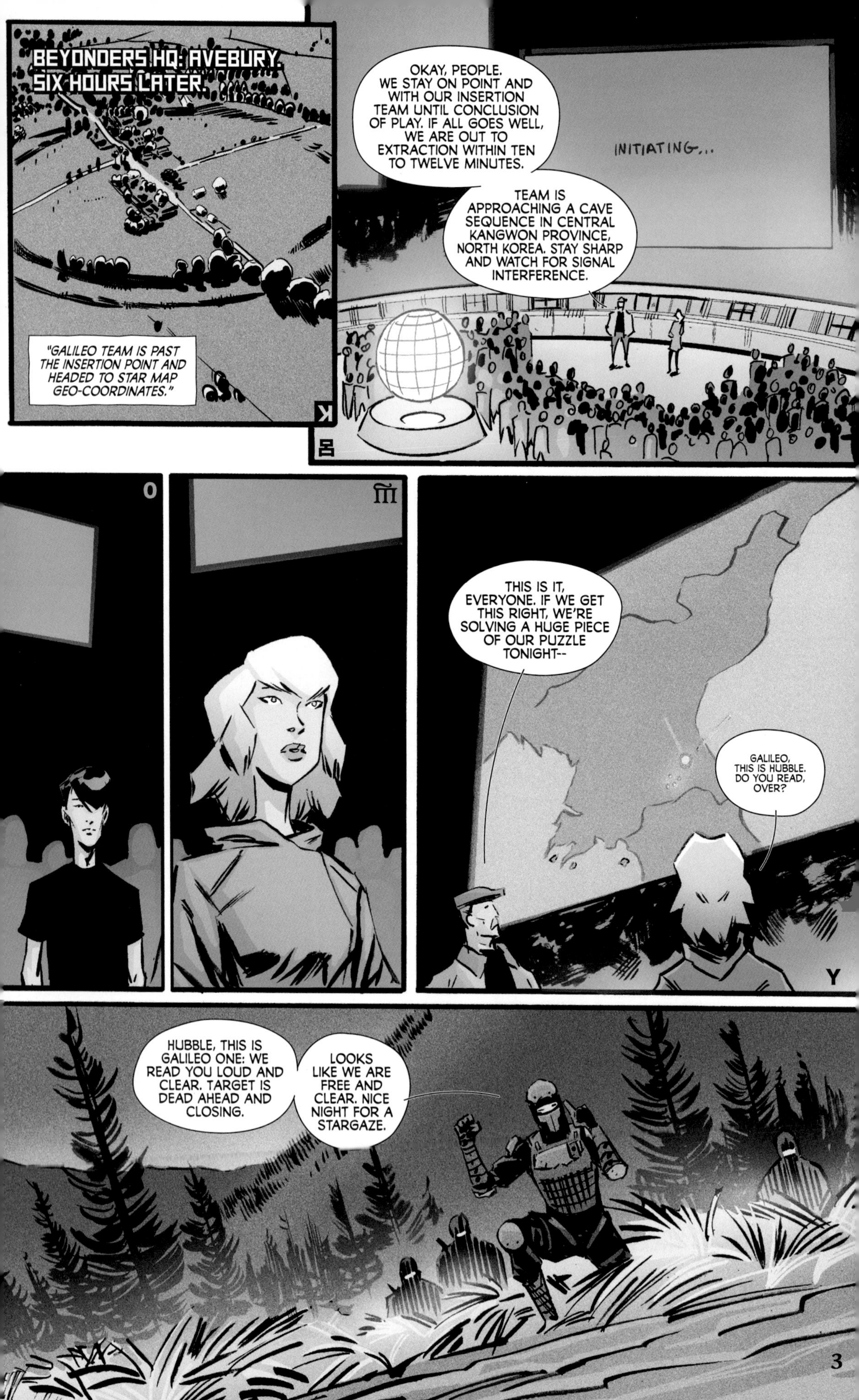
BEYONDERS HQ: AVEBURY. SIX HOURS LATER.
"GALILEO TEAM IS PAST THE INSERTION POINT AND HEADED TO STAR MAP GEO-COORDINATES."
OKAY, PEOPLE. WE STAY ON POINT AND WITH OUR INSERTION TEAM UNTIL CONCLUSION OF PLAY. IF ALL GOES WELL, WE ARE OUT TO EXTRACTION WITHIN TEN TO TWELVE MINUTES.
INITIATING...
TEAM IS APPROACHING A CAVE SEQUENCE IN CENTRAL KANGWON PROVINCE, NORTH KOREA. STAY SHARP AND WATCH FOR SIGNAL INTERFERENCE.
THIS IS IT, EVERYONE. IF WE GET THIS RIGHT, WE'RE SOLVING A HUGE PIECE OF OUR PUZZLE TONIGHT--
GALILEO, THIS IS HUBBLE. DO YOU READ, OVER?
HUBBLE, THIS IS GALILEO ONE: WE READ YOU LOUD AND CLEAR. TARGET IS DEAD AHEAD AND CLOSING.
LOOKS LIKE WE ARE FREE AND CLEAR. NICE NIGHT FOR A STARGAZE.

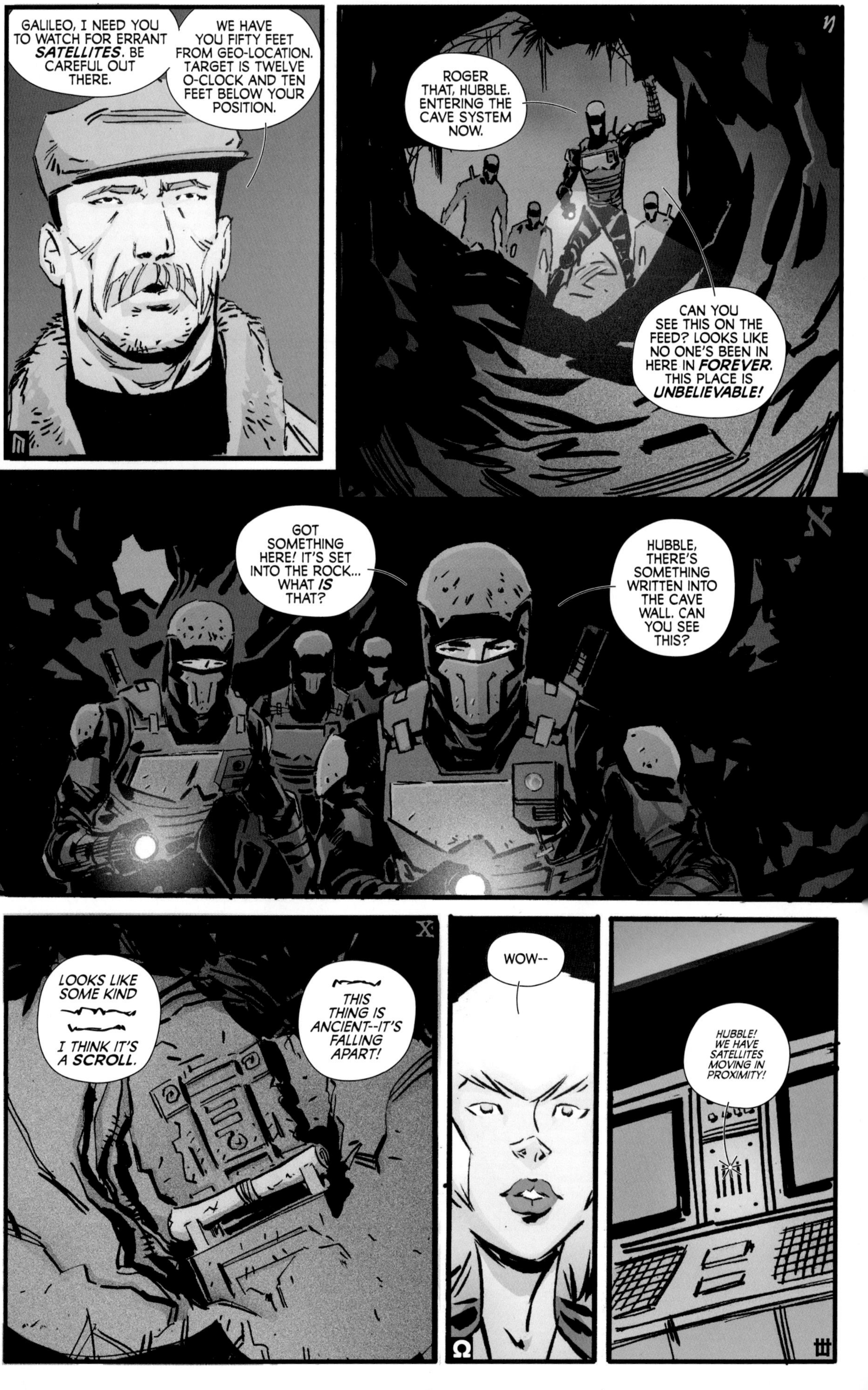
GALILEO, I NEED YOU TO WATCH FOR ERRANT SATELLITES. BE CAREFUL OUT THERE.
WE HAVE YOU FIFTY FEET FROM GEO-LOCATION. TARGET IS TWELVE O-CLOCK AND TEN FEET BELOW YOUR POSITION.
ROGER THAT, HUBBLE. ENTERING THE CAVE SYSTEM NOW.
CAN YOU SEE THIS ON THE FEED? LOOKS LIKE NO ONE'S BEEN IN HERE IN FOREVER. THIS PLACE IS UNBELIEVABLE!
GOT SOMETHING HERE! IT'S SET INTO THE ROCK... WHAT IS THAT?
HUBBLE, THERE'S SOMETHING WRITTEN INTO THE CAVE WALL. CAN YOU SEE THIS?
LOOKS LIKE SOME KIND
I THINK IT'S A SCROLL.
THIS THING IS ANCIENT--IT'S FALLING APART!
WOW--
HUBBLE! WE HAVE SATELLITES MOVING IN PROXIMITY!

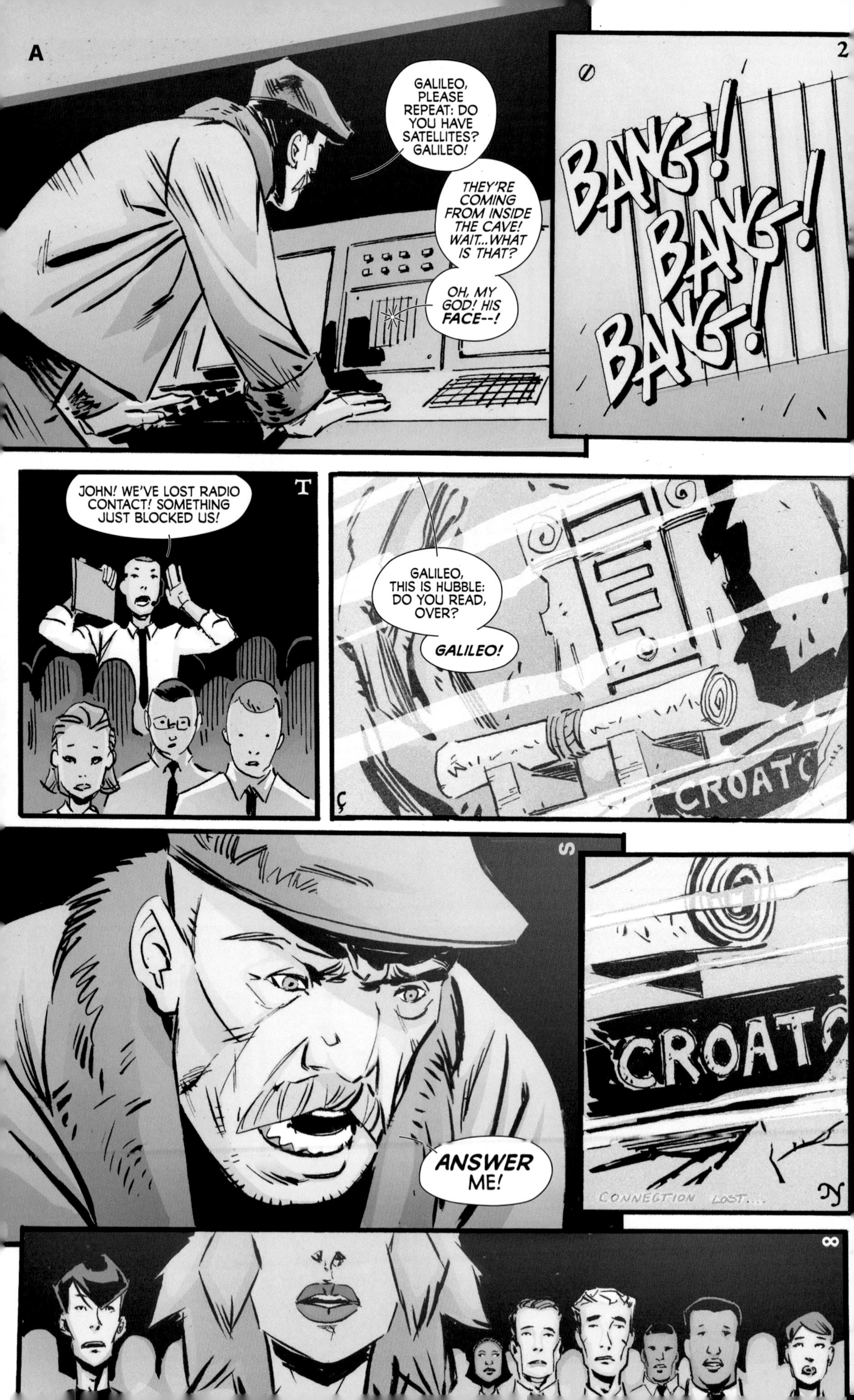
GALILEO, PLEASE REPEAT: DO YOU HAVE SATELLITES? GALILEO!
THEY'RE COMING FROM INSIDE THE CAVE! WAIT...WHAT IS THAT?
OH, MY GOD! HIS FACE--!
BANG! BANG! BANG!
JOHN! WE'VE LOST RADIO CONTACT! SOMETHING JUST BLOCKED US!
GALILEO, THIS IS HUBBLE: DO YOU READ, OVER?
GALILEO!
CROATO
ANSWER ME!
CROATO
CONNECTION LOST....

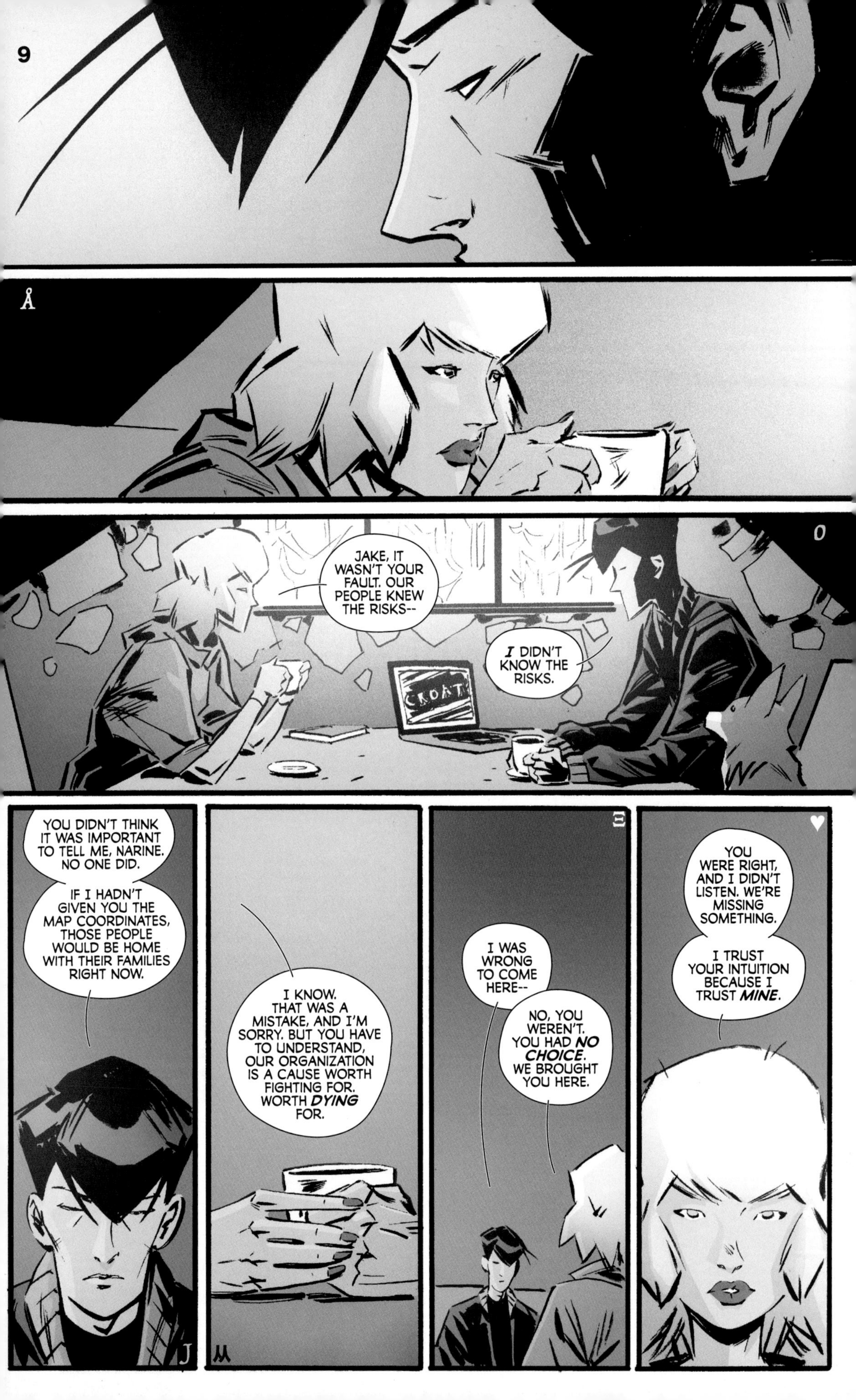
JAKE, IT WASN'T YOUR FAULT. OUR PEOPLE KNEW THE RISKS--
I DIDN'T KNOW THE RISKS.
YOU DIDN'T THINK IT WAS IMPORTANT TO TELL ME, NARINE. NO ONE DID.
IF I HADN'T GIVEN YOU THE MAP COORDINATES, THOSE PEOPLE WOULD BE HOME WITH THEIR FAMILIES RIGHT NOW.
I KNOW. THAT WAS A MISTAKE, AND I'M SORRY. BUT YOU HAVE TO UNDERSTAND, OUR ORGANIZATION IS A CAUSE WORTH FIGHTING FOR. WORTH DYING FOR.
I WAS WRONG TO COME HERE--
NO, YOU WEREN'T. YOU HAD NO CHOICE. WE BROUGHT YOU HERE.
YOU WERE RIGHT, AND I DIDN'T LISTEN. WE'RE MISSING SOMETHING.
I TRUST YOUR INTUITION BECAUSE I TRUST MINE.

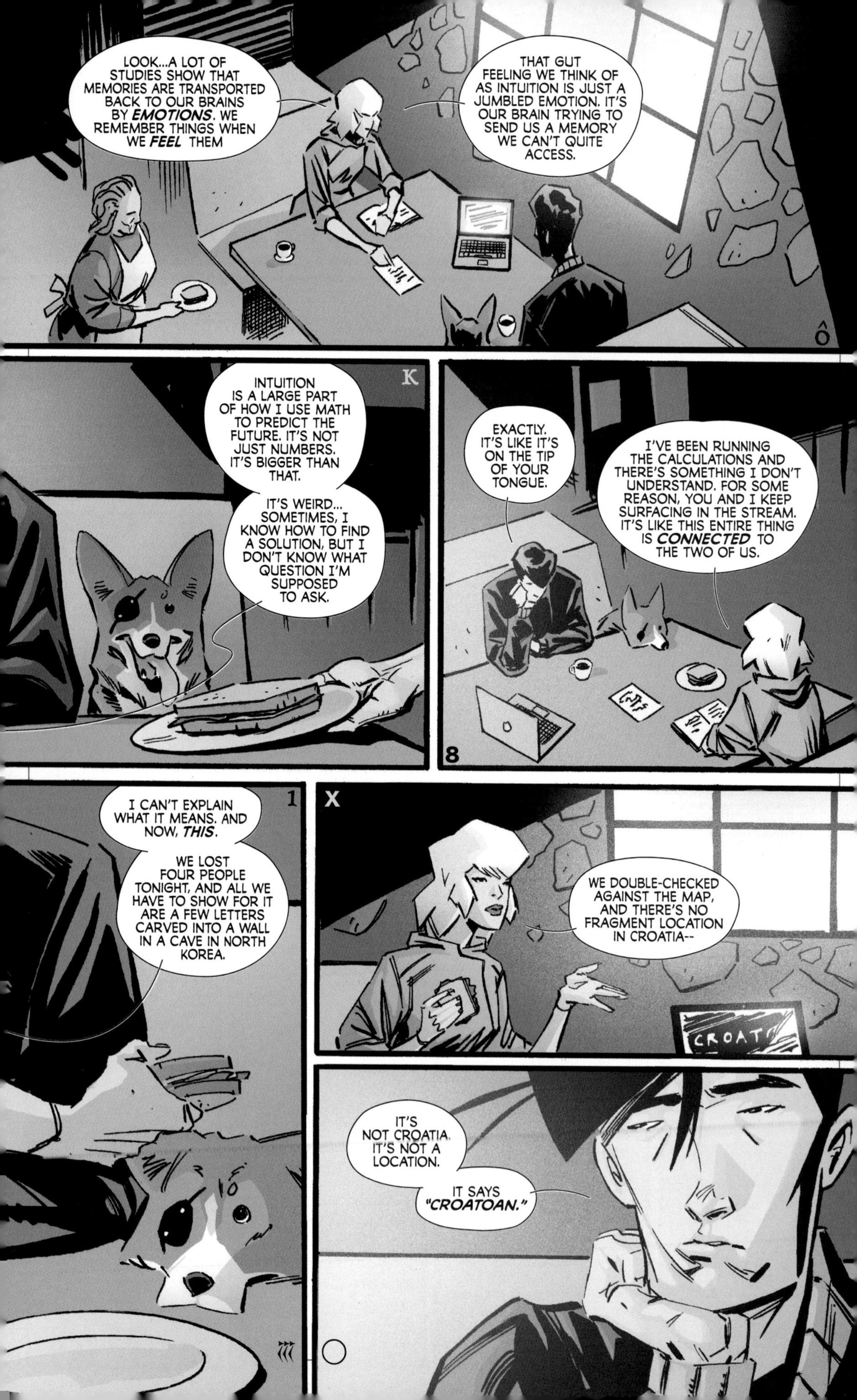
LOOK...A LOT OF STUDIES SHOW THAT MEMORIES ARE TRANSPORTED BACK TO OUR BRAINS BY ***EMOTIONS***. WE REMEMBER THINGS WHEN WE ***FEEL*** THEM
THAT GUT FEELING WE THINK OF AS INTUITION IS JUST A JUMBLED EMOTION. IT'S OUR BRAIN TRYING TO SEND US A MEMORY WE CAN'T QUITE ACCESS.
INTUITION IS A LARGE PART OF HOW I USE MATH TO PREDICT THE FUTURE. IT'S NOT JUST NUMBERS. IT'S BIGGER THAN THAT.
IT'S WEIRD... SOMETIMES, I KNOW HOW TO FIND A SOLUTION, BUT I DON'T KNOW WHAT QUESTION I'M SUPPOSED TO ASK.
EXACTLY. IT'S LIKE IT'S ON THE TIP OF YOUR TONGUE.
I'VE BEEN RUNNING THE CALCULATIONS AND THERE'S SOMETHING I DON'T UNDERSTAND. FOR SOME REASON, YOU AND I KEEP SURFACING IN THE STREAM. IT'S LIKE THIS ENTIRE THING IS ***CONNECTED*** TO THE TWO OF US.
I CAN'T EXPLAIN WHAT IT MEANS. AND NOW, ***THIS***.
WE LOST FOUR PEOPLE TONIGHT, AND ALL WE HAVE TO SHOW FOR IT ARE A FEW LETTERS CARVED INTO A WALL IN A CAVE IN NORTH KOREA.
WE DOUBLE-CHECKED AGAINST THE MAP, AND THERE'S NO FRAGMENT LOCATION IN CROATIA--
CROAT
IT'S NOT CROATIA. IT'S NOT A LOCATION.
IT SAYS ***"CROATOAN."***

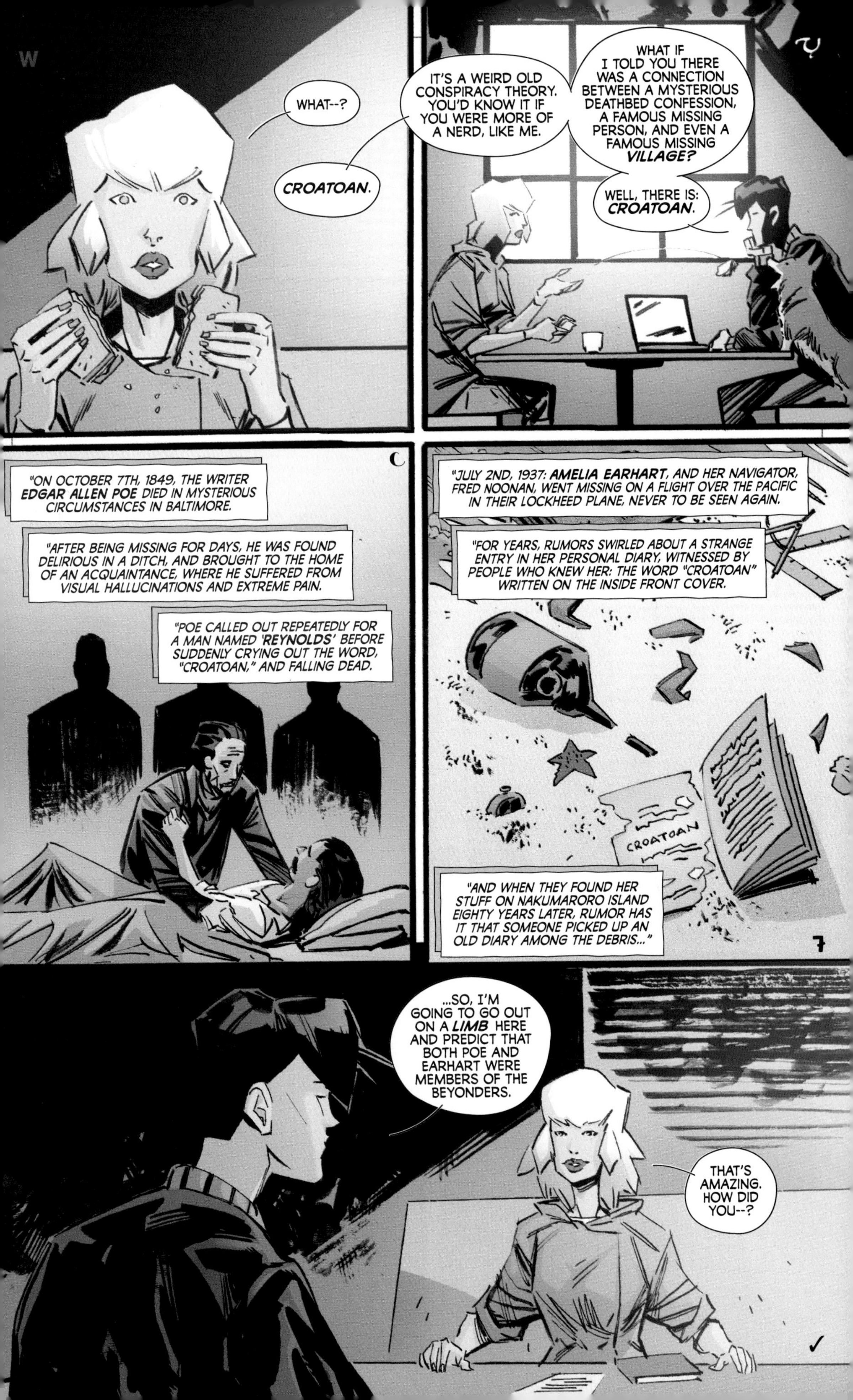
WHAT--?
CROATOAN.
IT'S A WEIRD OLD CONSPIRACY THEORY. YOU'D KNOW IT IF YOU WERE MORE OF A NERD, LIKE ME.
WHAT IF I TOLD YOU THERE WAS A CONNECTION BETWEEN A MYSTERIOUS DEATHBED CONFESSION, A FAMOUS MISSING PERSON, AND EVEN A FAMOUS MISSING VILLAGE?
WELL, THERE IS: CROATOAN.
"ON OCTOBER 7TH, 1849, THE WRITER EDGAR ALLEN POE DIED IN MYSTERIOUS CIRCUMSTANCES IN BALTIMORE.
"AFTER BEING MISSING FOR DAYS, HE WAS FOUND DELIRIOUS IN A DITCH, AND BROUGHT TO THE HOME OF AN ACQUAINTANCE, WHERE HE SUFFERED FROM VISUAL HALLUCINATIONS AND EXTREME PAIN.
"POE CALLED OUT REPEATEDLY FOR A MAN NAMED 'REYNOLDS' BEFORE SUDDENLY CRYING OUT THE WORD, "CROATOAN," AND FALLING DEAD.
"JULY 2ND, 1937: AMELIA EARHART, AND HER NAVIGATOR, FRED NOONAN, WENT MISSING ON A FLIGHT OVER THE PACIFIC IN THEIR LOCKHEED PLANE, NEVER TO BE SEEN AGAIN.
"FOR YEARS, RUMORS SWIRLED ABOUT A STRANGE ENTRY IN HER PERSONAL DIARY, WITNESSED BY PEOPLE WHO KNEW HER: THE WORD "CROATOAN" WRITTEN ON THE INSIDE FRONT COVER.
CROATOAN
"AND WHEN THEY FOUND HER STUFF ON NAKUMARORO ISLAND EIGHTY YEARS LATER, RUMOR HAS IT THAT SOMEONE PICKED UP AN OLD DIARY AMONG THE DEBRIS..."
...SO, I'M GOING TO GO OUT ON A LIMB HERE AND PREDICT THAT BOTH POE AND EARHART WERE MEMBERS OF THE BEYONDERS.
THAT'S AMAZING. HOW DID YOU--?

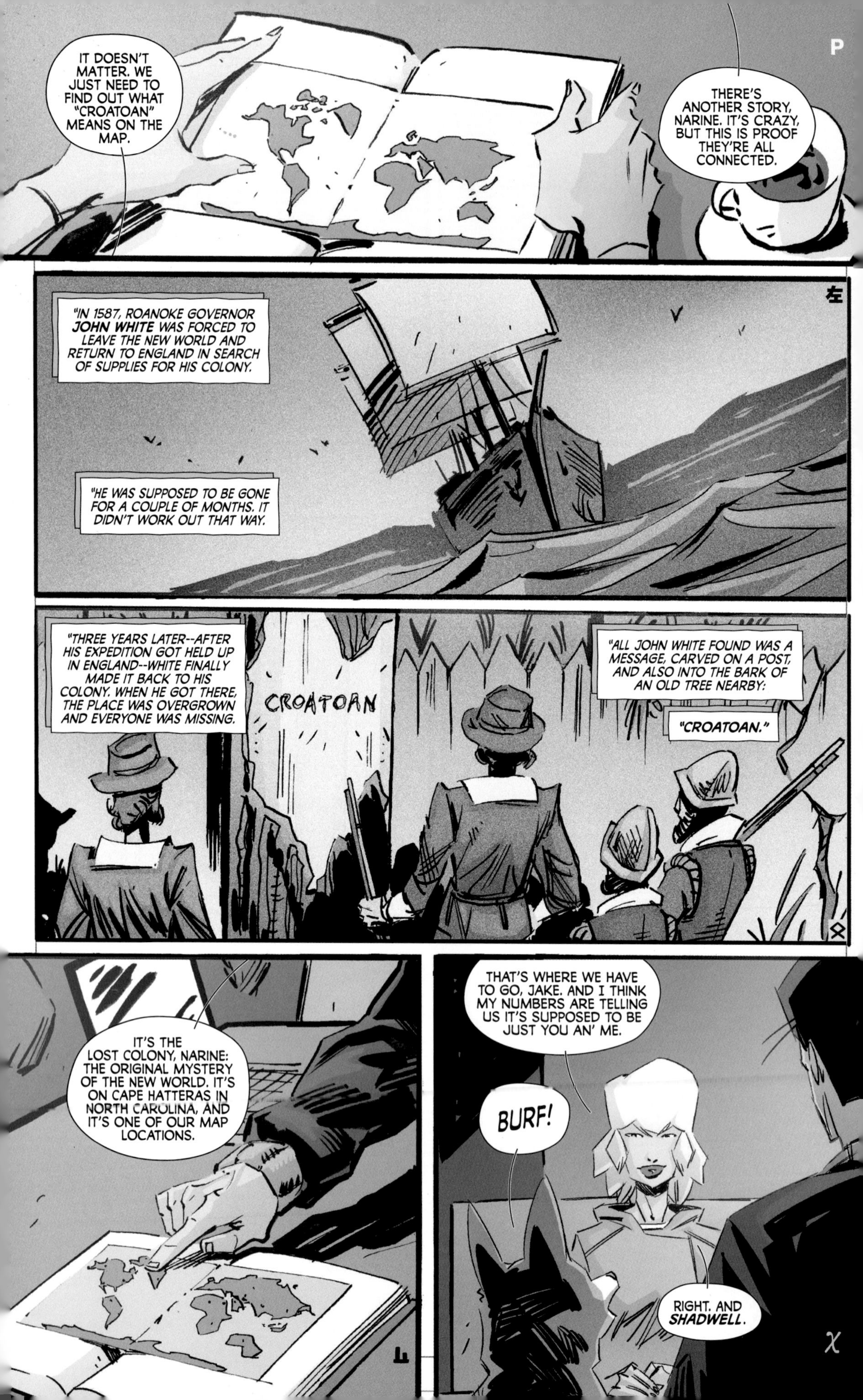
IT DOESN'T MATTER. WE JUST NEED TO FIND OUT WHAT "CROATOAN" MEANS ON THE MAP.
THERE'S ANOTHER STORY, NARINE. IT'S CRAZY, BUT THIS IS PROOF THEY'RE ALL CONNECTED.
"IN 1587, ROANOKE GOVERNOR JOHN WHITE WAS FORCED TO LEAVE THE NEW WORLD AND RETURN TO ENGLAND IN SEARCH OF SUPPLIES FOR HIS COLONY.
"HE WAS SUPPOSED TO BE GONE FOR A COUPLE OF MONTHS. IT DIDN'T WORK OUT THAT WAY.
"THREE YEARS LATER--AFTER HIS EXPEDITION GOT HELD UP IN ENGLAND--WHITE FINALLY MADE IT BACK TO HIS COLONY. WHEN HE GOT THERE, THE PLACE WAS OVERGROWN AND EVERYONE WAS MISSING.
CROATOAN
"ALL JOHN WHITE FOUND WAS A MESSAGE, CARVED ON A POST, AND ALSO INTO THE BARK OF AN OLD TREE NEARBY:
"CROATOAN."
IT'S THE LOST COLONY, NARINE: THE ORIGINAL MYSTERY OF THE NEW WORLD. IT'S ON CAPE HATTERAS IN NORTH CAROLINA, AND IT'S ONE OF OUR MAP LOCATIONS.
THAT'S WHERE WE HAVE TO GO, JAKE. AND I THINK MY NUMBERS ARE TELLING US IT'S SUPPOSED TO BE JUST YOU AN' ME.
BURF!
RIGHT. AND SHADWELL.

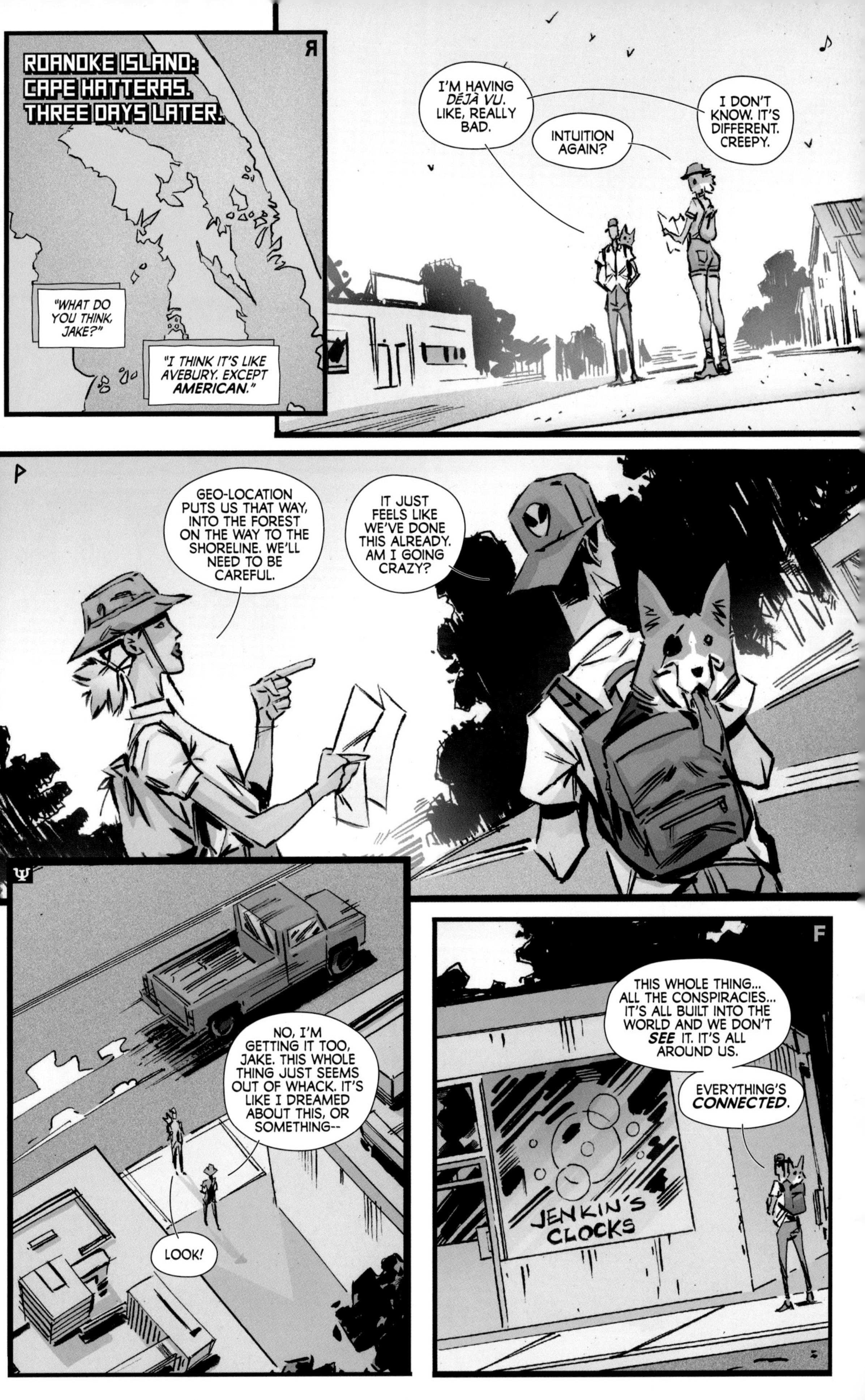
R
ROANOKE ISLAND: CAPE HATTERAS. THREE DAYS LATER.
"WHAT DO YOU THINK, JAKE?"
"I THINK IT'S LIKE AVEBURY. EXCEPT **AMERICAN**."
I'M HAVING *DÉJÀ VU*. LIKE, REALLY BAD.
INTUITION AGAIN?
I DON'T KNOW. IT'S DIFFERENT. CREEPY.
P
GEO-LOCATION PUTS US THAT WAY, INTO THE FOREST ON THE WAY TO THE SHORELINE. WE'LL NEED TO BE CAREFUL.
IT JUST FEELS LIKE WE'VE DONE THIS ALREADY. AM I GOING CRAZY?
Ψ
NO, I'M GETTING IT TOO, JAKE. THIS WHOLE THING JUST SEEMS OUT OF WHACK. IT'S LIKE I DREAMED ABOUT THIS, OR SOMETHING--
LOOK!
F
THIS WHOLE THING... ALL THE CONSPIRACIES... IT'S ALL BUILT INTO THE WORLD AND WE DON'T ***SEE*** IT. IT'S ALL AROUND US.
EVERYTHING'S ***CONNECTED***.
JENKIN'S CLOCKS

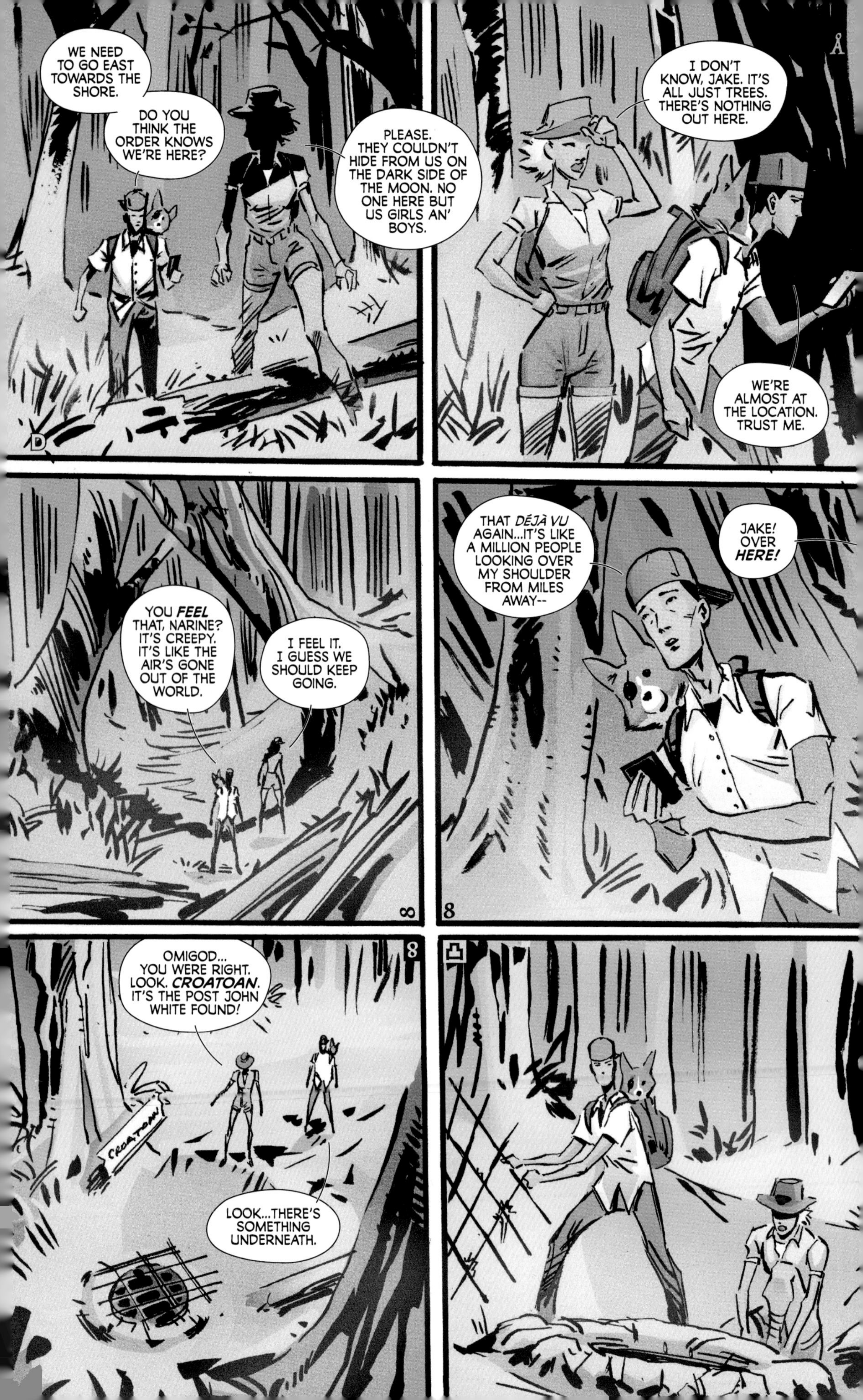

WE NEED TO GO EAST TOWARDS THE SHORE.
DO YOU THINK THE ORDER KNOWS WE'RE HERE?
PLEASE. THEY COULDN'T HIDE FROM US ON THE DARK SIDE OF THE MOON. NO ONE HERE BUT US GIRLS AN' BOYS.
I DON'T KNOW, JAKE. IT'S ALL JUST TREES. THERE'S NOTHING OUT HERE.
WE'RE ALMOST AT THE LOCATION. TRUST ME.
YOU *FEEL* THAT, NARINE? IT'S CREEPY. IT'S LIKE THE AIR'S GONE OUT OF THE WORLD.
I FEEL IT. I GUESS WE SHOULD KEEP GOING.
THAT *DÉJÀ VU* AGAIN...IT'S LIKE A MILLION PEOPLE LOOKING OVER MY SHOULDER FROM MILES AWAY--
JAKE! OVER ***HERE!***
OMIGOD... YOU WERE RIGHT. LOOK. ***CROATOAN***. IT'S THE POST JOHN WHITE FOUND!
CROATOAN
LOOK...THERE'S SOMETHING UNDERNEATH.

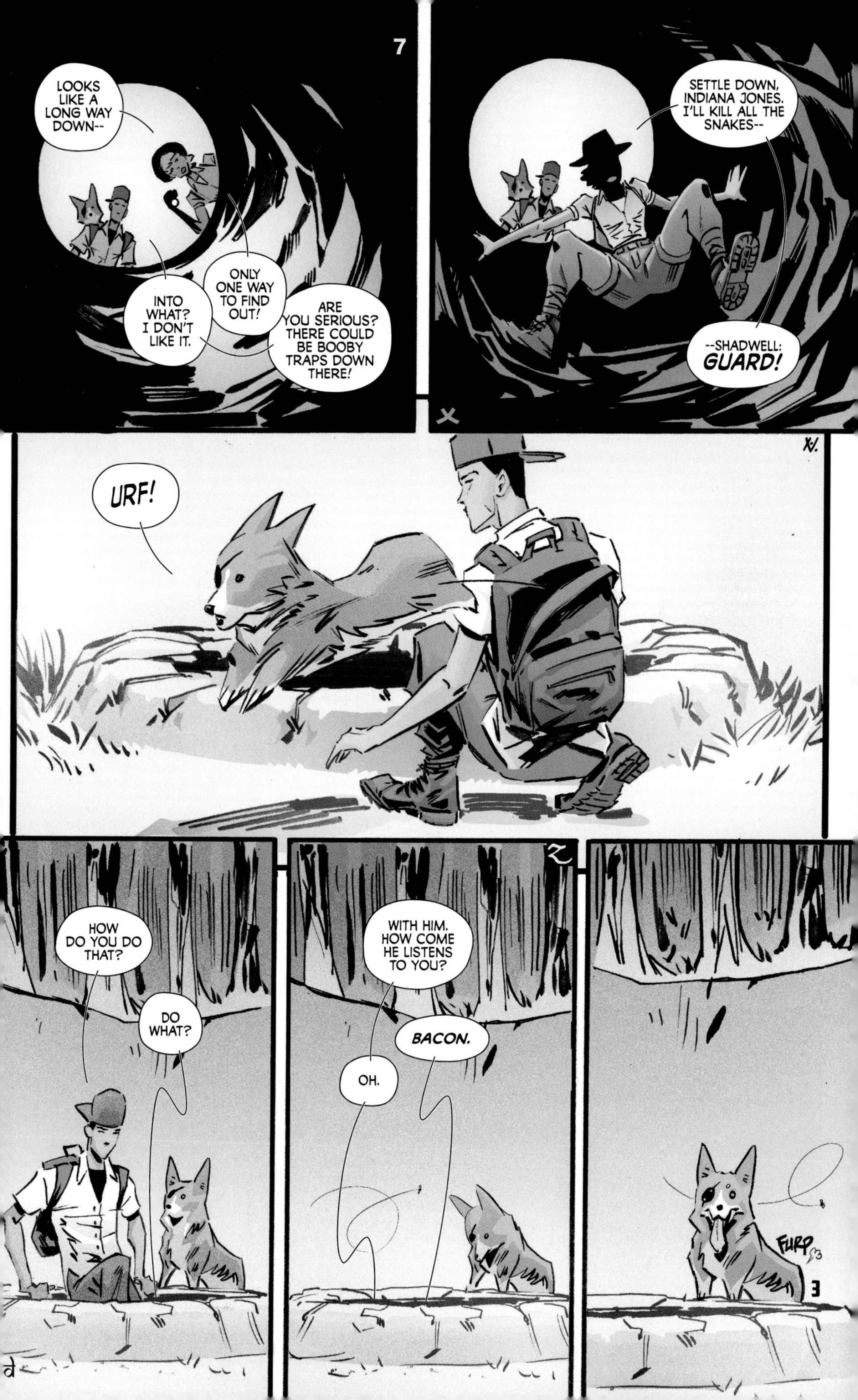
LOOKS LIKE A LONG WAY DOWN--
INTO WHAT? I DON'T LIKE IT.
ONLY ONE WAY TO FIND OUT!
ARE YOU SERIOUS? THERE COULD BE BOOBY TRAPS DOWN THERE!
SETTLE DOWN, INDIANA JONES. I'LL KILL ALL THE SNAKES--
--SHADWELL: GUARD!
URF!
HOW DO YOU DO THAT?
DO WHAT?
WITH HIM. HOW COME HE LISTENS TO YOU?
BACON.
OH.

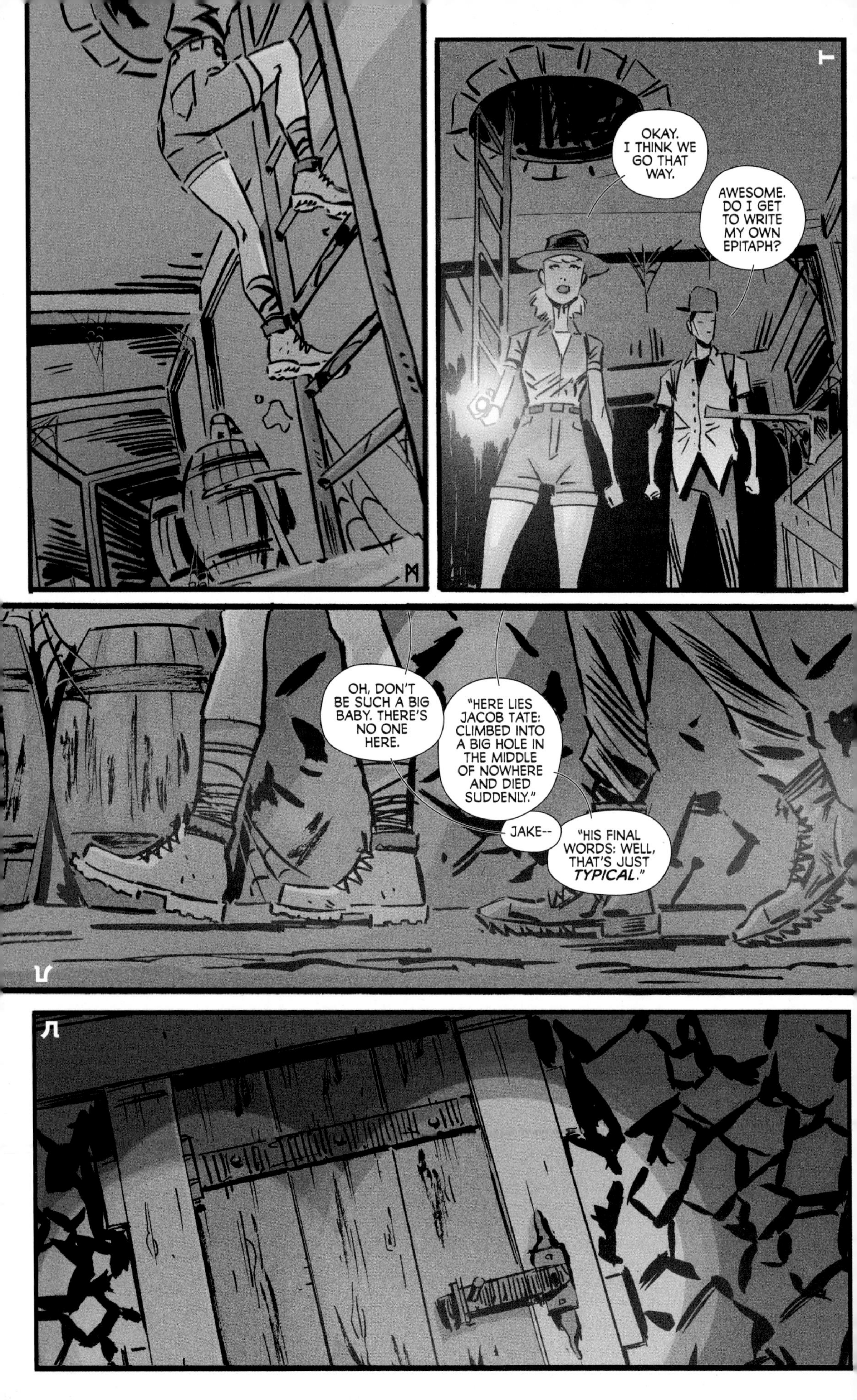
OKAY. I THINK WE GO THAT WAY.
AWESOME. DO I GET TO WRITE MY OWN EPITAPH?
OH, DON'T BE SUCH A BIG BABY. THERE'S NO ONE HERE.
"HERE LIES JACOB TATE: CLIMBED INTO A BIG HOLE IN THE MIDDLE OF NOWHERE AND DIED SUDDENLY."
JAKE--
"HIS FINAL WORDS: WELL, THAT'S JUST *TYPICAL*."

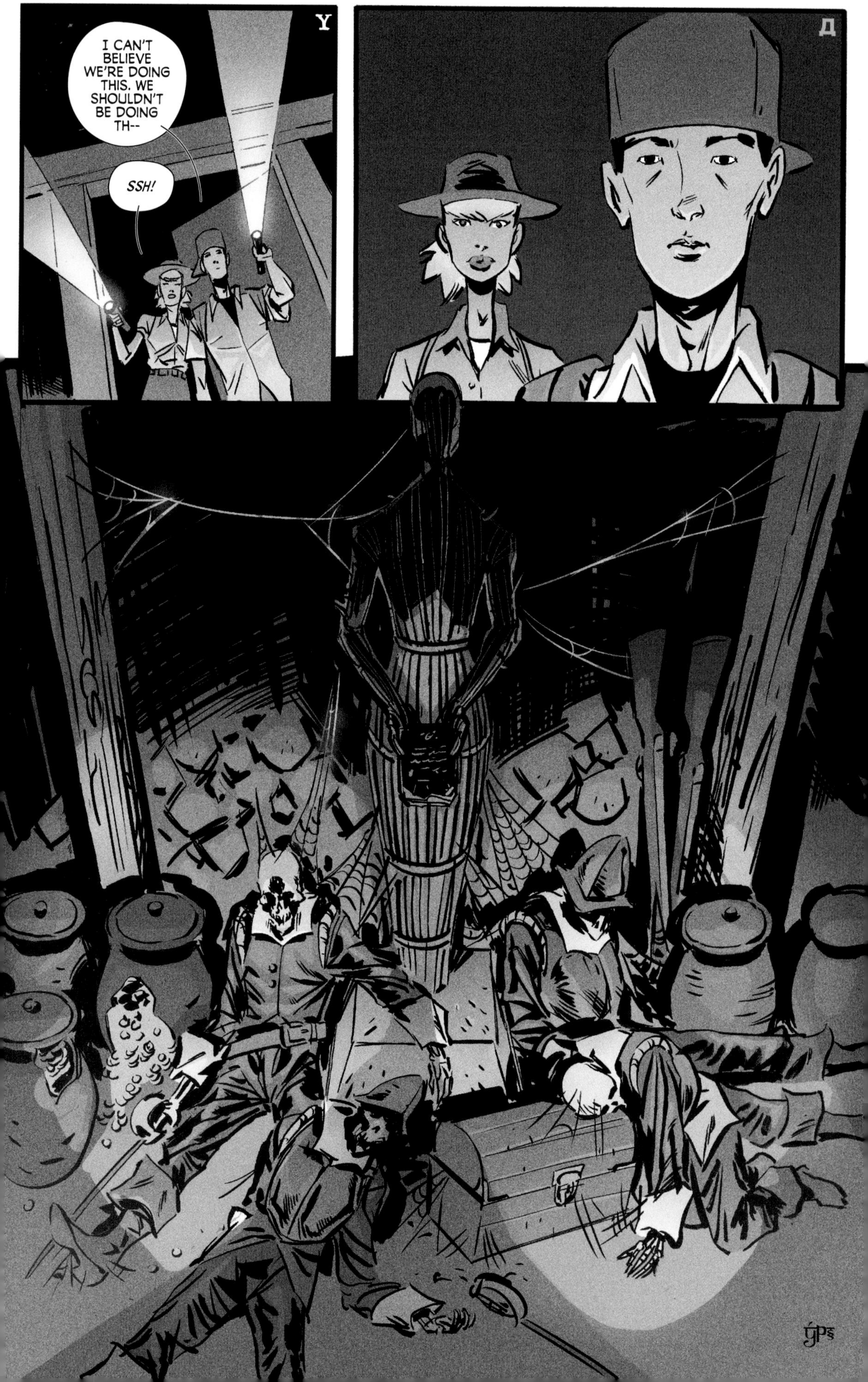
I CAN'T BELIEVE WE'RE DOING THIS. WE SHOULDN'T BE DOING TH--
SSH!

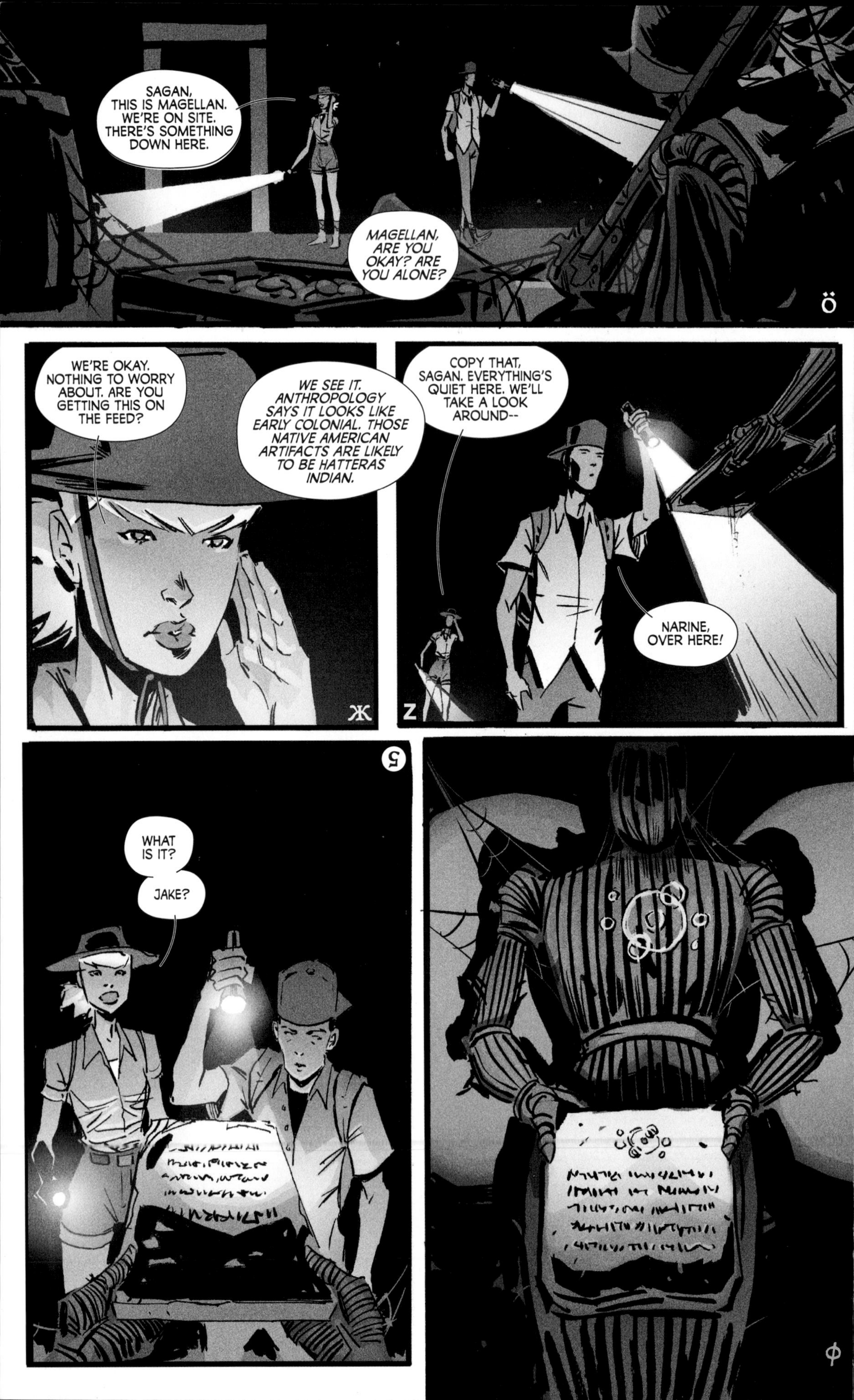
SAGAN, THIS IS MAGELLAN. WE'RE ON SITE. THERE'S SOMETHING DOWN HERE.
MAGELLAN, ARE YOU OKAY? ARE YOU ALONE?
WE'RE OKAY. NOTHING TO WORRY ABOUT. ARE YOU GETTING THIS ON THE FEED?
WE SEE IT. ANTHROPOLOGY SAYS IT LOOKS LIKE EARLY COLONIAL. THOSE NATIVE AMERICAN ARTIFACTS ARE LIKELY TO BE HATTERAS INDIAN.
COPY THAT, SAGAN. EVERYTHING'S QUIET HERE. WE'LL TAKE A LOOK AROUND--
NARINE, OVER HERE!
WHAT IS IT?
JAKE?

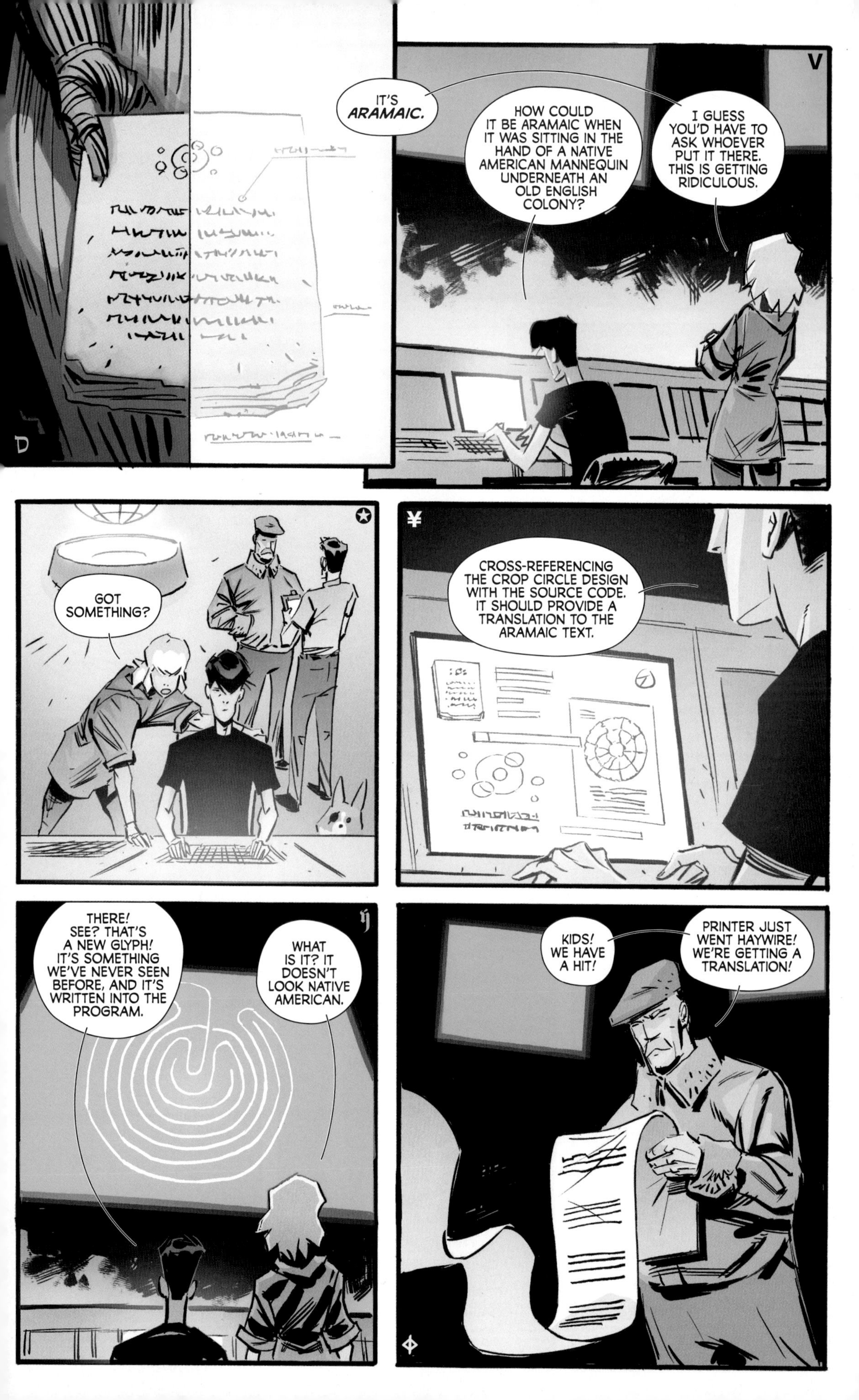
IT'S ARAMAIC.
HOW COULD IT BE ARAMAIC WHEN IT WAS SITTING IN THE HAND OF A NATIVE AMERICAN MANNEQUIN UNDERNEATH AN OLD ENGLISH COLONY?
I GUESS YOU'D HAVE TO ASK WHOEVER PUT IT THERE. THIS IS GETTING RIDICULOUS.
GOT SOMETHING?
CROSS-REFERENCING THE CROP CIRCLE DESIGN WITH THE SOURCE CODE. IT SHOULD PROVIDE A TRANSLATION TO THE ARAMAIC TEXT.
THERE! SEE? THAT'S A NEW GLYPH! IT'S SOMETHING WE'VE NEVER SEEN BEFORE, AND IT'S WRITTEN INTO THE PROGRAM.
WHAT IS IT? IT DOESN'T LOOK NATIVE AMERICAN.
KIDS! WE HAVE A HIT!
PRINTER JUST WENT HAYWIRE! WE'RE GETTING A TRANSLATION!

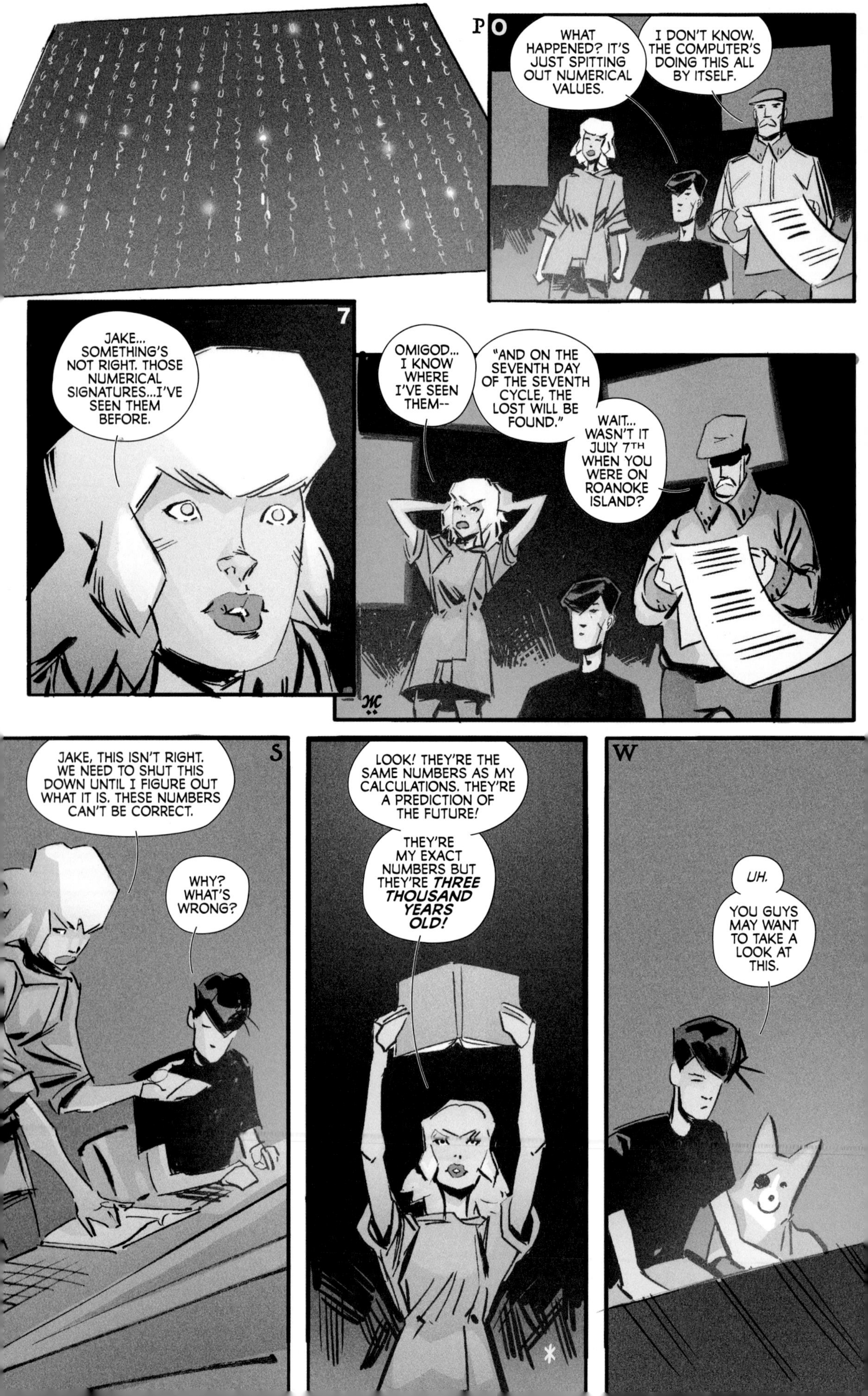
P O
WHAT HAPPENED? IT'S JUST SPITTING OUT NUMERICAL VALUES.
I DON'T KNOW. THE COMPUTER'S DOING THIS ALL BY ITSELF.
7
JAKE... SOMETHING'S NOT RIGHT. THOSE NUMERICAL SIGNATURES...I'VE SEEN THEM BEFORE.
OMIGOD... I KNOW WHERE I'VE SEEN THEM--
"AND ON THE SEVENTH DAY OF THE SEVENTH CYCLE, THE LOST WILL BE FOUND."
WAIT... WASN'T IT JULY 7TH WHEN YOU WERE ON ROANOKE ISLAND?
S
JAKE, THIS ISN'T RIGHT. WE NEED TO SHUT THIS DOWN UNTIL I FIGURE OUT WHAT IT IS. THESE NUMBERS CAN'T BE CORRECT.
WHY? WHAT'S WRONG?
LOOK! THEY'RE THE SAME NUMBERS AS MY CALCULATIONS. THEY'RE A PREDICTION OF THE FUTURE!
THEY'RE MY EXACT NUMBERS BUT THEY'RE THREE THOUSAND YEARS OLD!
W
UH.
YOU GUYS MAY WANT TO TAKE A LOOK AT THIS.

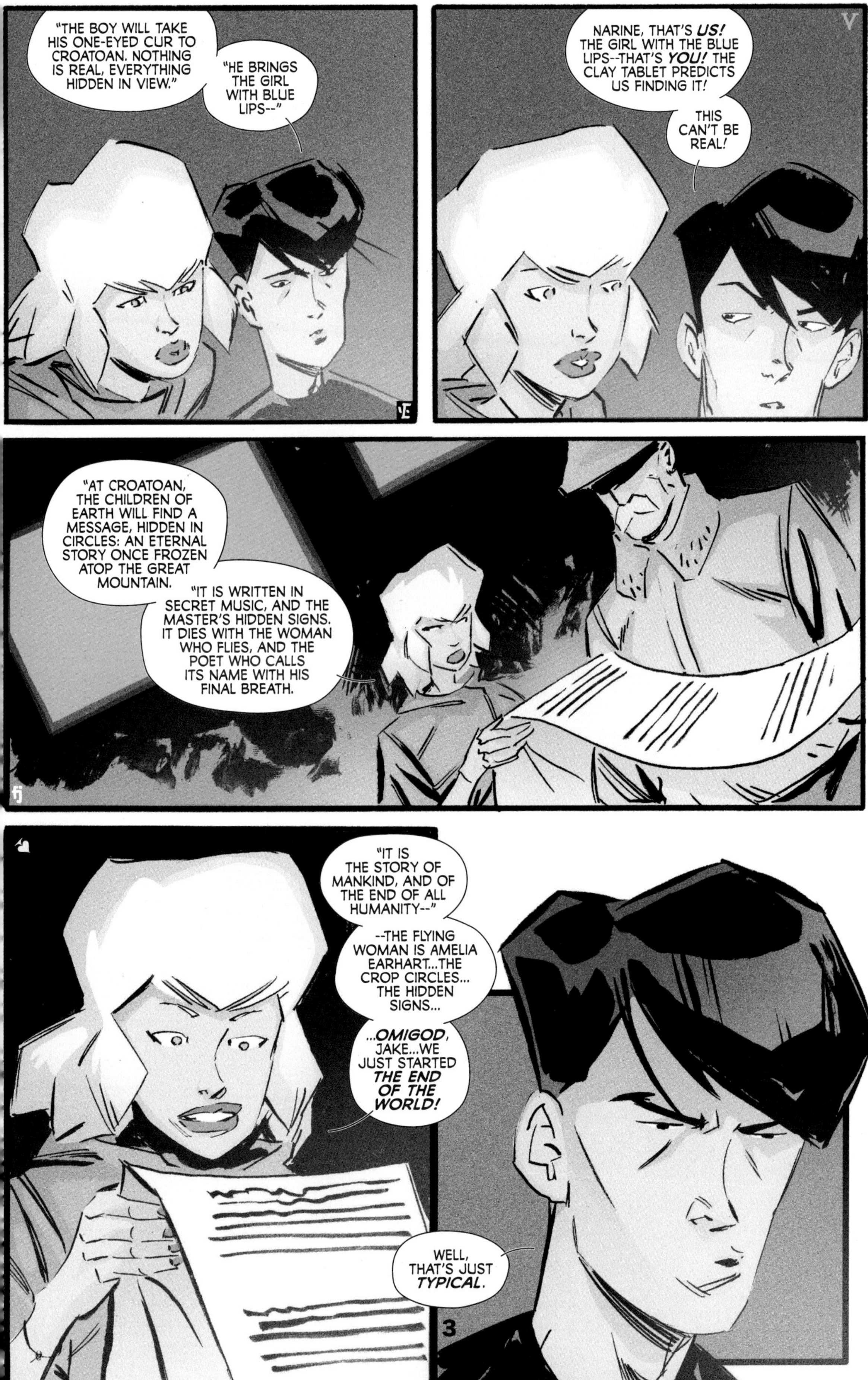
"THE BOY WILL TAKE HIS ONE-EYED CUR TO CROATOAN. NOTHING IS REAL, EVERYTHING HIDDEN IN VIEW."
"HE BRINGS THE GIRL WITH BLUE LIPS--"
NARINE, THAT'S ***US!*** THE GIRL WITH THE BLUE LIPS--THAT'S ***YOU!*** THE CLAY TABLET PREDICTS US FINDING IT!
THIS CAN'T BE REAL!
"AT CROATOAN, THE CHILDREN OF EARTH WILL FIND A MESSAGE, HIDDEN IN CIRCLES: AN ETERNAL STORY ONCE FROZEN ATOP THE GREAT MOUNTAIN.
"IT IS WRITTEN IN SECRET MUSIC, AND THE MASTER'S HIDDEN SIGNS. IT DIES WITH THE WOMAN WHO FLIES, AND THE POET WHO CALLS ITS NAME WITH HIS FINAL BREATH.
"IT IS THE STORY OF MANKIND, AND OF THE END OF ALL HUMANITY--"
--THE FLYING WOMAN IS AMELIA EARHART...THE CROP CIRCLES... THE HIDDEN SIGNS...
...***OMIGOD***, JAKE...WE JUST STARTED ***THE END OF THE WORLD!***
WELL, THAT'S JUST ***TYPICAL***.

4

EVERYTHING BLOWS UP

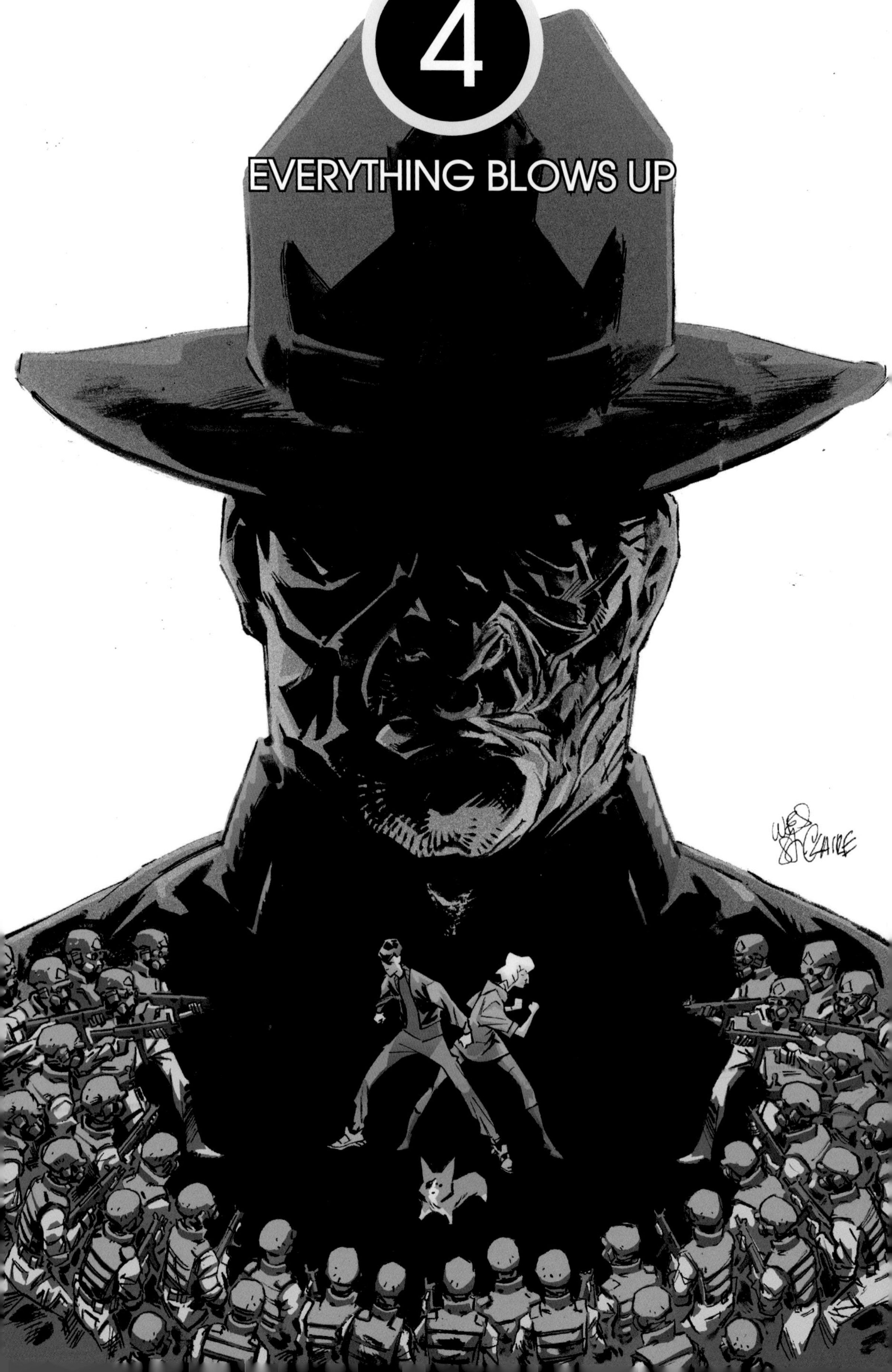

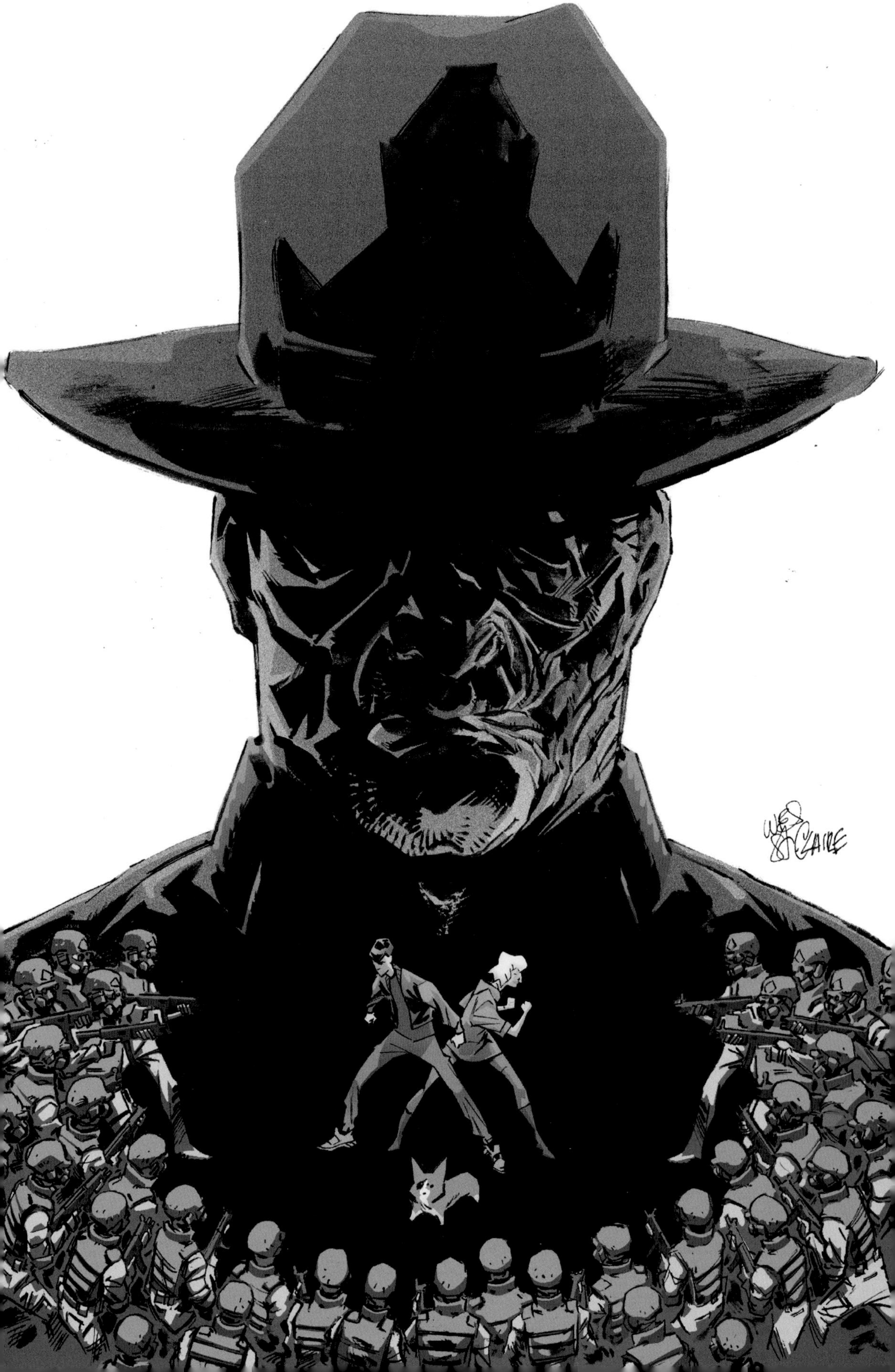

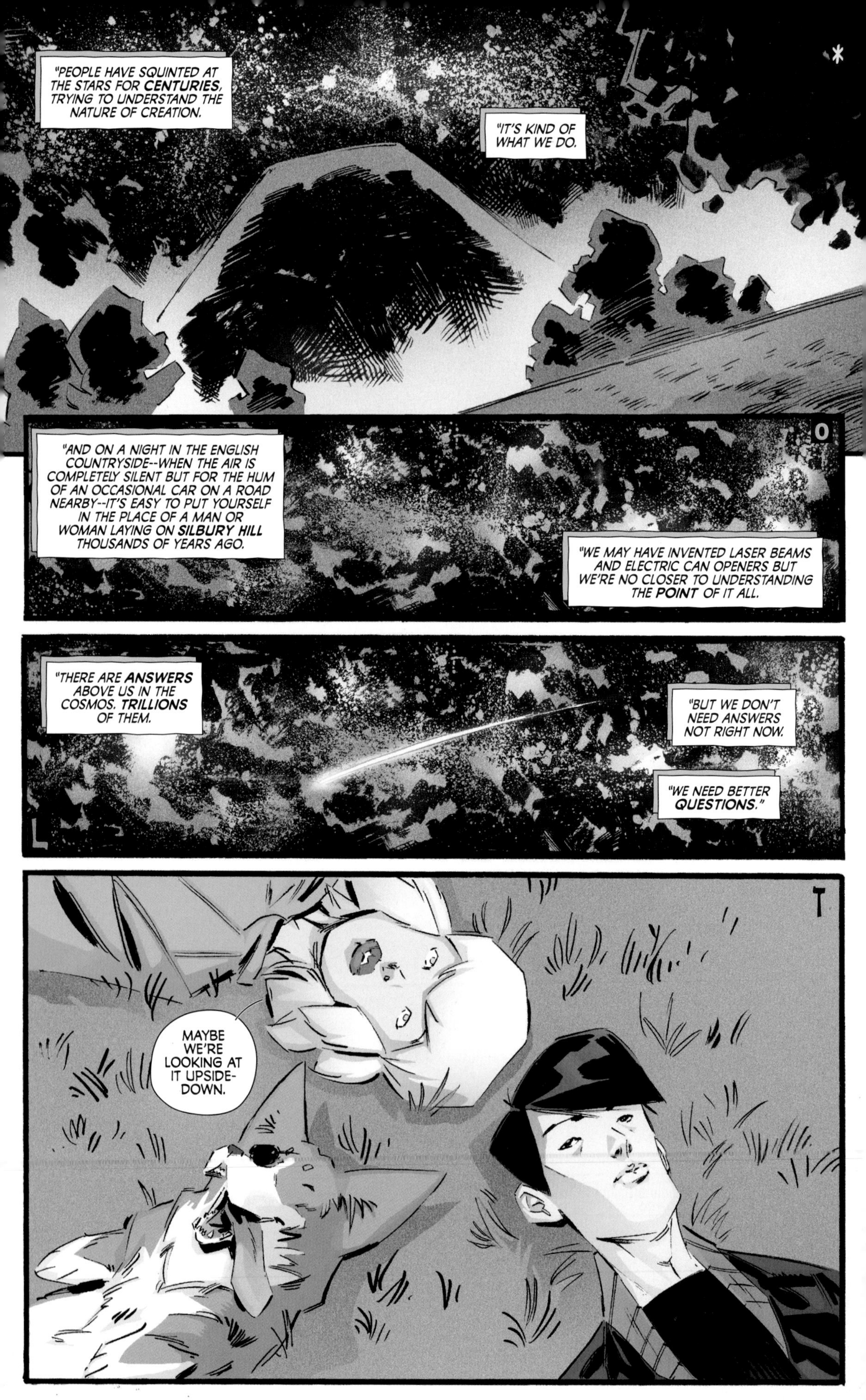
"PEOPLE HAVE SQUINTED AT THE STARS FOR CENTURIES, TRYING TO UNDERSTAND THE NATURE OF CREATION.
"IT'S KIND OF WHAT WE DO.
"AND ON A NIGHT IN THE ENGLISH COUNTRYSIDE--WHEN THE AIR IS COMPLETELY SILENT BUT FOR THE HUM OF AN OCCASIONAL CAR ON A ROAD NEARBY--IT'S EASY TO PUT YOURSELF IN THE PLACE OF A MAN OR WOMAN LAYING ON SILBURY HILL THOUSANDS OF YEARS AGO.
"WE MAY HAVE INVENTED LASER BEAMS AND ELECTRIC CAN OPENERS BUT WE'RE NO CLOSER TO UNDERSTANDING THE POINT OF IT ALL.
"THERE ARE ANSWERS ABOVE US IN THE COSMOS. TRILLIONS OF THEM.
"BUT WE DON'T NEED ANSWERS NOT RIGHT NOW.
"WE NEED BETTER QUESTIONS."
MAYBE WE'RE LOOKING AT IT UPSIDE-DOWN.

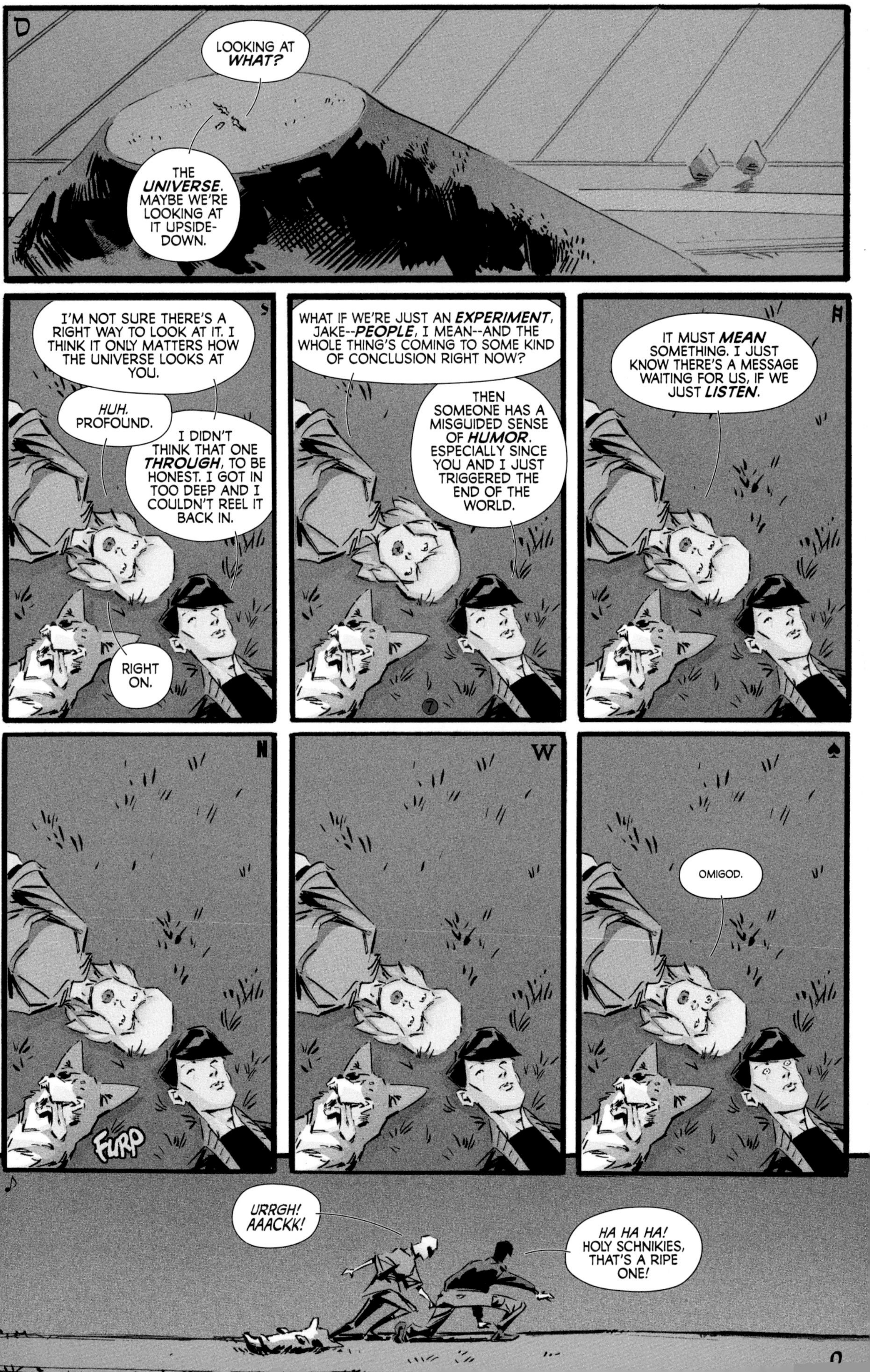
LOOKING AT WHAT?
THE UNIVERSE. MAYBE WE'RE LOOKING AT IT UPSIDE-DOWN.
I'M NOT SURE THERE'S A RIGHT WAY TO LOOK AT IT. I THINK IT ONLY MATTERS HOW THE UNIVERSE LOOKS AT YOU.
HUH. PROFOUND.
I DIDN'T THINK THAT ONE THROUGH, TO BE HONEST. I GOT IN TOO DEEP AND I COULDN'T REEL IT BACK IN.
RIGHT ON.
WHAT IF WE'RE JUST AN EXPERIMENT, JAKE--PEOPLE, I MEAN--AND THE WHOLE THING'S COMING TO SOME KIND OF CONCLUSION RIGHT NOW?
THEN SOMEONE HAS A MISGUIDED SENSE OF HUMOR. ESPECIALLY SINCE YOU AND I JUST TRIGGERED THE END OF THE WORLD.
IT MUST MEAN SOMETHING. I JUST KNOW THERE'S A MESSAGE WAITING FOR US, IF WE JUST LISTEN.
FURP
OMIGOD.
URRGH! AAACKK!
HA HA HA! HOLY SCHNIKIES, THAT'S A RIPE ONE!

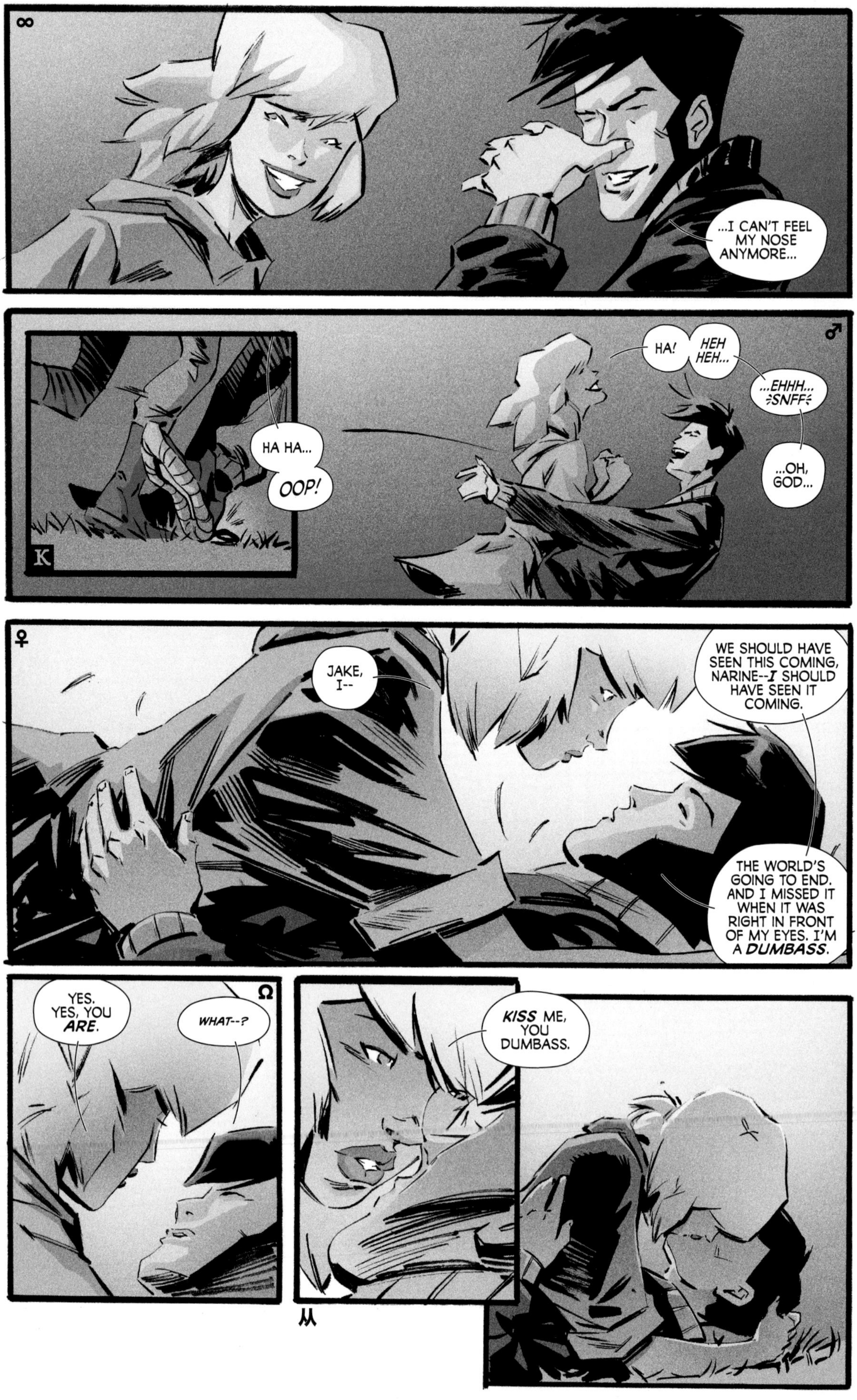
...I CAN'T FEEL MY NOSE ANYMORE...
HA HA... OOP!
HA!
HEH HEH...
...EHHH... SNFF
...OH, GOD...
JAKE, I--
WE SHOULD HAVE SEEN THIS COMING, NARINE--I SHOULD HAVE SEEN IT COMING.
THE WORLD'S GOING TO END. AND I MISSED IT WHEN IT WAS RIGHT IN FRONT OF MY EYES. I'M A DUMBASS.
YES. YES, YOU ARE.
WHAT--?
KISS ME, YOU DUMBASS.

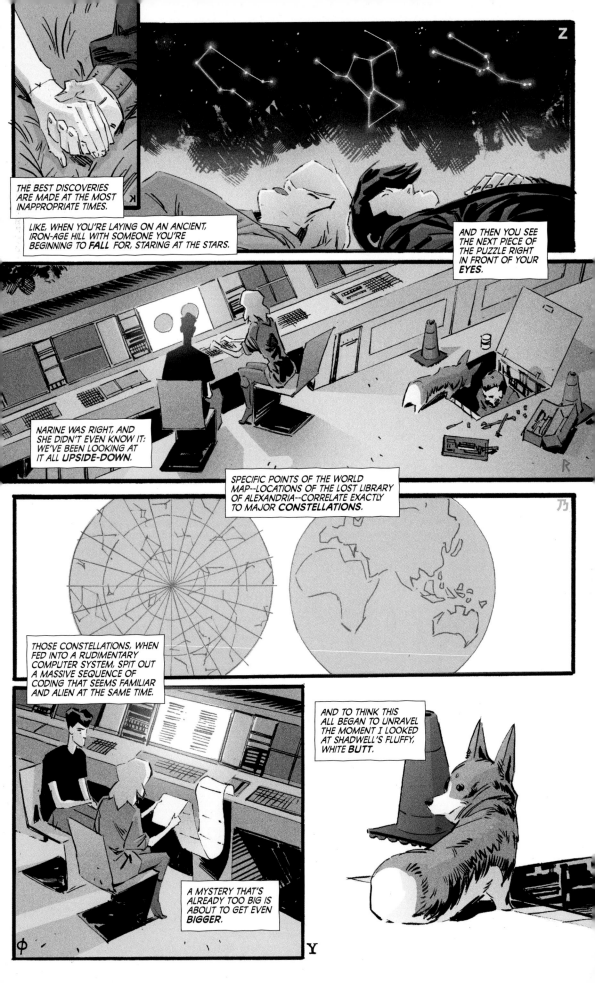

THE BEST DISCOVERIES ARE MADE AT THE MOST INAPPROPRIATE TIMES.

LIKE, WHEN YOU'RE LAYING ON AN ANCIENT, IRON-AGE HILL WITH SOMEONE YOU'RE BEGINNING TO **FALL** FOR, STARING AT THE STARS.

AND THEN YOU SEE THE NEXT PIECE OF THE PUZZLE RIGHT IN FRONT OF YOUR **EYES**.

NARINE WAS RIGHT, AND SHE DIDN'T EVEN KNOW IT: WE'VE BEEN LOOKING AT IT ALL **UPSIDE-DOWN**.

SPECIFIC POINTS OF THE WORLD MAP--LOCATIONS OF THE LOST LIBRARY OF ALEXANDRIA--CORRELATE EXACTLY TO MAJOR **CONSTELLATIONS**.

THOSE CONSTELLATIONS, WHEN FED INTO A RUDIMENTARY COMPUTER SYSTEM, SPIT OUT A MASSIVE SEQUENCE OF CODING THAT SEEMS FAMILIAR AND ALIEN AT THE SAME TIME.

AND TO THINK THIS ALL BEGAN TO UNRAVEL THE MOMENT I LOOKED AT SHADWELL'S FLUFFY, WHITE **BUTT**.

A MYSTERY THAT'S ALREADY TOO BIG IS ABOUT TO GET EVEN **BIGGER**.

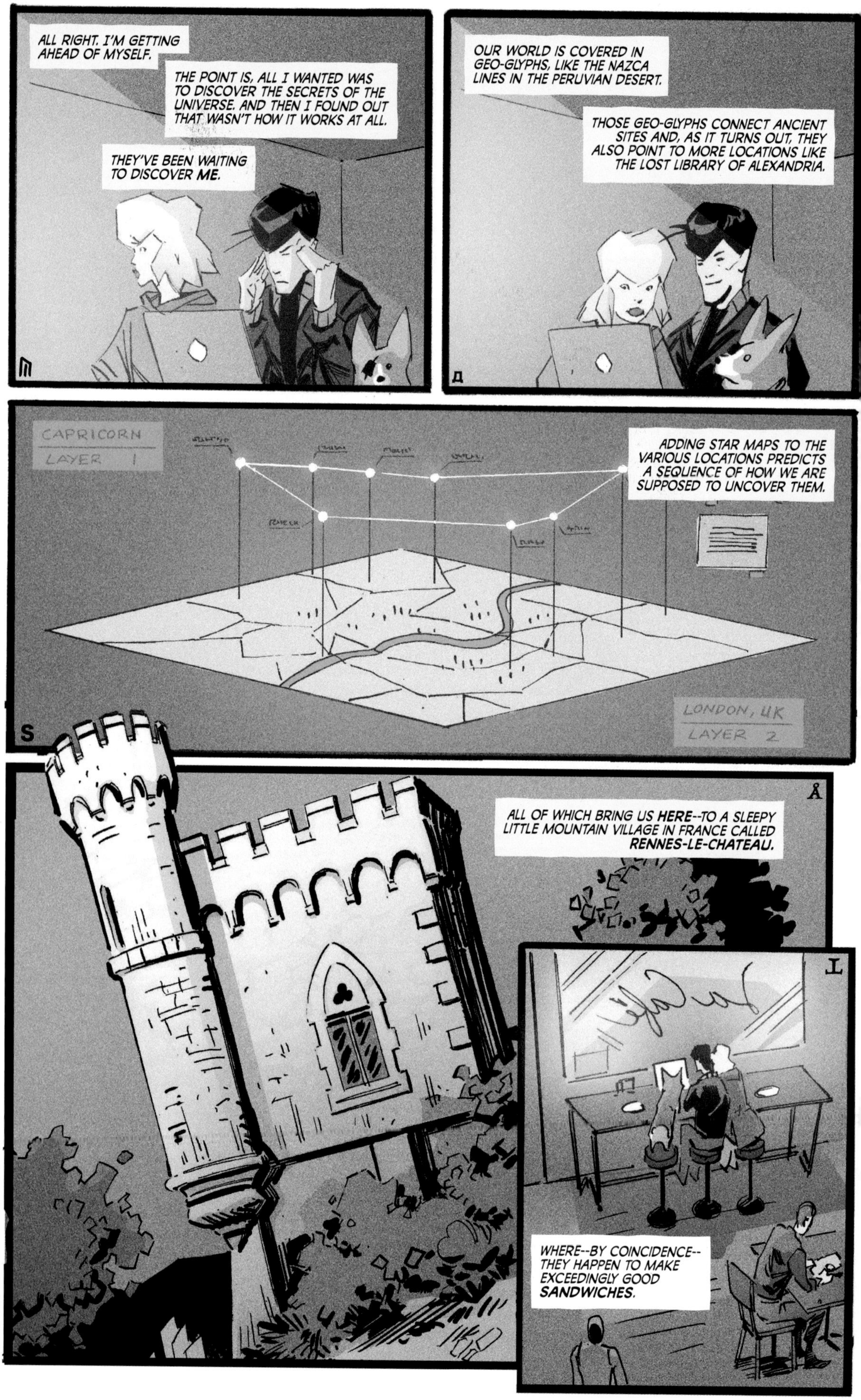
ALL RIGHT. I'M GETTING AHEAD OF MYSELF.
THE POINT IS, ALL I WANTED WAS TO DISCOVER THE SECRETS OF THE UNIVERSE. AND THEN I FOUND OUT THAT WASN'T HOW IT WORKS AT ALL.
THEY'VE BEEN WAITING TO DISCOVER **ME**.
OUR WORLD IS COVERED IN GEO-GLYPHS, LIKE THE NAZCA LINES IN THE PERUVIAN DESERT.
THOSE GEO-GLYPHS CONNECT ANCIENT SITES AND, AS IT TURNS OUT, THEY ALSO POINT TO MORE LOCATIONS LIKE THE LOST LIBRARY OF ALEXANDRIA.
CAPRICORN
LAYER 1
ADDING STAR MAPS TO THE VARIOUS LOCATIONS PREDICTS A SEQUENCE OF HOW WE ARE SUPPOSED TO UNCOVER THEM.
LONDON, UK
LAYER 2
ALL OF WHICH BRING US **HERE**--TO A SLEEPY LITTLE MOUNTAIN VILLAGE IN FRANCE CALLED **RENNES-LE-CHATEAU.**
WHERE--BY COINCIDENCE--THEY HAPPEN TO MAKE EXCEEDINGLY GOOD **SANDWICHES**.

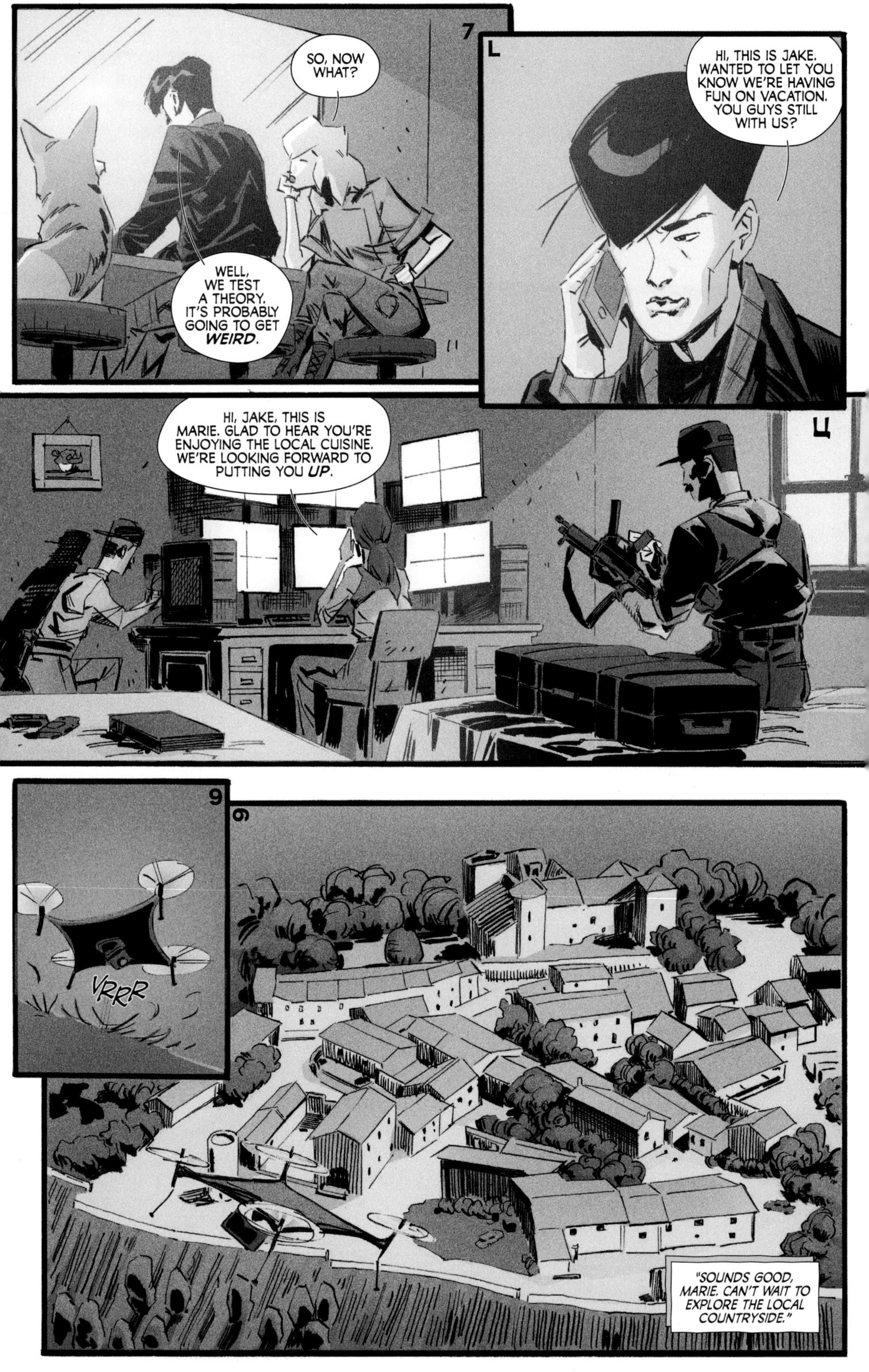
SO, NOW WHAT?
WELL, WE TEST A THEORY. IT'S PROBABLY GOING TO GET *WEIRD*.
HI, THIS IS JAKE. WANTED TO LET YOU KNOW WE'RE HAVING FUN ON VACATION. YOU GUYS STILL WITH US?
HI, JAKE, THIS IS MARIE. GLAD TO HEAR YOU'RE ENJOYING THE LOCAL CUISINE. WE'RE LOOKING FORWARD TO PUTTING YOU *UP*.
VRRR
"SOUNDS GOOD, MARIE. CAN'T WAIT TO EXPLORE THE LOCAL COUNTRYSIDE."

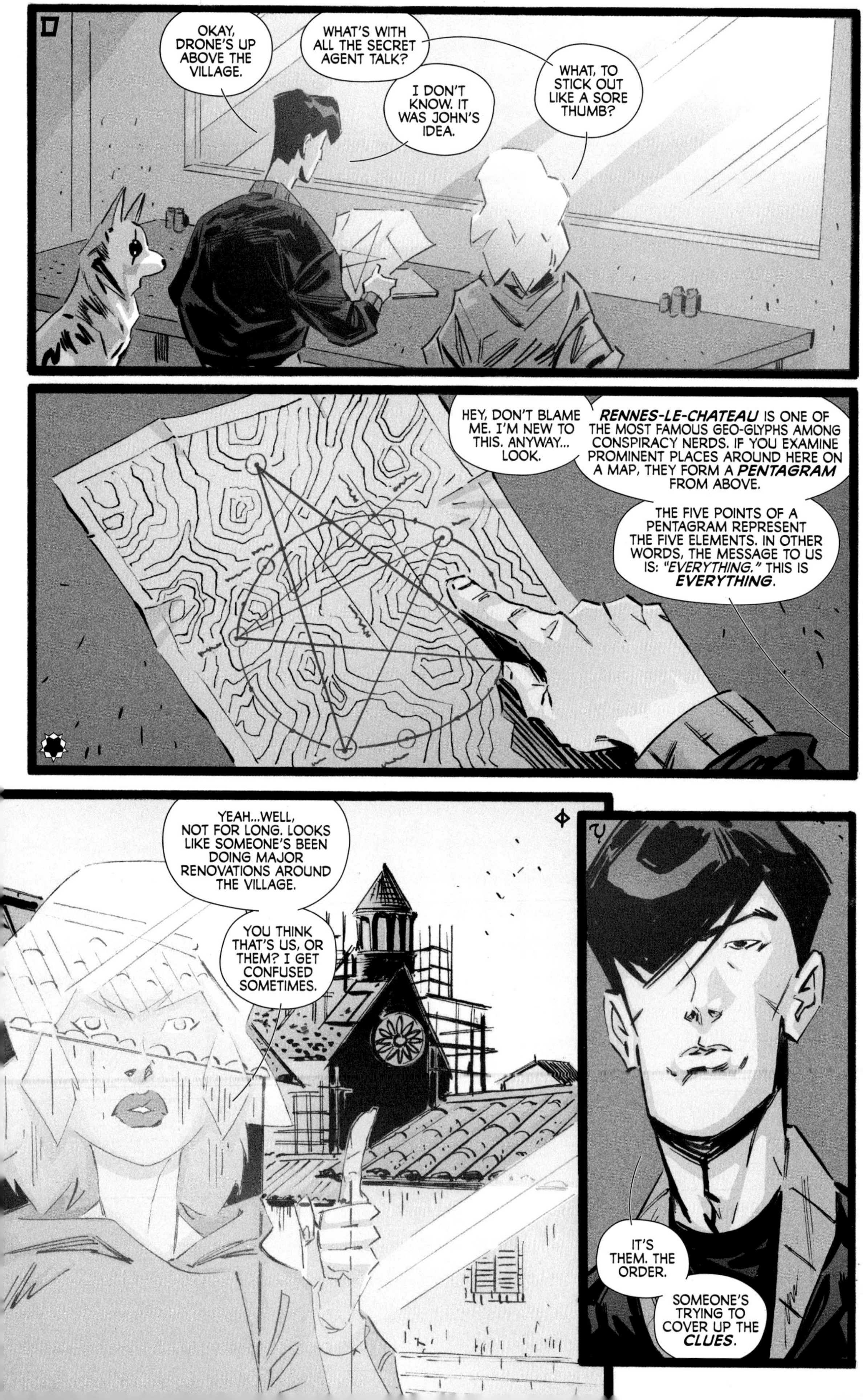
OKAY, DRONE'S UP ABOVE THE VILLAGE.
WHAT'S WITH ALL THE SECRET AGENT TALK?
I DON'T KNOW. IT WAS JOHN'S IDEA.
WHAT, TO STICK OUT LIKE A SORE THUMB?
HEY, DON'T BLAME ME. I'M NEW TO THIS. ANYWAY... LOOK.
RENNES-LE-CHATEAU IS ONE OF THE MOST FAMOUS GEO-GLYPHS AMONG CONSPIRACY NERDS. IF YOU EXAMINE PROMINENT PLACES AROUND HERE ON A MAP, THEY FORM A PENTAGRAM FROM ABOVE.
THE FIVE POINTS OF A PENTAGRAM REPRESENT THE FIVE ELEMENTS. IN OTHER WORDS, THE MESSAGE TO US IS: "EVERYTHING." THIS IS EVERYTHING.
YEAH...WELL, NOT FOR LONG. LOOKS LIKE SOMEONE'S BEEN DOING MAJOR RENOVATIONS AROUND THE VILLAGE.
YOU THINK THAT'S US, OR THEM? I GET CONFUSED SOMETIMES.
IT'S THEM. THE ORDER.
SOMEONE'S TRYING TO COVER UP THE CLUES.

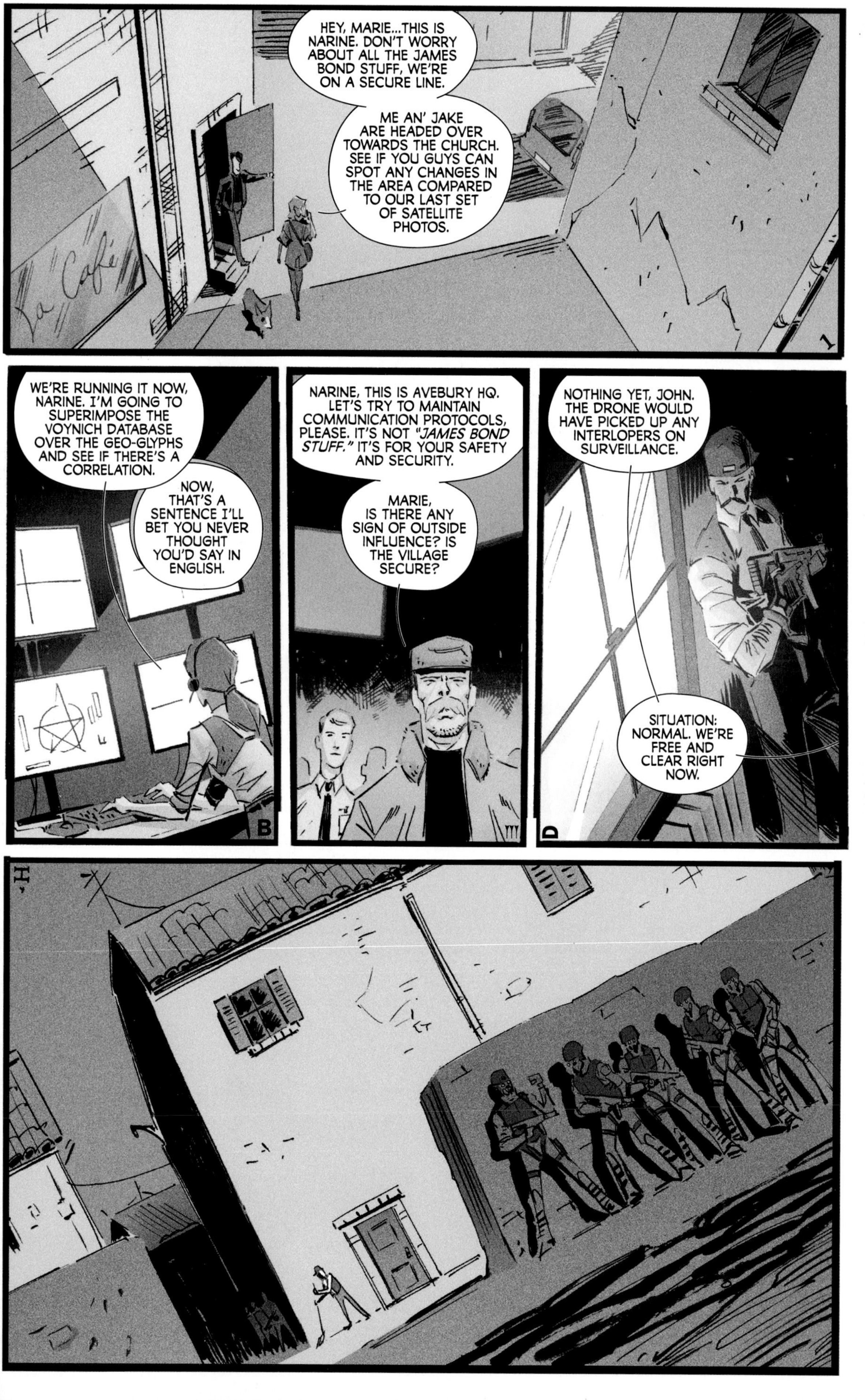
HEY, MARIE...THIS IS NARINE. DON'T WORRY ABOUT ALL THE JAMES BOND STUFF, WE'RE ON A SECURE LINE.
ME AN' JAKE ARE HEADED OVER TOWARDS THE CHURCH. SEE IF YOU GUYS CAN SPOT ANY CHANGES IN THE AREA COMPARED TO OUR LAST SET OF SATELLITE PHOTOS.
La Café
WE'RE RUNNING IT NOW, NARINE. I'M GOING TO SUPERIMPOSE THE VOYNICH DATABASE OVER THE GEO-GLYPHS AND SEE IF THERE'S A CORRELATION.
NOW, THAT'S A SENTENCE I'LL BET YOU NEVER THOUGHT YOU'D SAY IN ENGLISH.
NARINE, THIS IS AVEBURY HQ. LET'S TRY TO MAINTAIN COMMUNICATION PROTOCOLS, PLEASE. IT'S NOT *"JAMES BOND STUFF."* IT'S FOR YOUR SAFETY AND SECURITY.
MARIE, IS THERE ANY SIGN OF OUTSIDE INFLUENCE? IS THE VILLAGE SECURE?
NOTHING YET, JOHN. THE DRONE WOULD HAVE PICKED UP ANY INTERLOPERS ON SURVEILLANCE.
SITUATION: NORMAL. WE'RE FREE AND CLEAR RIGHT NOW.

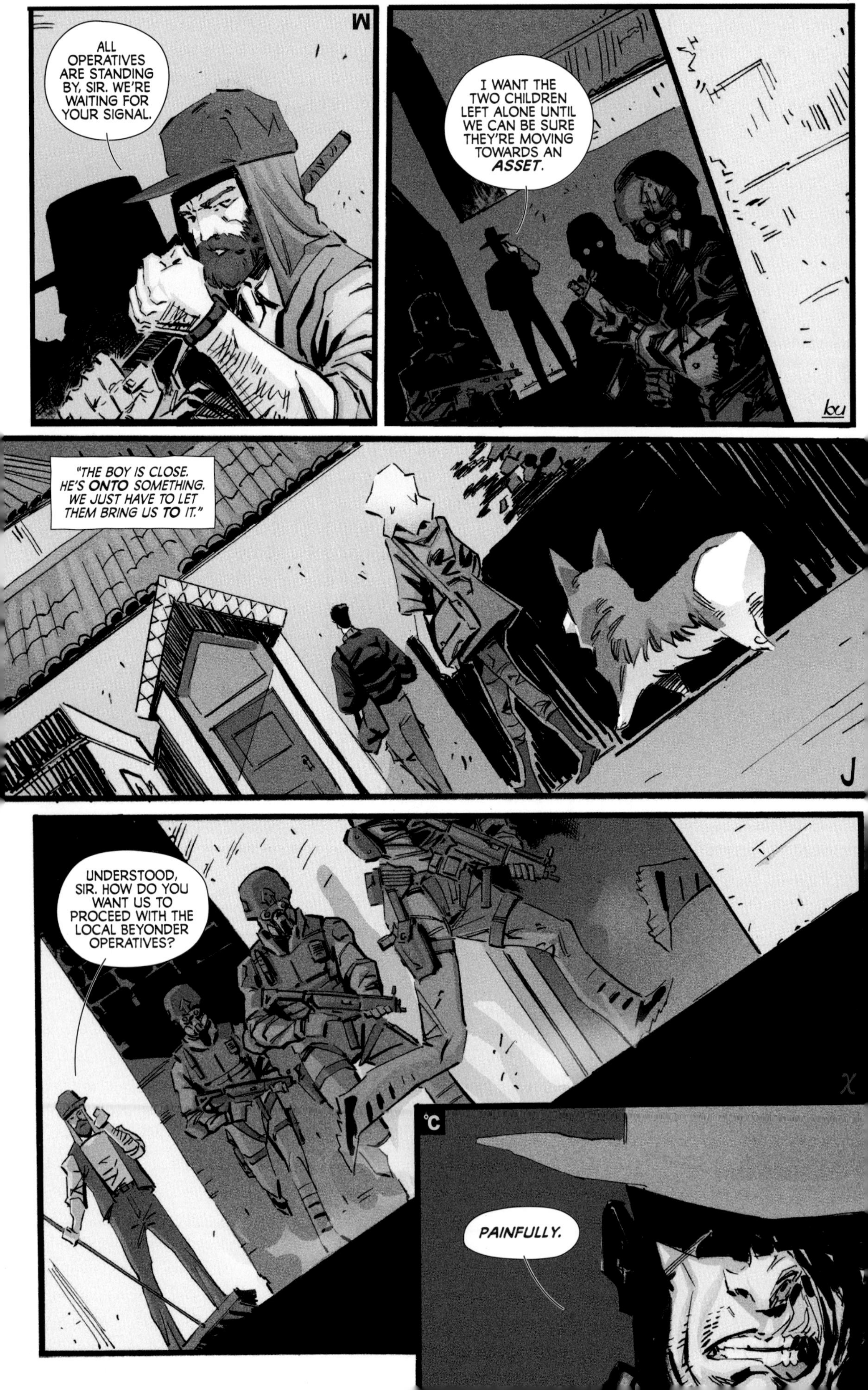
ALL OPERATIVES ARE STANDING BY, SIR. WE'RE WAITING FOR YOUR SIGNAL.
I WANT THE TWO CHILDREN LEFT ALONE UNTIL WE CAN BE SURE THEY'RE MOVING TOWARDS AN ASSET.
"THE BOY IS CLOSE. HE'S ONTO SOMETHING. WE JUST HAVE TO LET THEM BRING US TO IT."
UNDERSTOOD, SIR. HOW DO YOU WANT US TO PROCEED WITH THE LOCAL BEYONDER OPERATIVES?
PAINFULLY.

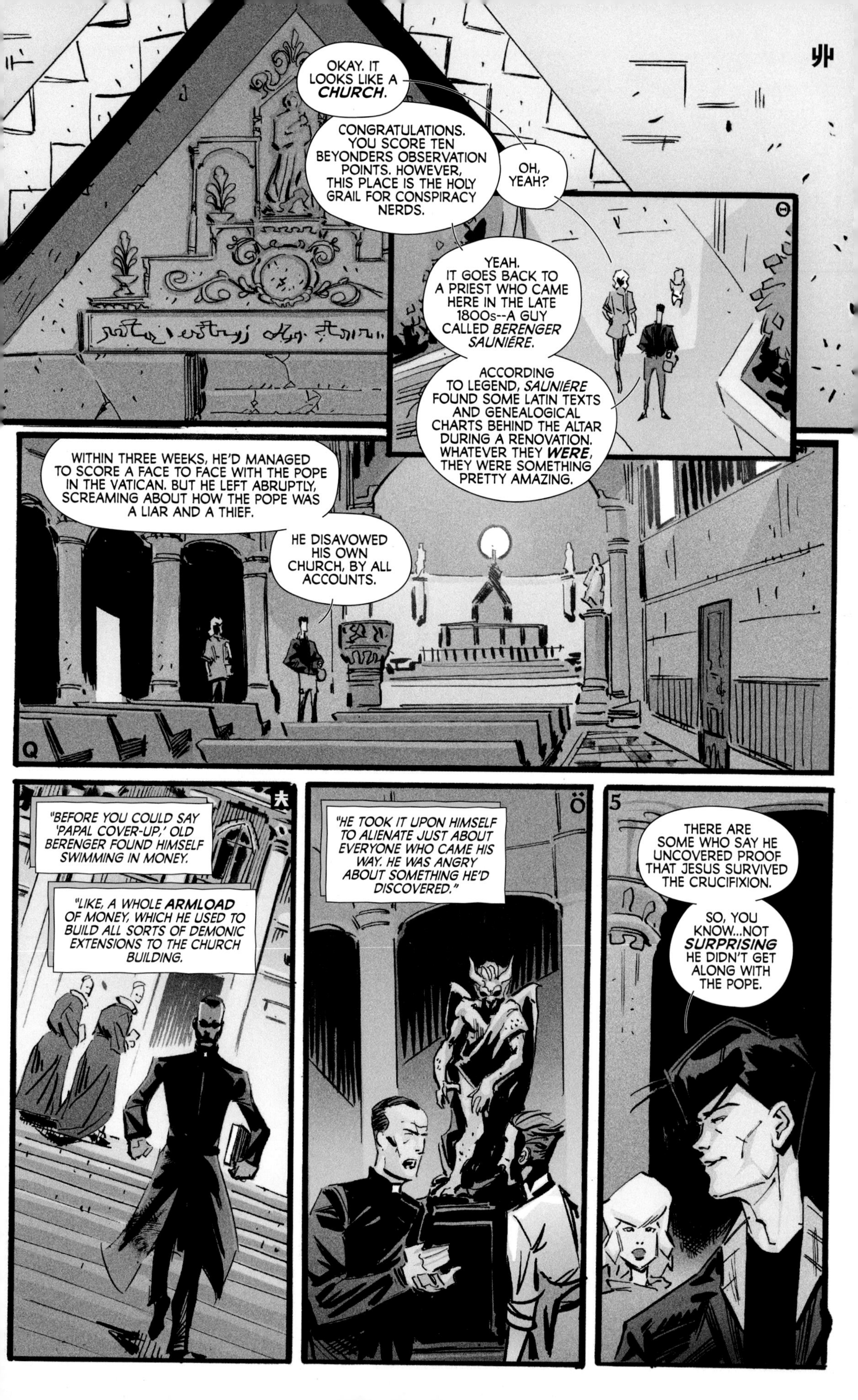
OKAY. IT LOOKS LIKE A ***CHURCH***.
CONGRATULATIONS. YOU SCORE TEN BEYONDERS OBSERVATION POINTS. HOWEVER, THIS PLACE IS THE HOLY GRAIL FOR CONSPIRACY NERDS.
OH, YEAH?
YEAH. IT GOES BACK TO A PRIEST WHO CAME HERE IN THE LATE 1800s--A GUY CALLED *BERENGER SAUNIÉRE*.
ACCORDING TO LEGEND, *SAUNIÉRE* FOUND SOME LATIN TEXTS AND GENEALOGICAL CHARTS BEHIND THE ALTAR DURING A RENOVATION. WHATEVER THEY ***WERE***, THEY WERE SOMETHING PRETTY AMAZING.
WITHIN THREE WEEKS, HE'D MANAGED TO SCORE A FACE TO FACE WITH THE POPE IN THE VATICAN. BUT HE LEFT ABRUPTLY, SCREAMING ABOUT HOW THE POPE WAS A LIAR AND A THIEF.
HE DISAVOWED HIS OWN CHURCH, BY ALL ACCOUNTS.
"BEFORE YOU COULD SAY 'PAPAL COVER-UP,' OLD BERENGER FOUND HIMSELF SWIMMING IN MONEY.
"LIKE, A WHOLE ***ARMLOAD*** *OF MONEY, WHICH HE USED TO BUILD ALL SORTS OF DEMONIC EXTENSIONS TO THE CHURCH BUILDING.*
"HE TOOK IT UPON HIMSELF TO ALIENATE JUST ABOUT EVERYONE WHO CAME HIS WAY. HE WAS ANGRY ABOUT SOMETHING HE'D DISCOVERED."
THERE ARE SOME WHO SAY HE UNCOVERED PROOF THAT JESUS SURVIVED THE CRUCIFIXION.
SO, YOU KNOW...NOT ***SURPRISING*** HE DIDN'T GET ALONG WITH THE POPE.

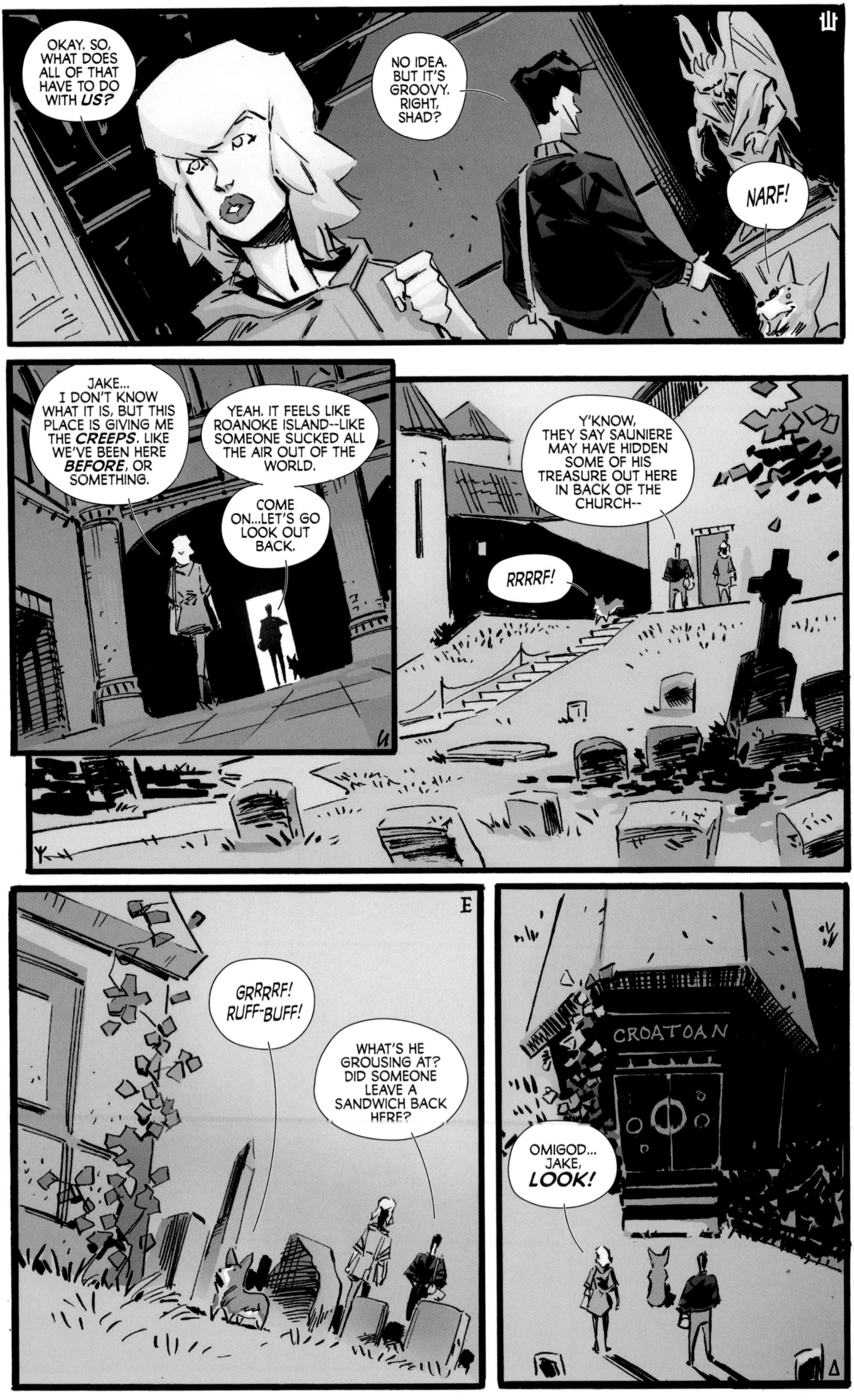
OKAY. SO, WHAT DOES ALL OF THAT HAVE TO DO WITH *US?*
NO IDEA. BUT IT'S GROOVY. RIGHT, SHAD?
NARF!
JAKE... I DON'T KNOW WHAT IT IS, BUT THIS PLACE IS GIVING ME THE ***CREEPS***. LIKE WE'VE BEEN HERE ***BEFORE***, OR SOMETHING.
YEAH. IT FEELS LIKE ROANOKE ISLAND--LIKE SOMEONE SUCKED ALL THE AIR OUT OF THE WORLD.
COME ON...LET'S GO LOOK OUT BACK.
Y'KNOW, THEY SAY SAUNIERE MAY HAVE HIDDEN SOME OF HIS TREASURE OUT HERE IN BACK OF THE CHURCH--
RRRRF!
GRRRRF! RUFF-BUFF!
WHAT'S HE GROUSING AT? DID SOMEONE LEAVE A SANDWICH BACK HERE?
CROATOAN
OMIGOD... JAKE, ***LOOK!***

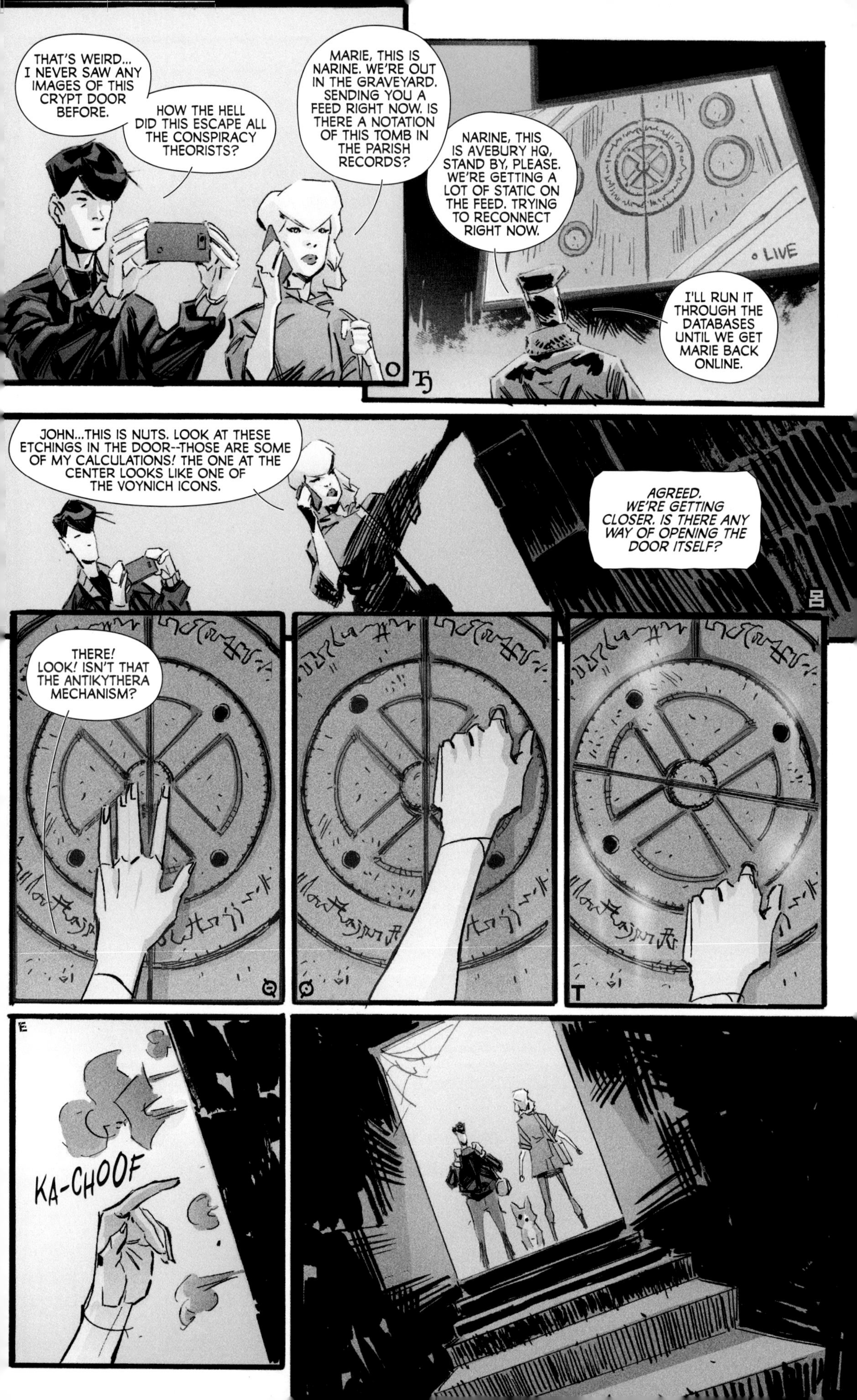

THAT'S WEIRD... I NEVER SAW ANY IMAGES OF THIS CRYPT DOOR BEFORE.
HOW THE HELL DID THIS ESCAPE ALL THE CONSPIRACY THEORISTS?
MARIE, THIS IS NARINE. WE'RE OUT IN THE GRAVEYARD. SENDING YOU A FEED RIGHT NOW. IS THERE A NOTATION OF THIS TOMB IN THE PARISH RECORDS?
NARINE, THIS IS AVEBURY HQ, STAND BY, PLEASE. WE'RE GETTING A LOT OF STATIC ON THE FEED. TRYING TO RECONNECT RIGHT NOW.
LIVE
I'LL RUN IT THROUGH THE DATABASES UNTIL WE GET MARIE BACK ONLINE.
JOHN...THIS IS NUTS. LOOK AT THESE ETCHINGS IN THE DOOR--THOSE ARE SOME OF MY CALCULATIONS! THE ONE AT THE CENTER LOOKS LIKE ONE OF THE VOYNICH ICONS.
AGREED. WE'RE GETTING CLOSER. IS THERE ANY WAY OF OPENING THE DOOR ITSELF?
THERE! LOOK! ISN'T THAT THE ANTIKYTHERA MECHANISM?
KA-CHOOF

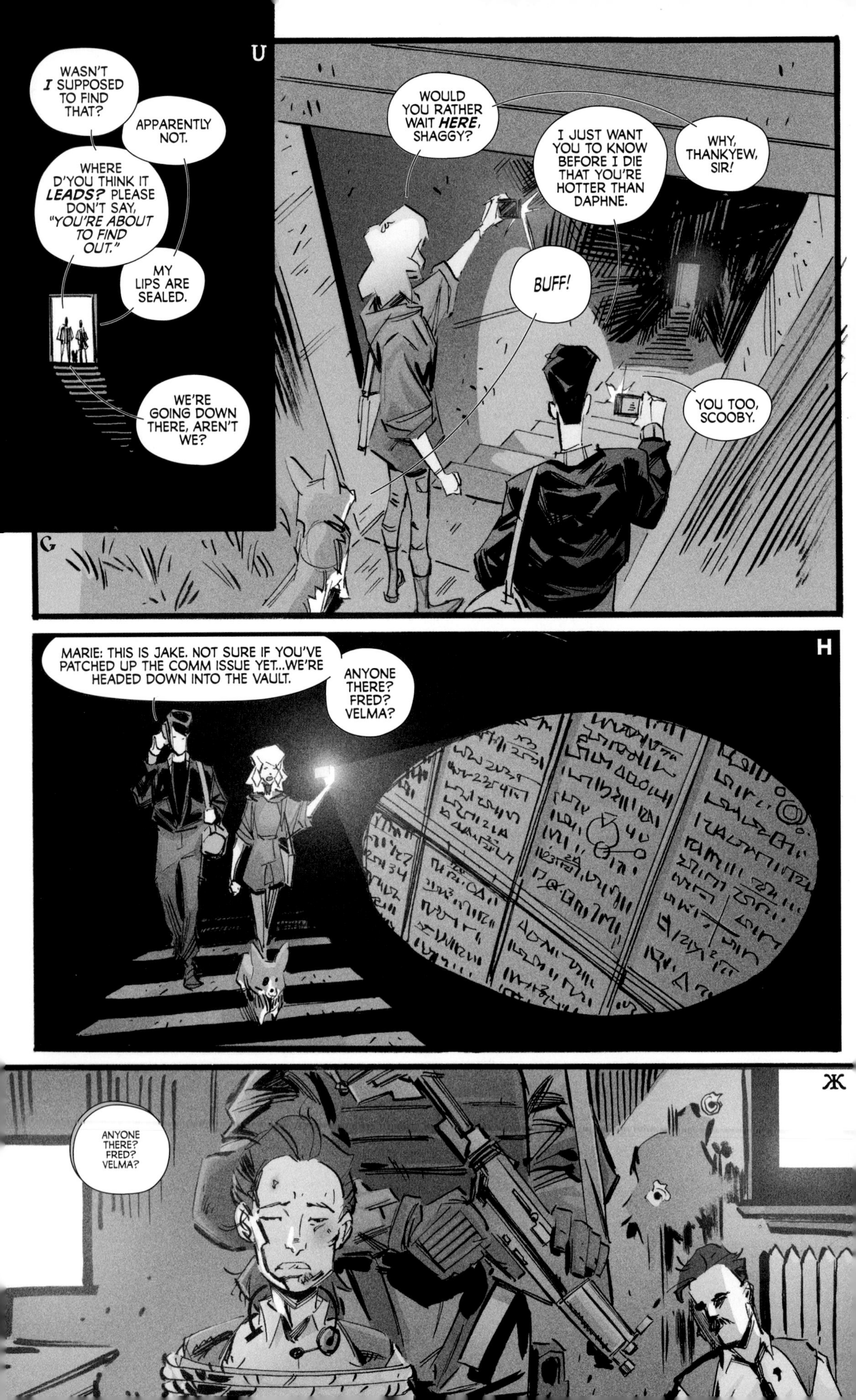
U
WASN'T *I* SUPPOSED TO FIND THAT?
APPARENTLY NOT.
WHERE D'YOU THINK IT *LEADS?* PLEASE DON'T SAY, *"YOU'RE ABOUT TO FIND OUT."*
MY LIPS ARE SEALED.
WE'RE GOING DOWN THERE, AREN'T WE?
WOULD YOU RATHER WAIT ***HERE***, SHAGGY?
WHY, THANKYEW, SIR!
I JUST WANT YOU TO KNOW BEFORE I DIE THAT YOU'RE HOTTER THAN DAPHNE.
BUFF!
YOU TOO, SCOOBY.
G
H
MARIE: THIS IS JAKE. NOT SURE IF YOU'VE PATCHED UP THE COMM ISSUE YET...WE'RE HEADED DOWN INTO THE VAULT.
ANYONE THERE? FRED? VELMA?
Ж
ANYONE THERE? FRED? VELMA?

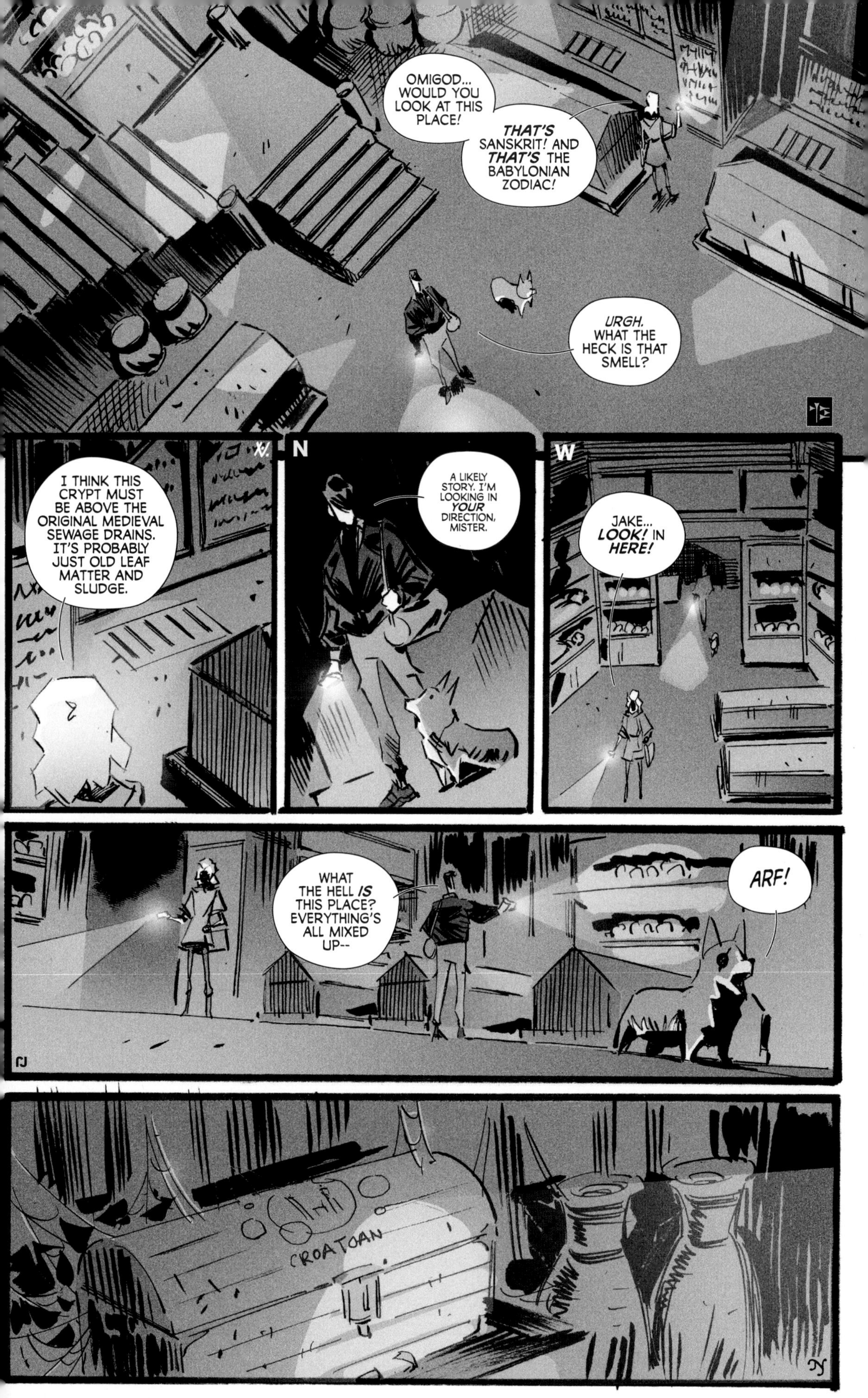
OMIGOD... WOULD YOU LOOK AT THIS PLACE!
THAT'S SANSKRIT! AND THAT'S THE BABYLONIAN ZODIAC!
URGH. WHAT THE HECK IS THAT SMELL?
I THINK THIS CRYPT MUST BE ABOVE THE ORIGINAL MEDIEVAL SEWAGE DRAINS. IT'S PROBABLY JUST OLD LEAF MATTER AND SLUDGE.
N
A LIKELY STORY. I'M LOOKING IN YOUR DIRECTION, MISTER.
W
JAKE... LOOK! IN HERE!
WHAT THE HELL IS THIS PLACE? EVERYTHING'S ALL MIXED UP--
ARF!
CROATOAN

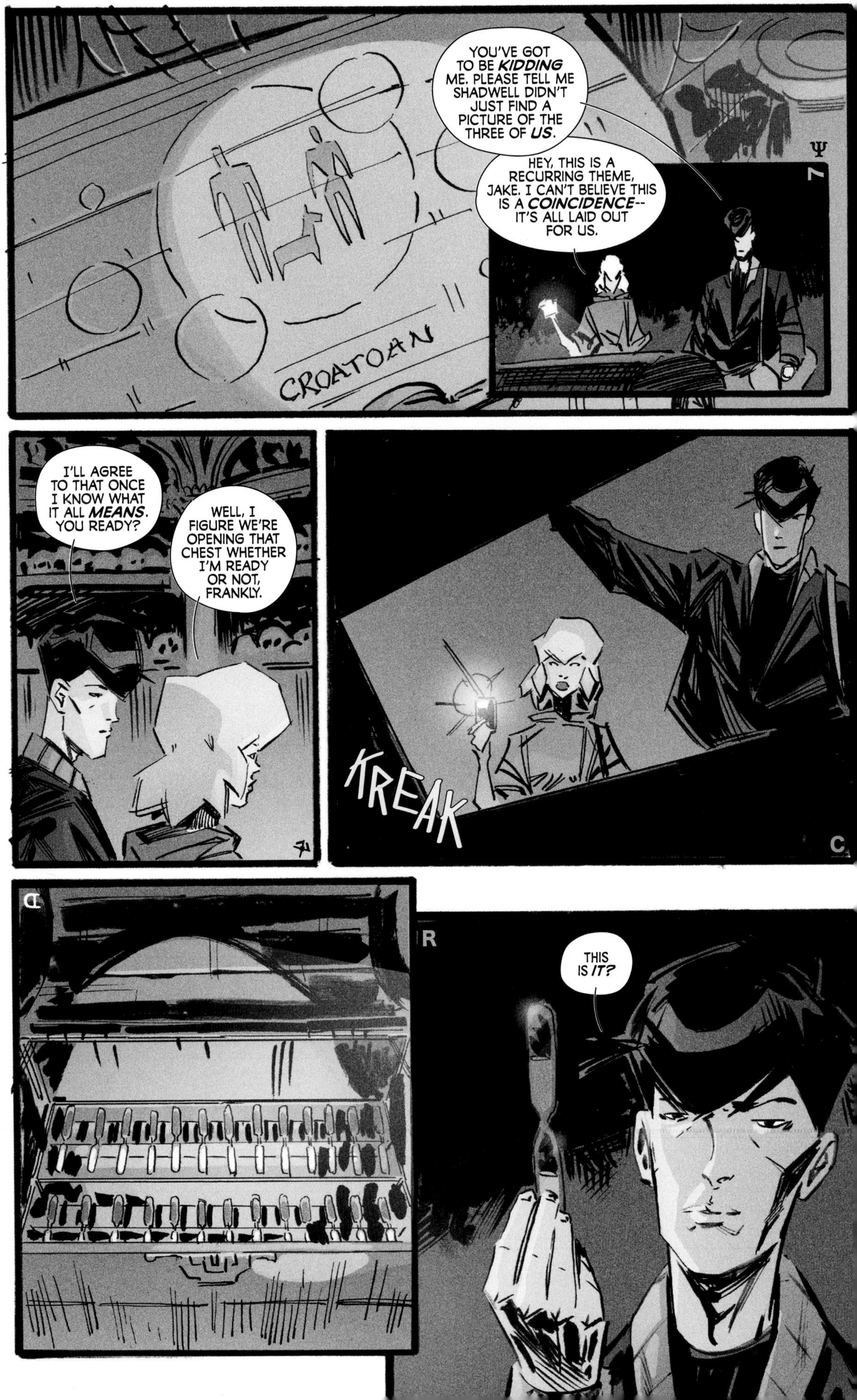
CROATOAN
YOU'VE GOT TO BE KIDDING ME. PLEASE TELL ME SHADWELL DIDN'T JUST FIND A PICTURE OF THE THREE OF US.
HEY, THIS IS A RECURRING THEME, JAKE. I CAN'T BELIEVE THIS IS A COINCIDENCE-- IT'S ALL LAID OUT FOR US.
I'LL AGREE TO THAT ONCE I KNOW WHAT IT ALL MEANS. YOU READY?
WELL, I FIGURE WE'RE OPENING THAT CHEST WHETHER I'M READY OR NOT, FRANKLY.
KREAK
THIS IS IT?

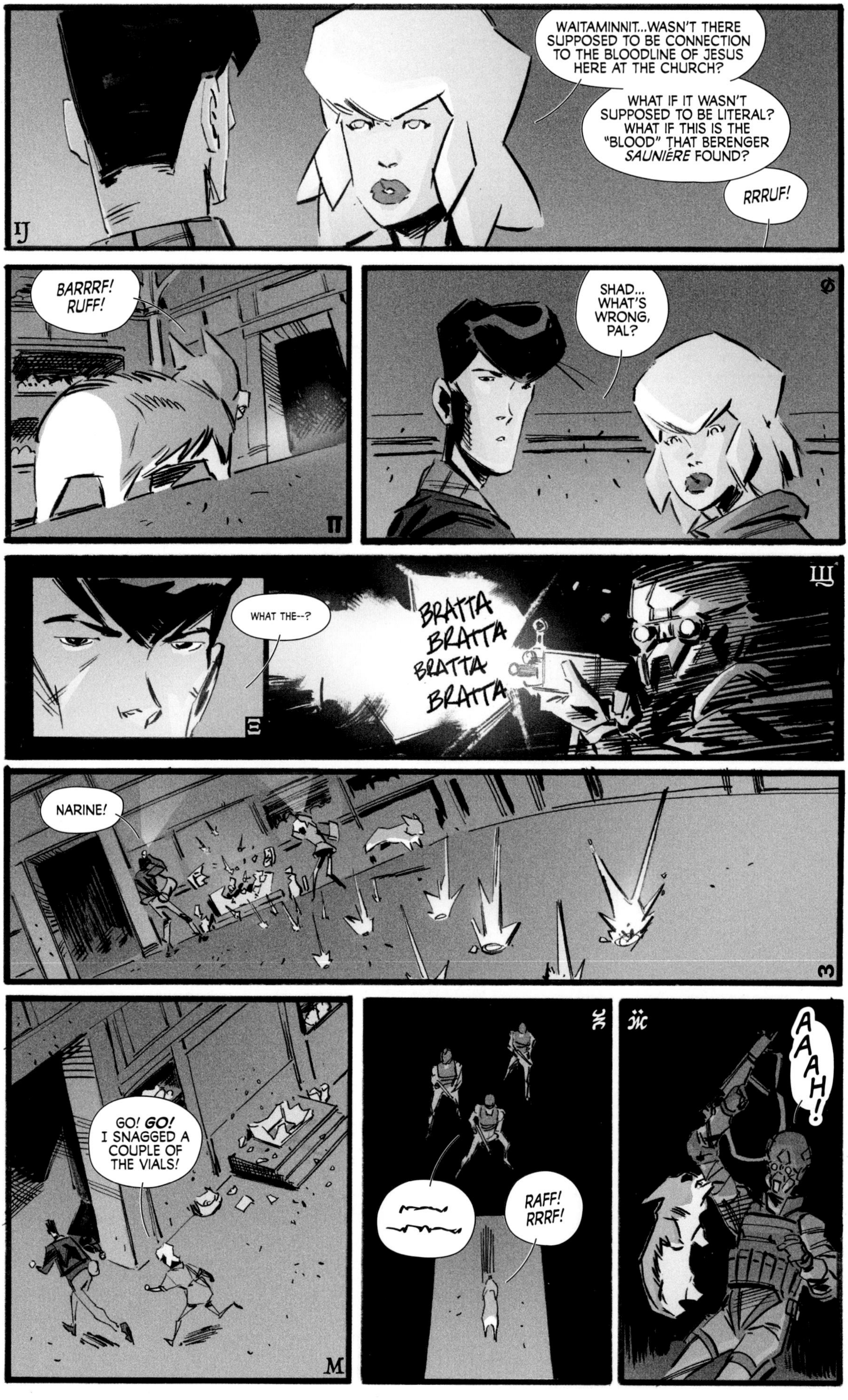
WAITAMINNIT...WASN'T THERE SUPPOSED TO BE CONNECTION TO THE BLOODLINE OF JESUS HERE AT THE CHURCH?
WHAT IF IT WASN'T SUPPOSED TO BE LITERAL? WHAT IF THIS IS THE "BLOOD" THAT BERENGER *SAUNIÉRE* FOUND?
RRRUF!
BARRRF! RUFF!
SHAD... WHAT'S WRONG, PAL?
WHAT THE--?
BRATTA BRATTA BRATTA BRATTA
NARINE!
GO! **GO!** I SNAGGED A COUPLE OF THE VIALS!
RAFF! RRRF!
AAAH!

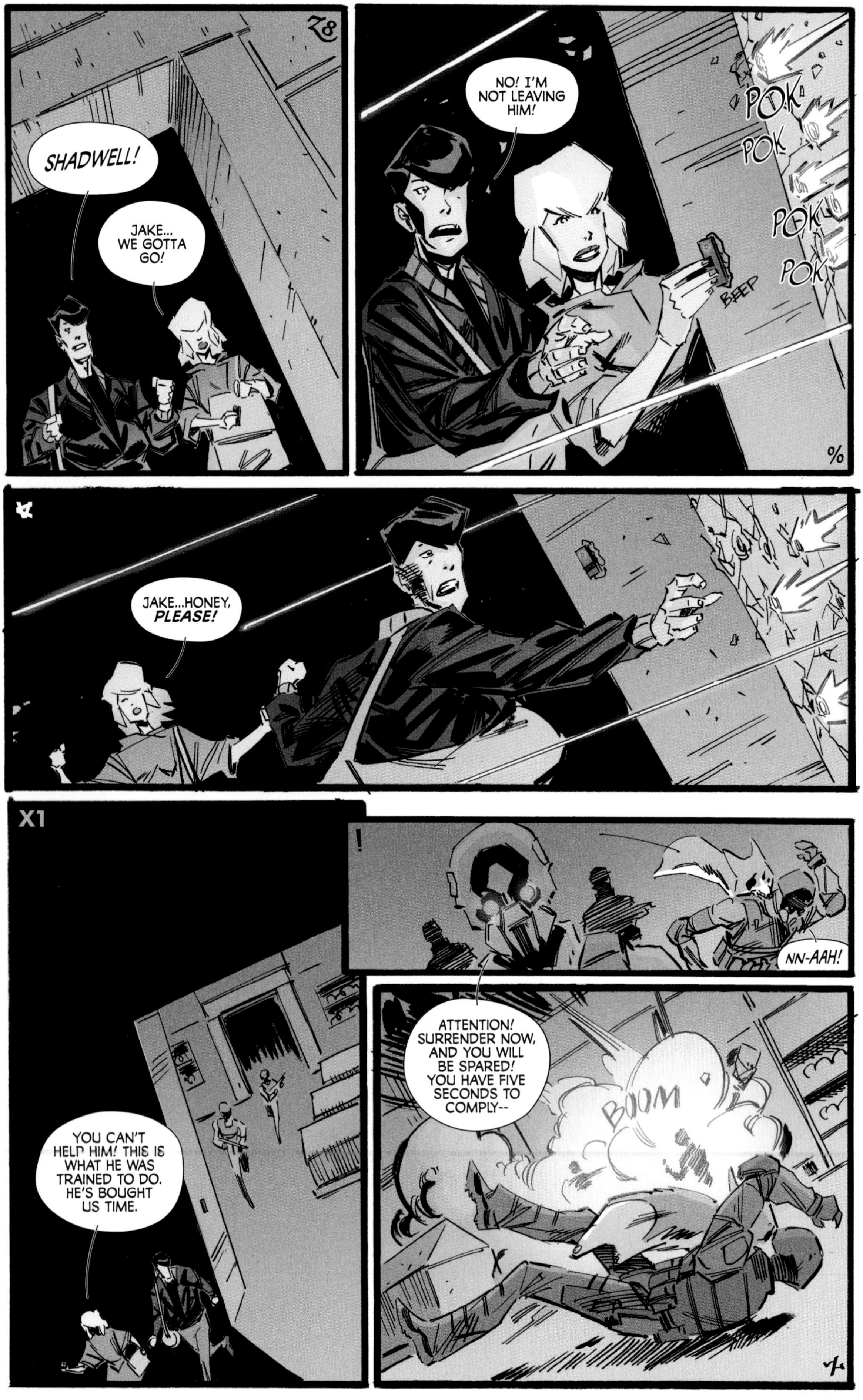
28
SHADWELL!
JAKE... WE GOTTA GO!
NO! I'M NOT LEAVING HIM!
POK
POK
POK
POK
BEEP
%
JAKE...HONEY, PLEASE!
X1
!
NN-AAH!
ATTENTION! SURRENDER NOW, AND YOU WILL BE SPARED! YOU HAVE FIVE SECONDS TO COMPLY--
BOOM
YOU CAN'T HELP HIM! THIS IS WHAT HE WAS TRAINED TO DO. HE'S BOUGHT US TIME.

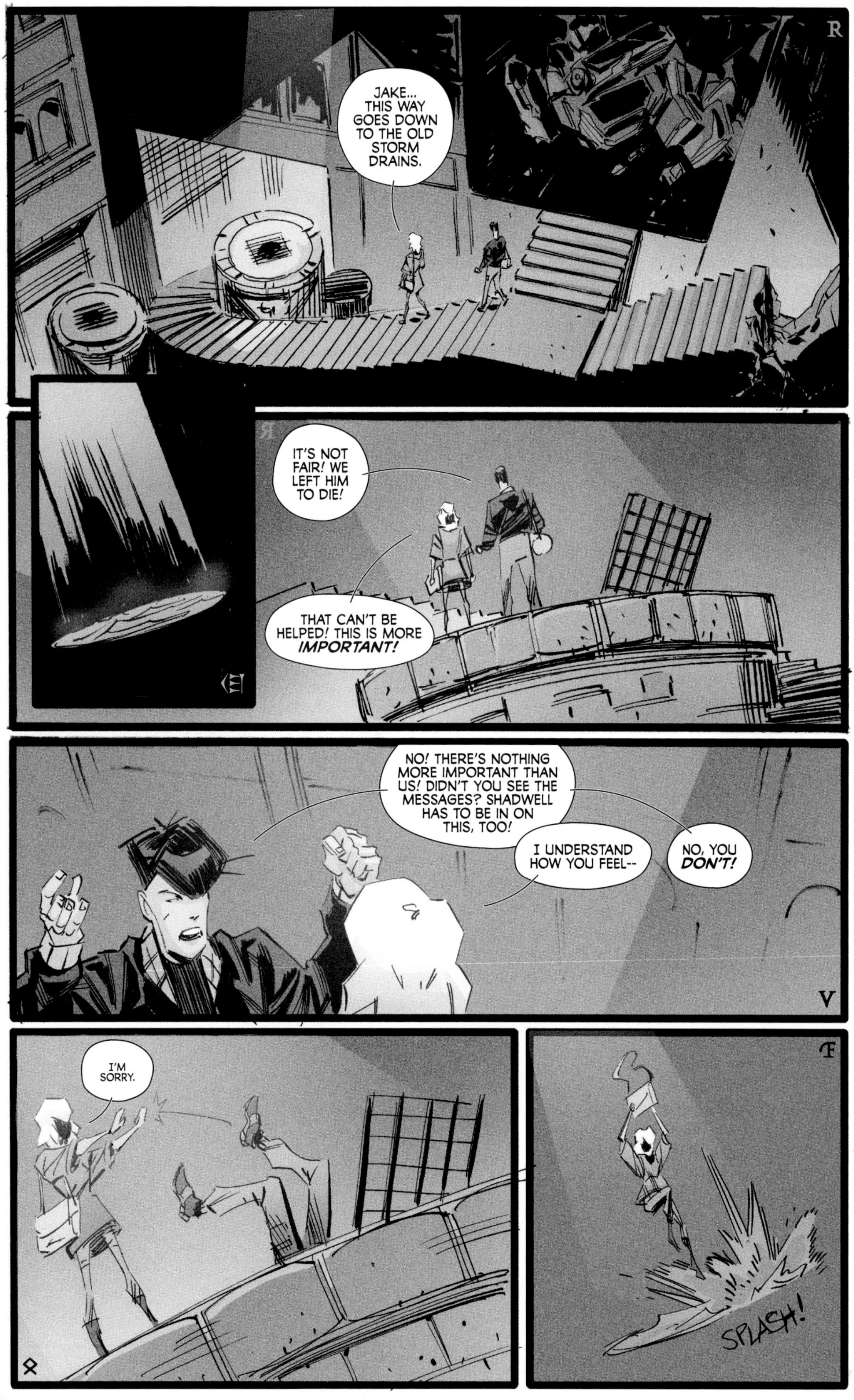
JAKE... THIS WAY GOES DOWN TO THE OLD STORM DRAINS.
IT'S NOT FAIR! WE LEFT HIM TO DIE!
THAT CAN'T BE HELPED! THIS IS MORE *IMPORTANT!*
NO! THERE'S NOTHING MORE IMPORTANT THAN US! DIDN'T YOU SEE THE MESSAGES? SHADWELL HAS TO BE IN ON THIS, TOO!
I UNDERSTAND HOW YOU FEEL--
NO, YOU *DON'T!*
I'M SORRY.
SPLASH!

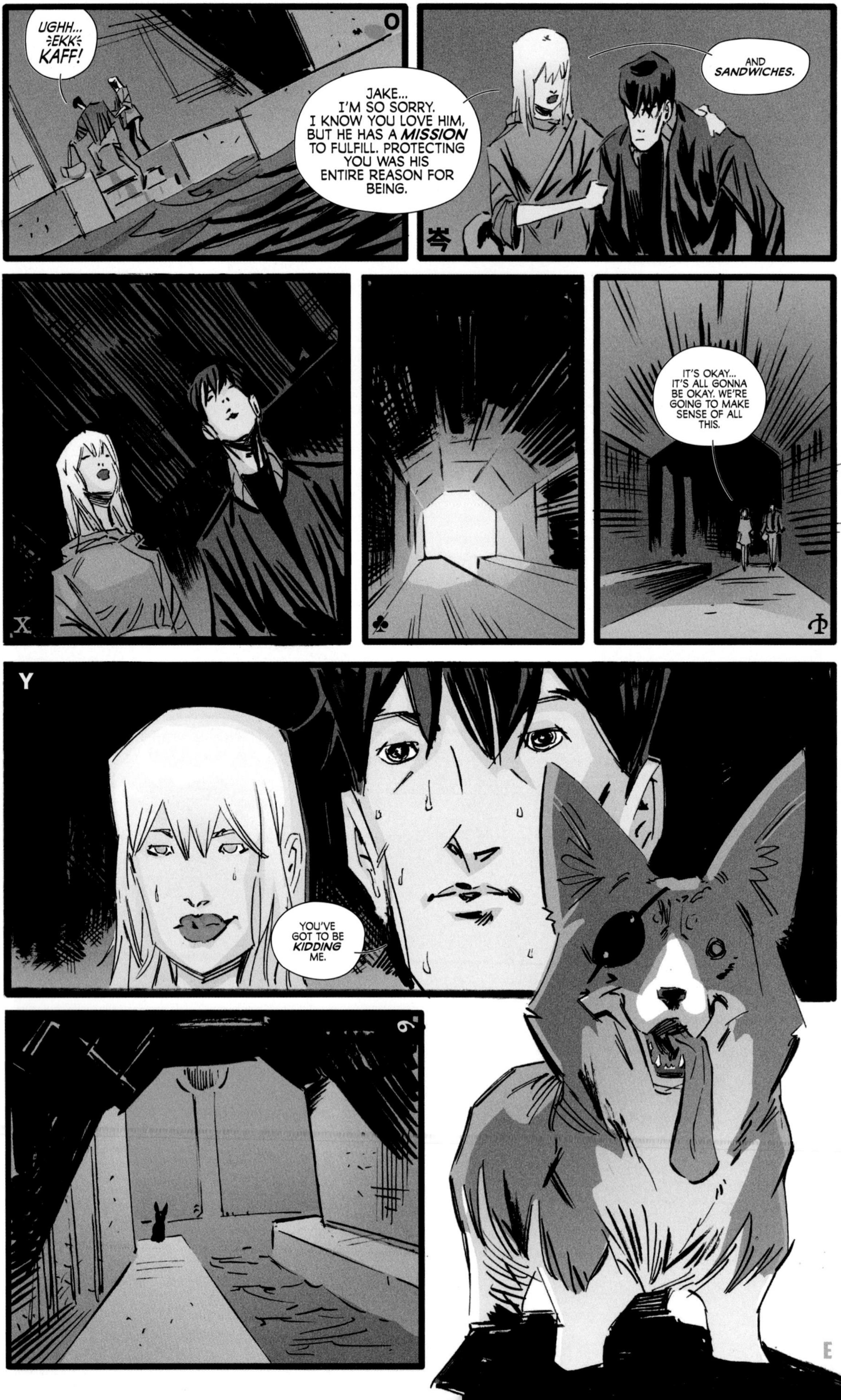
UGHH... EKK KAFF!
JAKE... I'M SO SORRY. I KNOW YOU LOVE HIM, BUT HE HAS A MISSION TO FULFILL. PROTECTING YOU WAS HIS ENTIRE REASON FOR BEING.
AND SANDWICHES.
IT'S OKAY... IT'S ALL GONNA BE OKAY. WE'RE GOING TO MAKE SENSE OF ALL THIS.
YOU'VE GOT TO BE KIDDING ME.

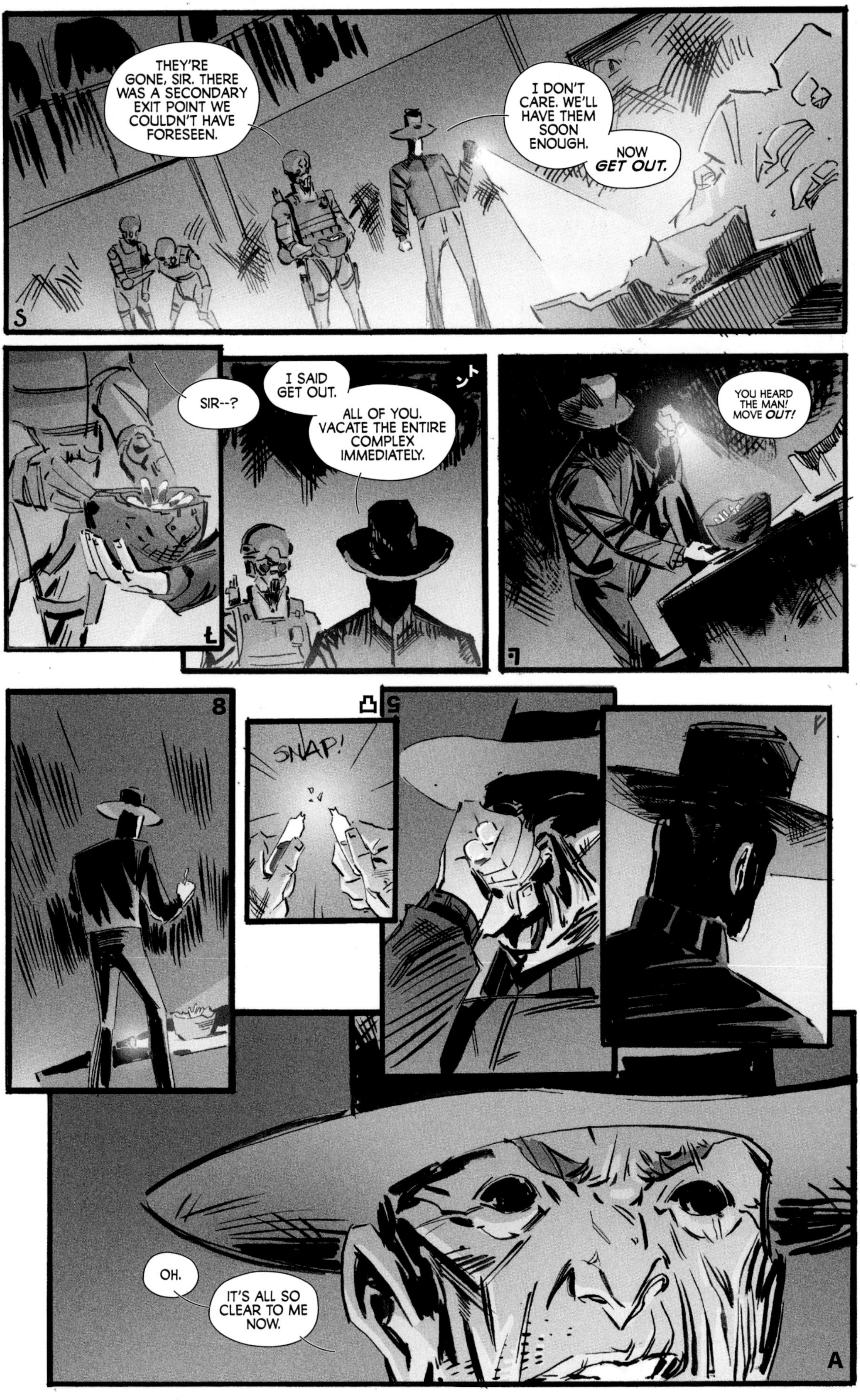
THEY'RE GONE, SIR. THERE WAS A SECONDARY EXIT POINT WE COULDN'T HAVE FORESEEN.
I DON'T CARE. WE'LL HAVE THEM SOON ENOUGH.
NOW GET OUT.
SIR--?
I SAID GET OUT.
ALL OF YOU. VACATE THE ENTIRE COMPLEX IMMEDIATELY.
YOU HEARD THE MAN! MOVE OUT!
SNAP!
OH.
IT'S ALL SO CLEAR TO ME NOW.

5

EVERYTHING IS EXPLAINED

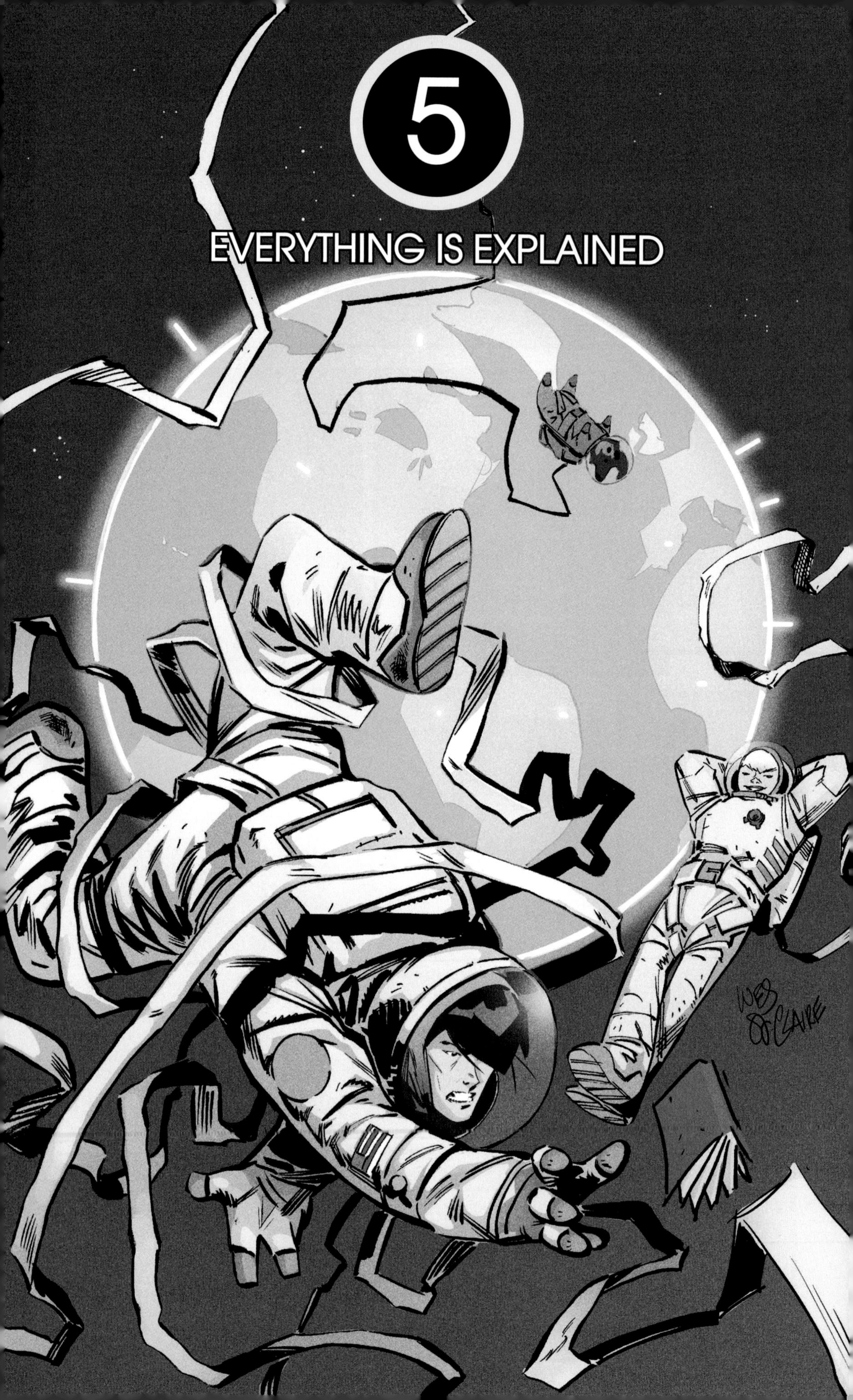

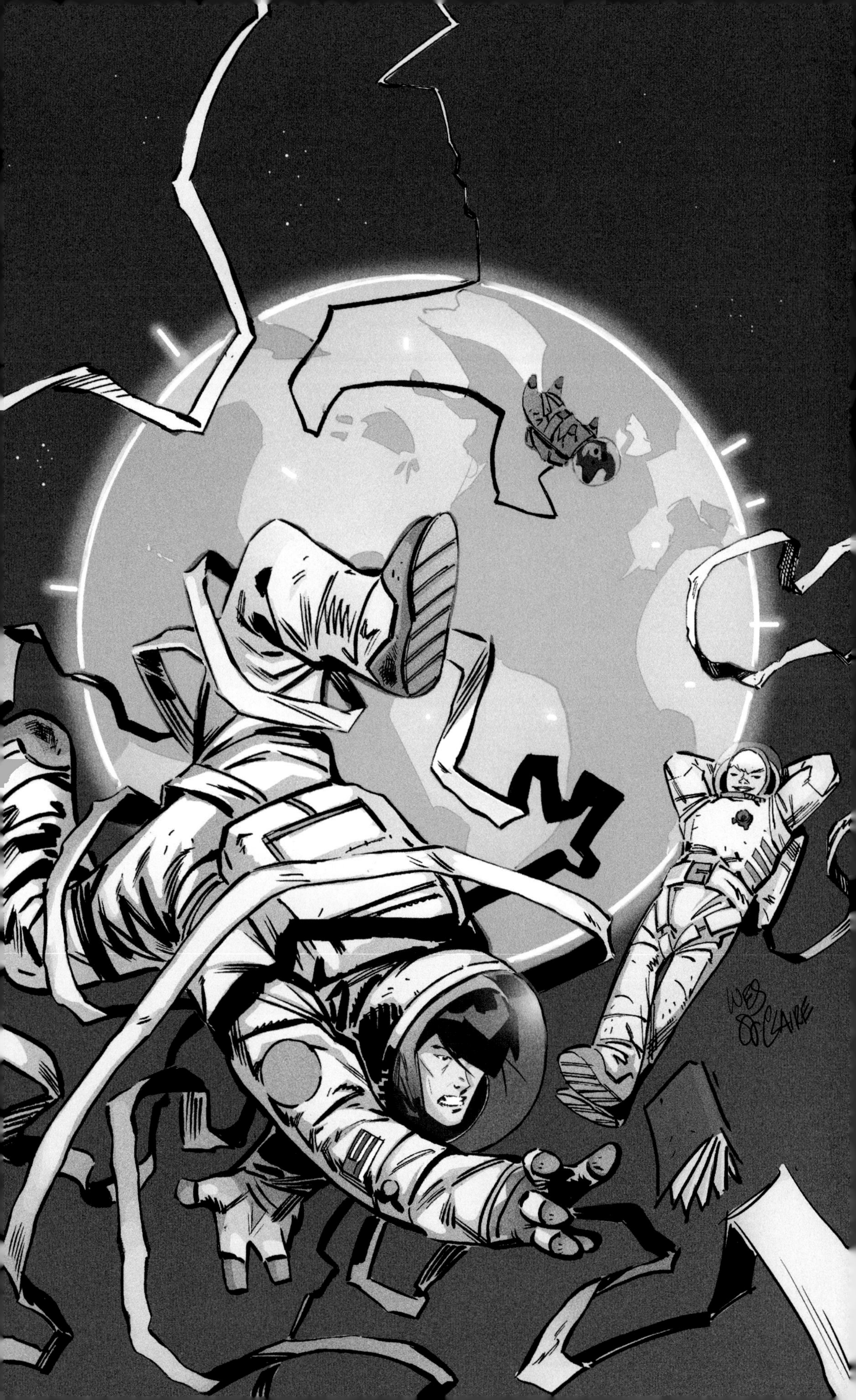
WES
O'CLAIRE

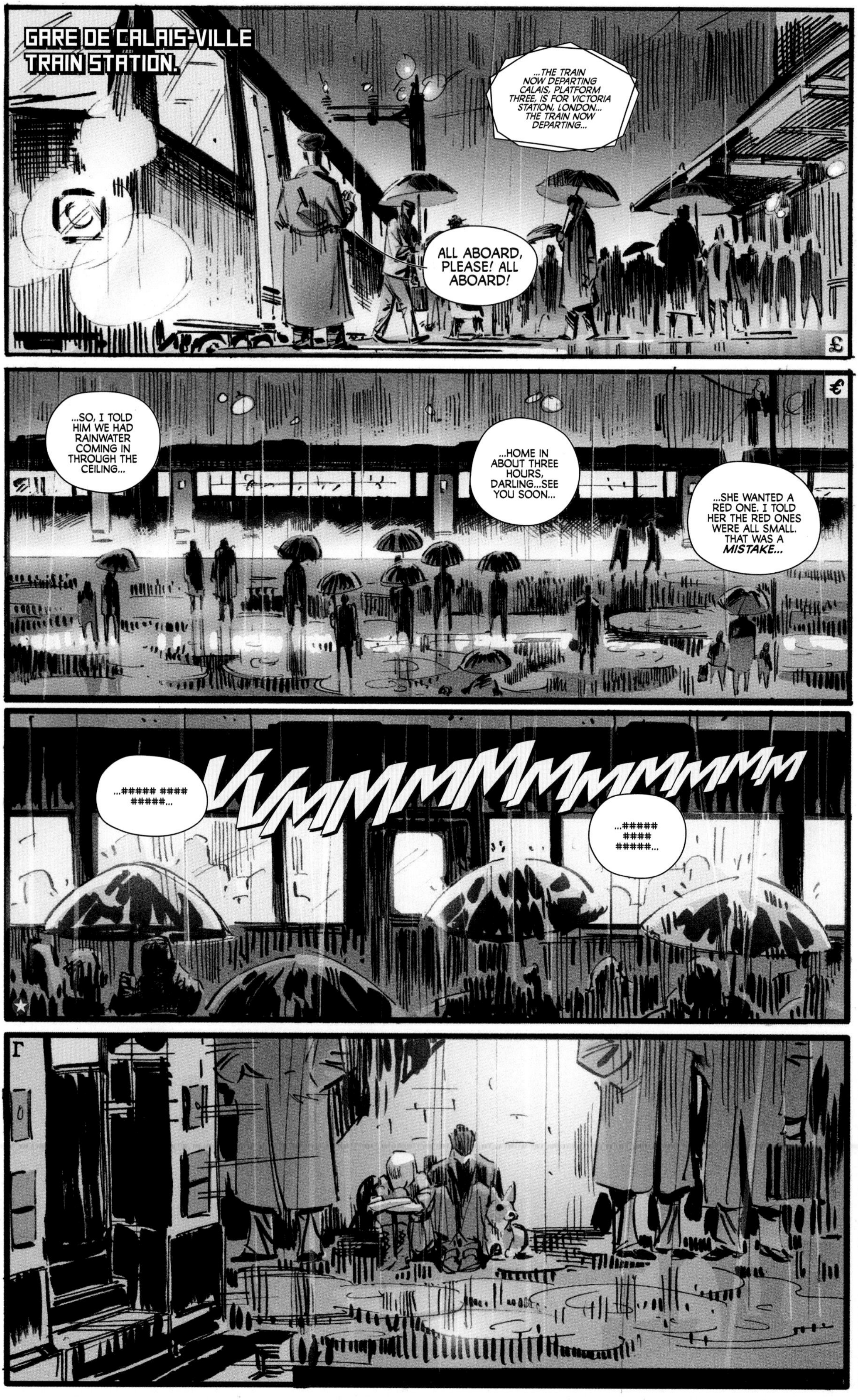
GARE DE CALAIS-VILLE TRAIN STATION.
...THE TRAIN NOW DEPARTING CALAIS, PLATFORM THREE, IS FOR VICTORIA STATION, LONDON... THE TRAIN NOW DEPARTING...
ALL ABOARD, PLEASE! ALL ABOARD!
£
€
...SO, I TOLD HIM WE HAD RAINWATER COMING IN THROUGH THE CEILING...
...HOME IN ABOUT THREE HOURS, DARLING...SEE YOU SOON...
...SHE WANTED A RED ONE. I TOLD HER THE RED ONES WERE ALL SMALL. THAT WAS A *MISTAKE...*
...##### #### #####...
VVMMMMMMMMMMMM
...##### #### #####...

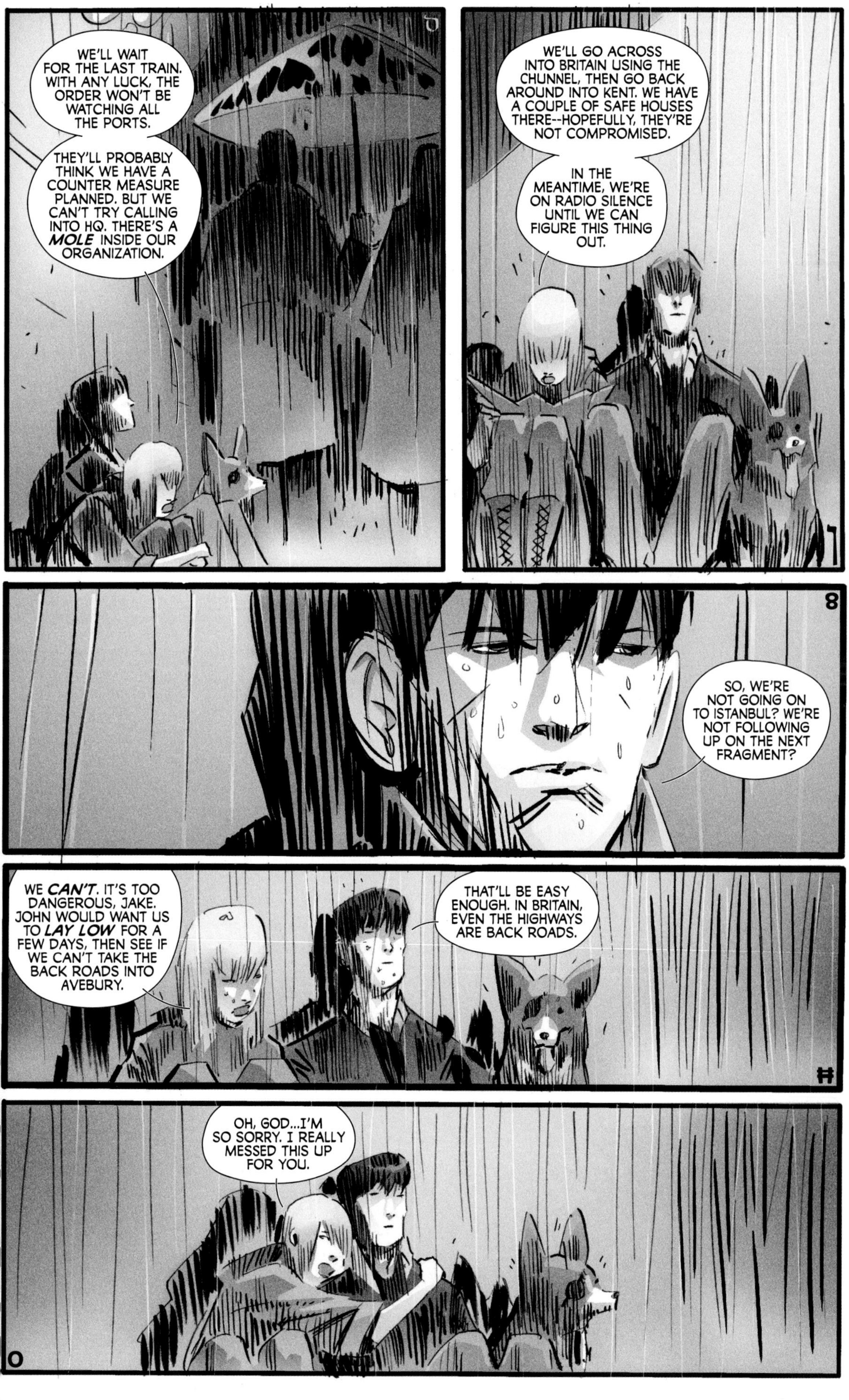
WE'LL WAIT FOR THE LAST TRAIN. WITH ANY LUCK, THE ORDER WON'T BE WATCHING ALL THE PORTS.
THEY'LL PROBABLY THINK WE HAVE A COUNTER MEASURE PLANNED. BUT WE CAN'T TRY CALLING INTO HQ. THERE'S A *MOLE* INSIDE OUR ORGANIZATION.
WE'LL GO ACROSS INTO BRITAIN USING THE CHUNNEL, THEN GO BACK AROUND INTO KENT. WE HAVE A COUPLE OF SAFE HOUSES THERE--HOPEFULLY, THEY'RE NOT COMPROMISED.
IN THE MEANTIME, WE'RE ON RADIO SILENCE UNTIL WE CAN FIGURE THIS THING OUT.
SO, WE'RE NOT GOING ON TO ISTANBUL? WE'RE NOT FOLLOWING UP ON THE NEXT FRAGMENT?
WE *CAN'T*. IT'S TOO DANGEROUS, JAKE. JOHN WOULD WANT US TO *LAY LOW* FOR A FEW DAYS, THEN SEE IF WE CAN'T TAKE THE BACK ROADS INTO AVEBURY.
THAT'LL BE EASY ENOUGH. IN BRITAIN, EVEN THE HIGHWAYS ARE BACK ROADS.
OH, GOD...I'M SO SORRY. I REALLY MESSED THIS UP FOR YOU.

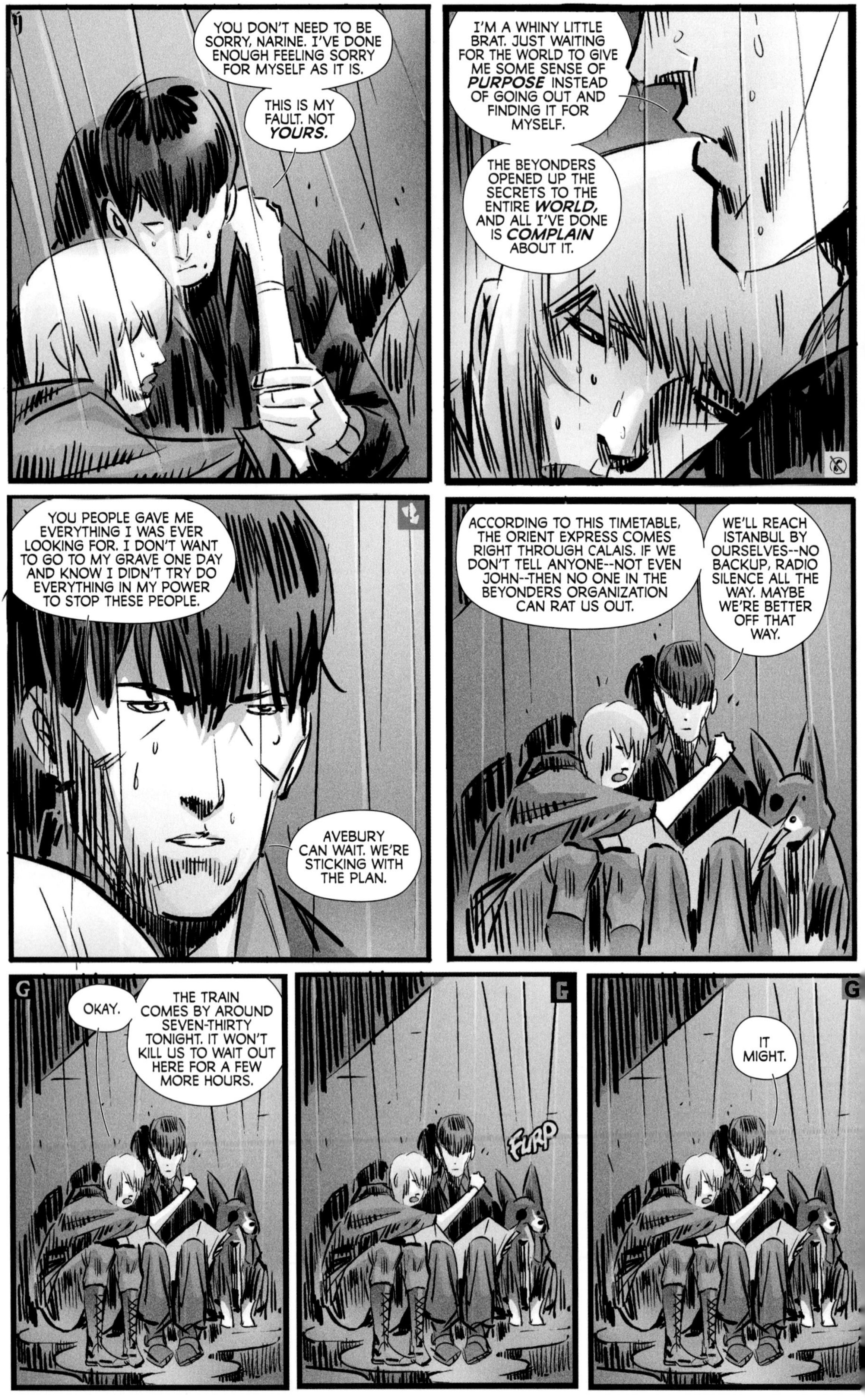
YOU DON'T NEED TO BE SORRY, NARINE. I'VE DONE ENOUGH FEELING SORRY FOR MYSELF AS IT IS.
THIS IS MY FAULT. NOT YOURS.
I'M A WHINY LITTLE BRAT. JUST WAITING FOR THE WORLD TO GIVE ME SOME SENSE OF PURPOSE INSTEAD OF GOING OUT AND FINDING IT FOR MYSELF.
THE BEYONDERS OPENED UP THE SECRETS TO THE ENTIRE WORLD, AND ALL I'VE DONE IS COMPLAIN ABOUT IT.
YOU PEOPLE GAVE ME EVERYTHING I WAS EVER LOOKING FOR. I DON'T WANT TO GO TO MY GRAVE ONE DAY AND KNOW I DIDN'T TRY DO EVERYTHING IN MY POWER TO STOP THESE PEOPLE.
AVEBURY CAN WAIT. WE'RE STICKING WITH THE PLAN.
ACCORDING TO THIS TIMETABLE, THE ORIENT EXPRESS COMES RIGHT THROUGH CALAIS. IF WE DON'T TELL ANYONE--NOT EVEN JOHN--THEN NO ONE IN THE BEYONDERS ORGANIZATION CAN RAT US OUT.
WE'LL REACH ISTANBUL BY OURSELVES--NO BACKUP, RADIO SILENCE ALL THE WAY. MAYBE WE'RE BETTER OFF THAT WAY.
OKAY.
THE TRAIN COMES BY AROUND SEVEN-THIRTY TONIGHT. IT WON'T KILL US TO WAIT OUT HERE FOR A FEW MORE HOURS.
FLRP
IT MIGHT.

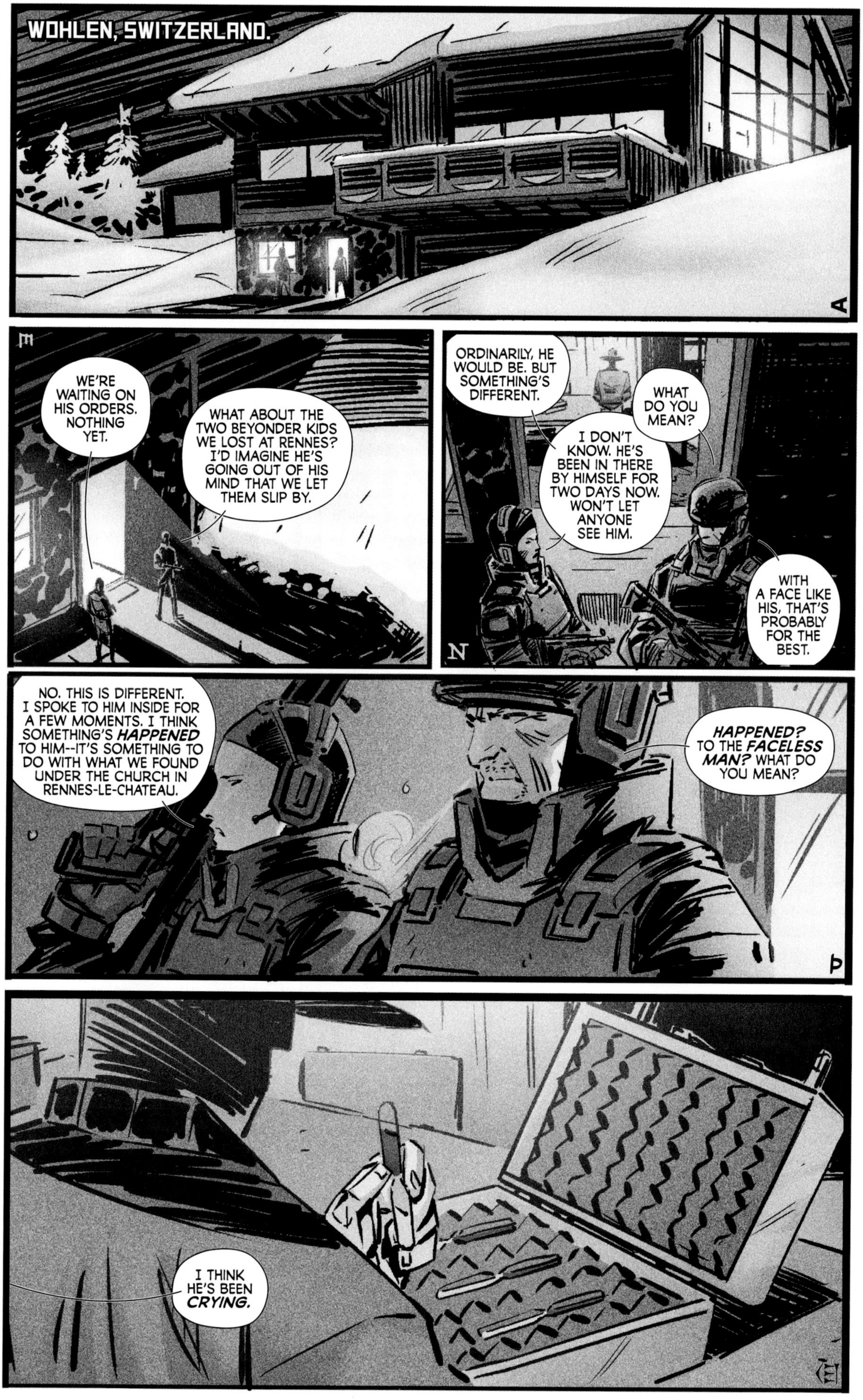
WOHLEN, SWITZERLAND.
WE'RE WAITING ON HIS ORDERS. NOTHING YET.
WHAT ABOUT THE TWO BEYONDER KIDS WE LOST AT RENNES? I'D IMAGINE HE'S GOING OUT OF HIS MIND THAT WE LET THEM SLIP BY.
ORDINARILY, HE WOULD BE. BUT SOMETHING'S DIFFERENT.
WHAT DO YOU MEAN?
I DON'T KNOW. HE'S BEEN IN THERE BY HIMSELF FOR TWO DAYS NOW. WON'T LET ANYONE SEE HIM.
WITH A FACE LIKE HIS, THAT'S PROBABLY FOR THE BEST.
NO. THIS IS DIFFERENT. I SPOKE TO HIM INSIDE FOR A FEW MOMENTS. I THINK SOMETHING'S ***HAPPENED*** TO HIM--IT'S SOMETHING TO DO WITH WHAT WE FOUND UNDER THE CHURCH IN RENNES-LE-CHATEAU.
HAPPENED? TO THE ***FACELESS MAN?*** WHAT DO YOU MEAN?
I THINK HE'S BEEN ***CRYING.***

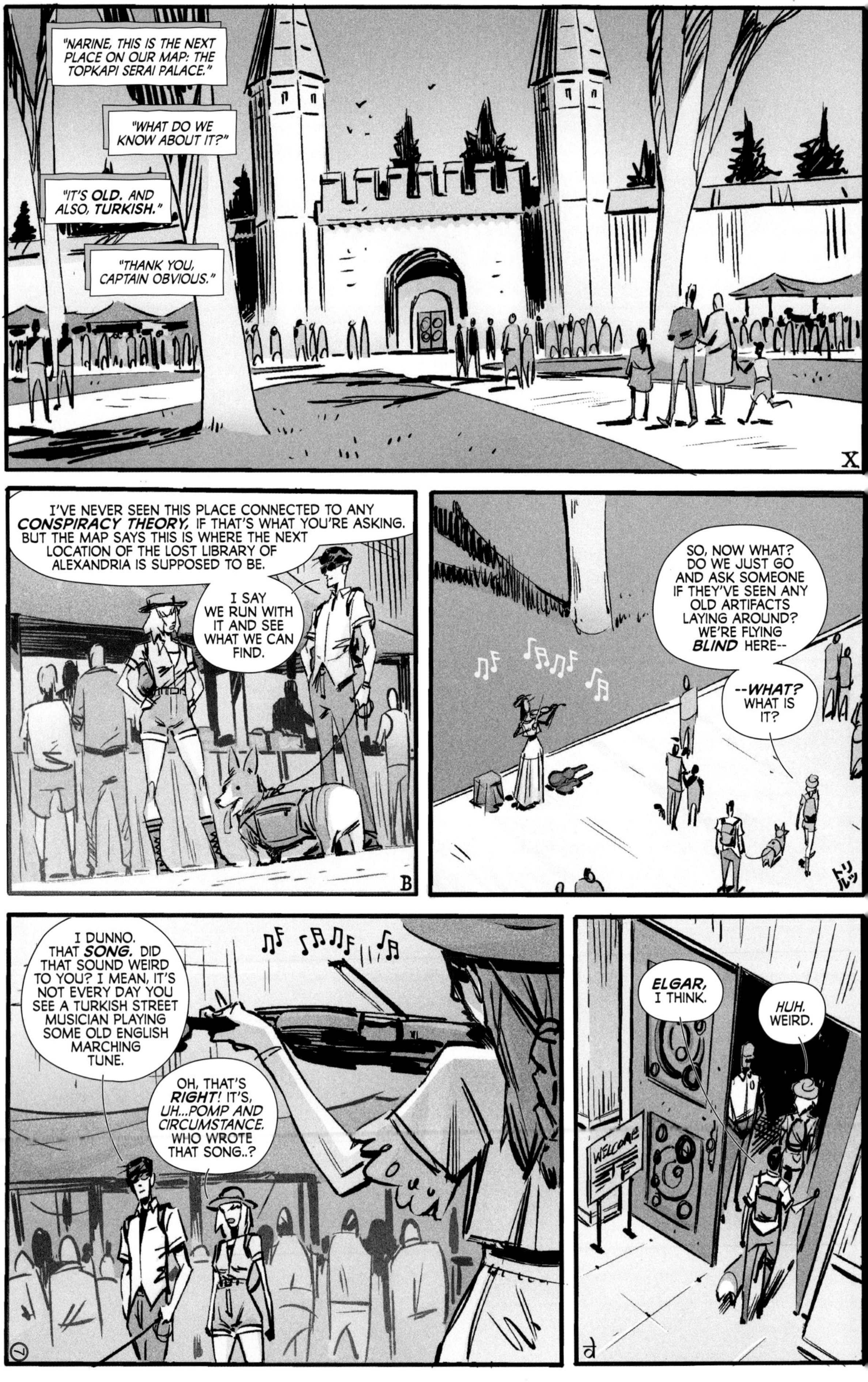
"NARINE, THIS IS THE NEXT PLACE ON OUR MAP: THE TOPKAPI SERAI PALACE."
"WHAT DO WE KNOW ABOUT IT?"
"IT'S OLD. AND ALSO, TURKISH."
"THANK YOU, CAPTAIN OBVIOUS."
I'VE NEVER SEEN THIS PLACE CONNECTED TO ANY CONSPIRACY THEORY, IF THAT'S WHAT YOU'RE ASKING. BUT THE MAP SAYS THIS IS WHERE THE NEXT LOCATION OF THE LOST LIBRARY OF ALEXANDRIA IS SUPPOSED TO BE.
I SAY WE RUN WITH IT AND SEE WHAT WE CAN FIND.
SO, NOW WHAT? DO WE JUST GO AND ASK SOMEONE IF THEY'VE SEEN ANY OLD ARTIFACTS LAYING AROUND? WE'RE FLYING BLIND HERE--
--WHAT? WHAT IS IT?
I DUNNO. THAT SONG. DID THAT SOUND WEIRD TO YOU? I MEAN, IT'S NOT EVERY DAY YOU SEE A TURKISH STREET MUSICIAN PLAYING SOME OLD ENGLISH MARCHING TUNE.
OH, THAT'S RIGHT! IT'S, UH...POMP AND CIRCUMSTANCE. WHO WROTE THAT SONG..?
ELGAR, I THINK.
HUH. WEIRD.
WELCOME

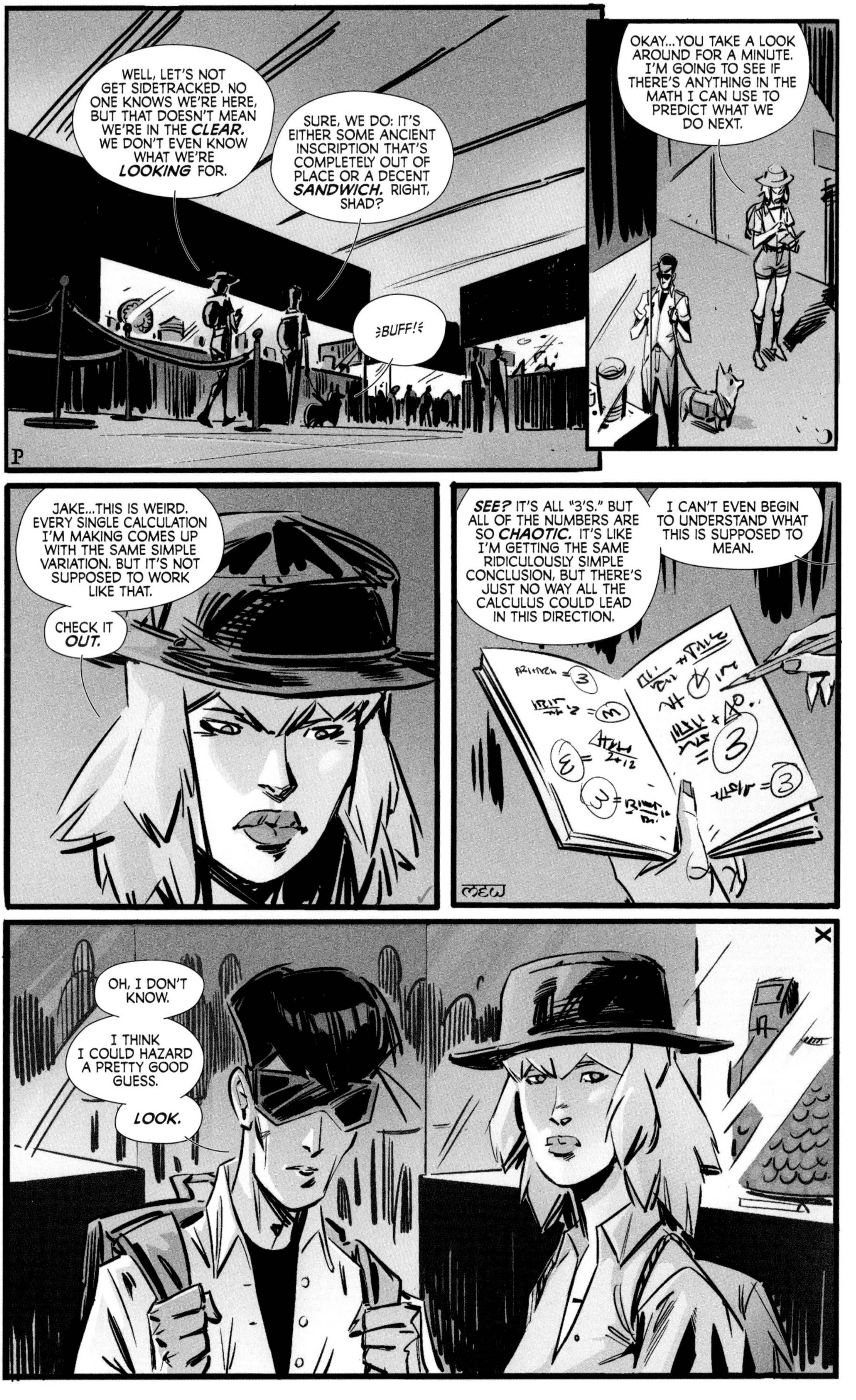
WELL, LET'S NOT GET SIDETRACKED. NO ONE KNOWS WE'RE HERE, BUT THAT DOESN'T MEAN WE'RE IN THE CLEAR. WE DON'T EVEN KNOW WHAT WE'RE LOOKING FOR.
SURE, WE DO: IT'S EITHER SOME ANCIENT INSCRIPTION THAT'S COMPLETELY OUT OF PLACE OR A DECENT SANDWICH. RIGHT, SHAD?
BUFF!
OKAY...YOU TAKE A LOOK AROUND FOR A MINUTE. I'M GOING TO SEE IF THERE'S ANYTHING IN THE MATH I CAN USE TO PREDICT WHAT WE DO NEXT.
JAKE...THIS IS WEIRD. EVERY SINGLE CALCULATION I'M MAKING COMES UP WITH THE SAME SIMPLE VARIATION. BUT IT'S NOT SUPPOSED TO WORK LIKE THAT.
CHECK IT OUT.
SEE? IT'S ALL "3'S." BUT ALL OF THE NUMBERS ARE SO CHAOTIC. IT'S LIKE I'M GETTING THE SAME RIDICULOUSLY SIMPLE CONCLUSION, BUT THERE'S JUST NO WAY ALL THE CALCULUS COULD LEAD IN THIS DIRECTION.
I CAN'T EVEN BEGIN TO UNDERSTAND WHAT THIS IS SUPPOSED TO MEAN.
MEW
OH, I DON'T KNOW.
I THINK I COULD HAZARD A PRETTY GOOD GUESS.
LOOK.

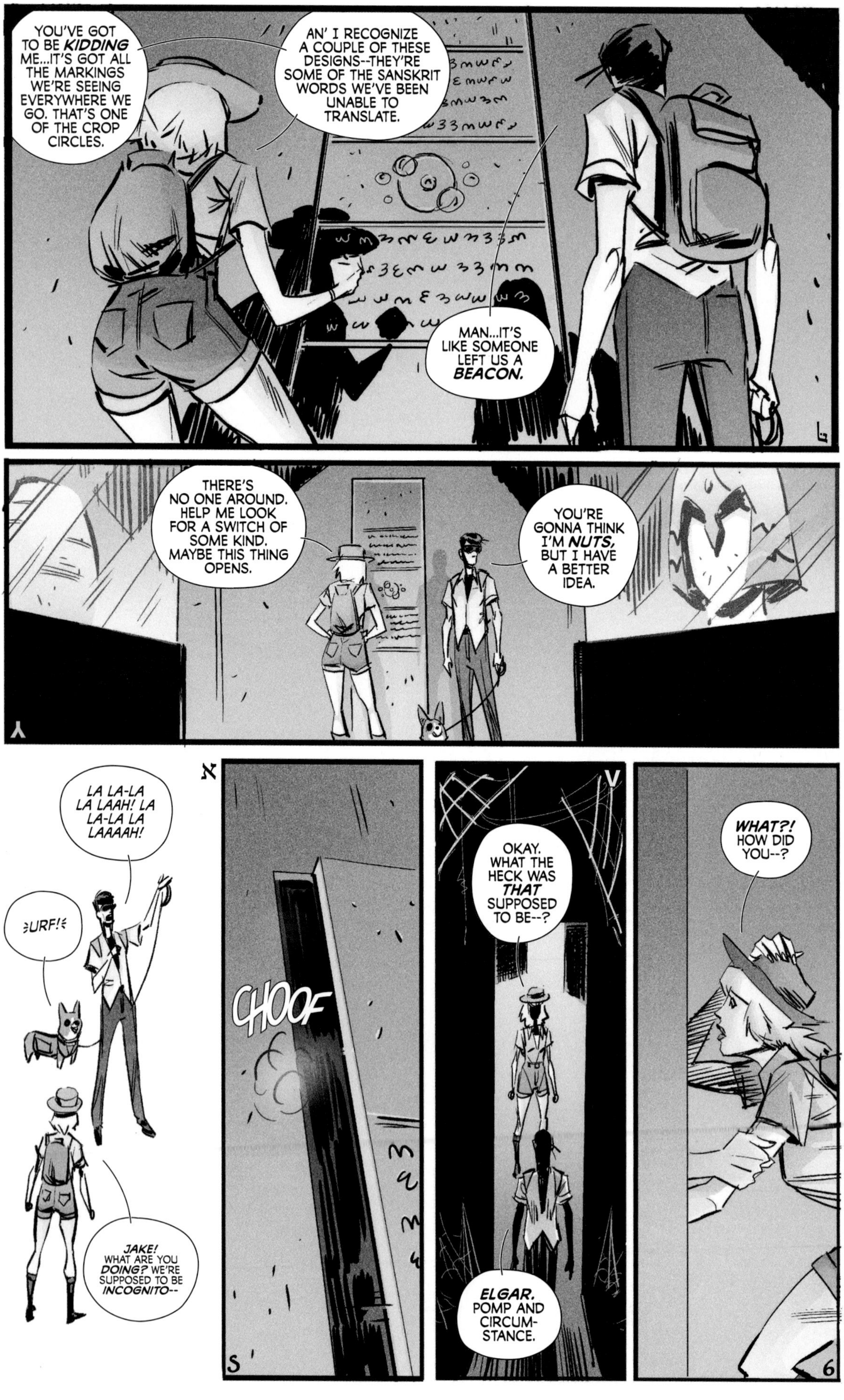
YOU'VE GOT TO BE KIDDING ME...IT'S GOT ALL THE MARKINGS WE'RE SEEING EVERYWHERE WE GO. THAT'S ONE OF THE CROP CIRCLES.
AN' I RECOGNIZE A COUPLE OF THESE DESIGNS--THEY'RE SOME OF THE SANSKRIT WORDS WE'VE BEEN UNABLE TO TRANSLATE.
MAN...IT'S LIKE SOMEONE LEFT US A BEACON.
THERE'S NO ONE AROUND. HELP ME LOOK FOR A SWITCH OF SOME KIND. MAYBE THIS THING OPENS.
YOU'RE GONNA THINK I'M NUTS, BUT I HAVE A BETTER IDEA.
LA LA-LA LA LAAH! LA LA-LA LA LAAAAH!
URF!
JAKE! WHAT ARE YOU DOING? WE'RE SUPPOSED TO BE INCOGNITO--
CHOOF
OKAY. WHAT THE HECK WAS THAT SUPPOSED TO BE--?
ELGAR. POMP AND CIRCUM-STANCE.
WHAT?! HOW DID YOU--?

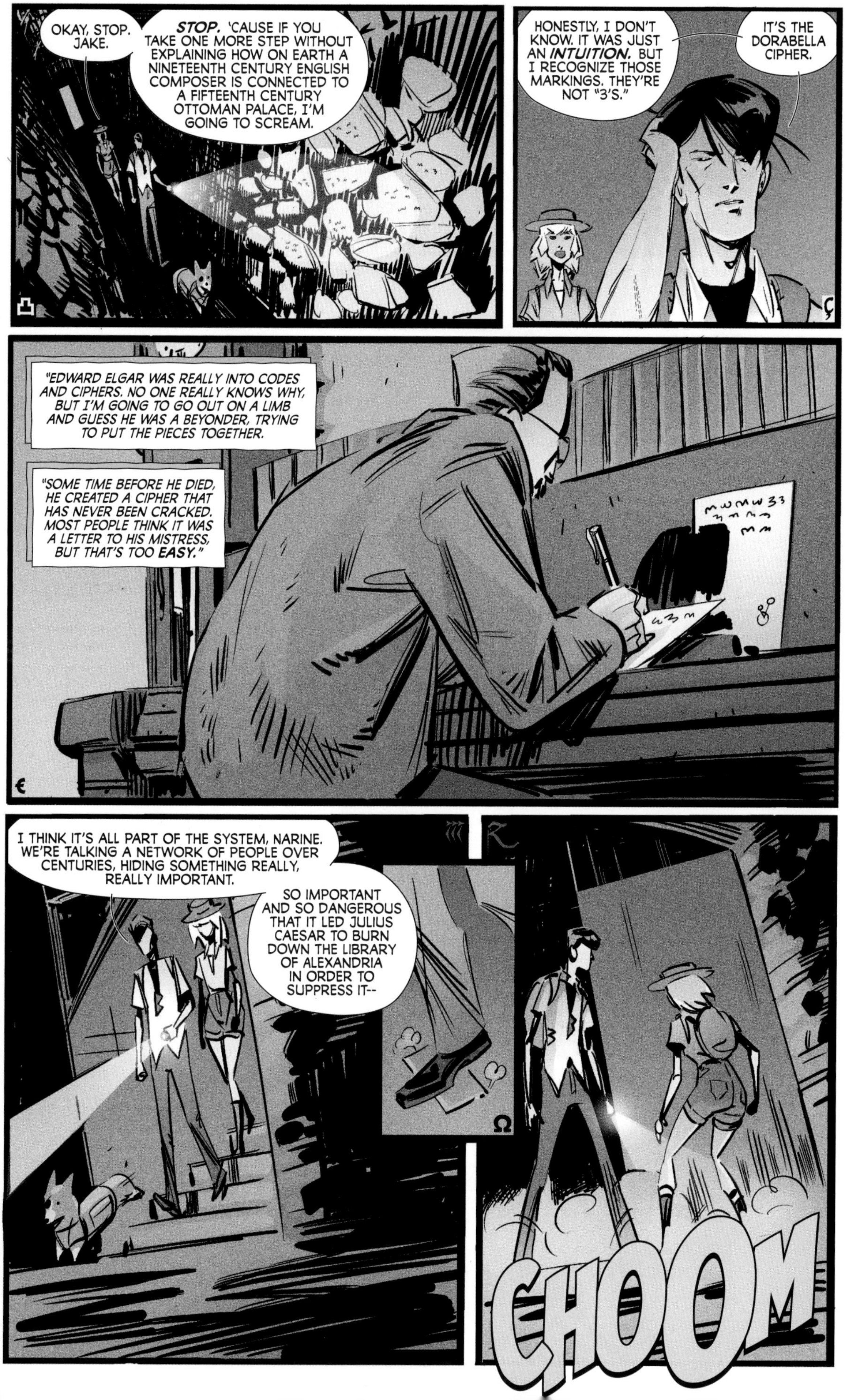
OKAY, STOP. JAKE.
STOP. 'CAUSE IF YOU TAKE ONE MORE STEP WITHOUT EXPLAINING HOW ON EARTH A NINETEENTH CENTURY ENGLISH COMPOSER IS CONNECTED TO A FIFTEENTH CENTURY OTTOMAN PALACE, I'M GOING TO SCREAM.
HONESTLY, I DON'T KNOW. IT WAS JUST AN INTUITION. BUT I RECOGNIZE THOSE MARKINGS. THEY'RE NOT "3'S."
IT'S THE DORABELLA CIPHER.
"EDWARD ELGAR WAS REALLY INTO CODES AND CIPHERS. NO ONE REALLY KNOWS WHY, BUT I'M GOING TO GO OUT ON A LIMB AND GUESS HE WAS A BEYONDER, TRYING TO PUT THE PIECES TOGETHER.
"SOME TIME BEFORE HE DIED, HE CREATED A CIPHER THAT HAS NEVER BEEN CRACKED. MOST PEOPLE THINK IT WAS A LETTER TO HIS MISTRESS, BUT THAT'S TOO EASY."
I THINK IT'S ALL PART OF THE SYSTEM, NARINE. WE'RE TALKING A NETWORK OF PEOPLE OVER CENTURIES, HIDING SOMETHING REALLY, REALLY IMPORTANT.
SO IMPORTANT AND SO DANGEROUS THAT IT LED JULIUS CAESAR TO BURN DOWN THE LIBRARY OF ALEXANDRIA IN ORDER TO SUPPRESS IT--
CHOOM

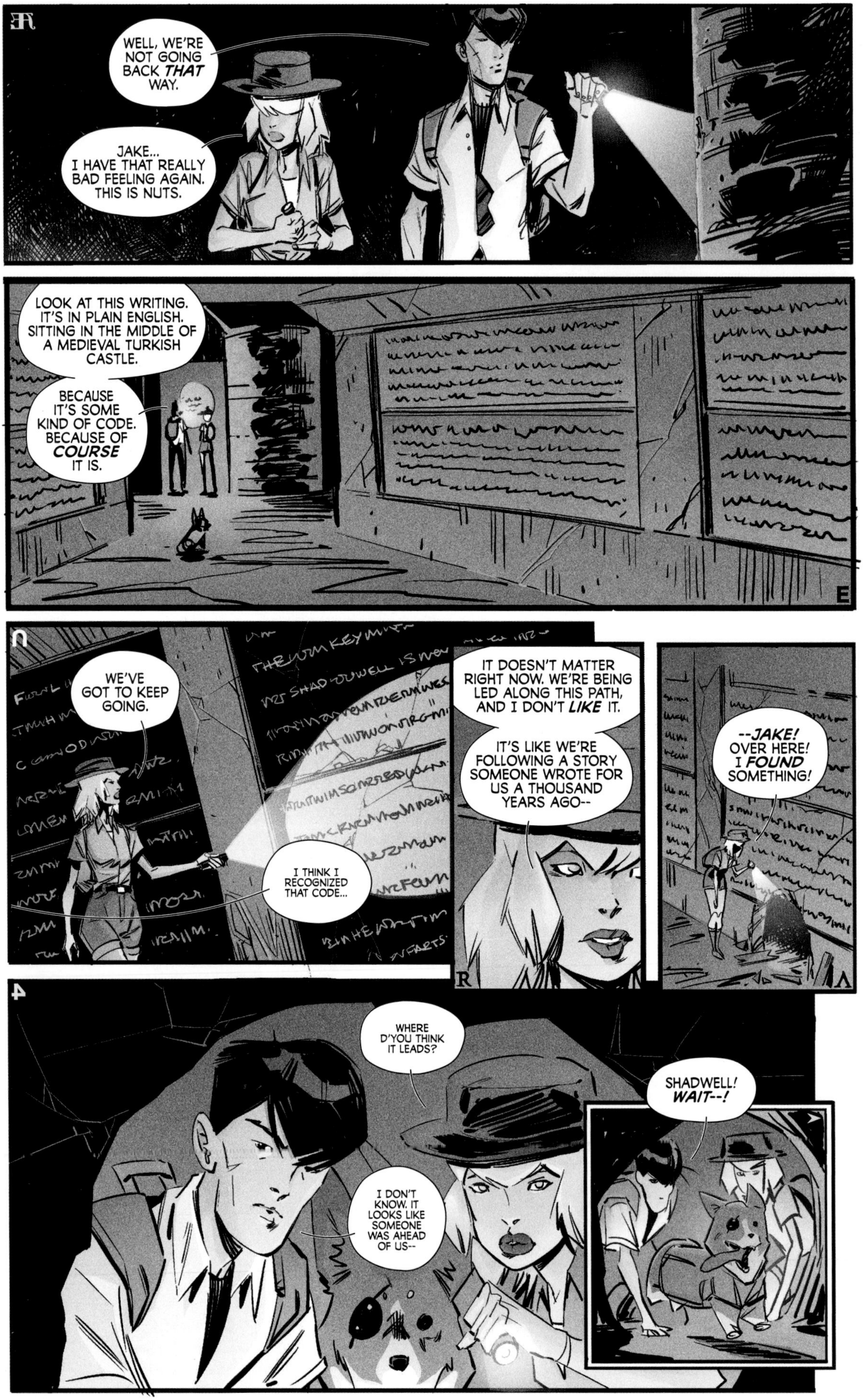
WELL, WE'RE NOT GOING BACK THAT WAY.
JAKE... I HAVE THAT REALLY BAD FEELING AGAIN. THIS IS NUTS.
LOOK AT THIS WRITING. IT'S IN PLAIN ENGLISH. SITTING IN THE MIDDLE OF A MEDIEVAL TURKISH CASTLE.
BECAUSE IT'S SOME KIND OF CODE. BECAUSE OF COURSE IT IS.
WE'VE GOT TO KEEP GOING.
I THINK I RECOGNIZED THAT CODE...
IT DOESN'T MATTER RIGHT NOW. WE'RE BEING LED ALONG THIS PATH, AND I DON'T LIKE IT.
IT'S LIKE WE'RE FOLLOWING A STORY SOMEONE WROTE FOR US A THOUSAND YEARS AGO--
--JAKE! OVER HERE! I FOUND SOMETHING!
WHERE D'YOU THINK IT LEADS?
I DON'T KNOW. IT LOOKS LIKE SOMEONE WAS AHEAD OF US--
SHADWELL! WAIT--!

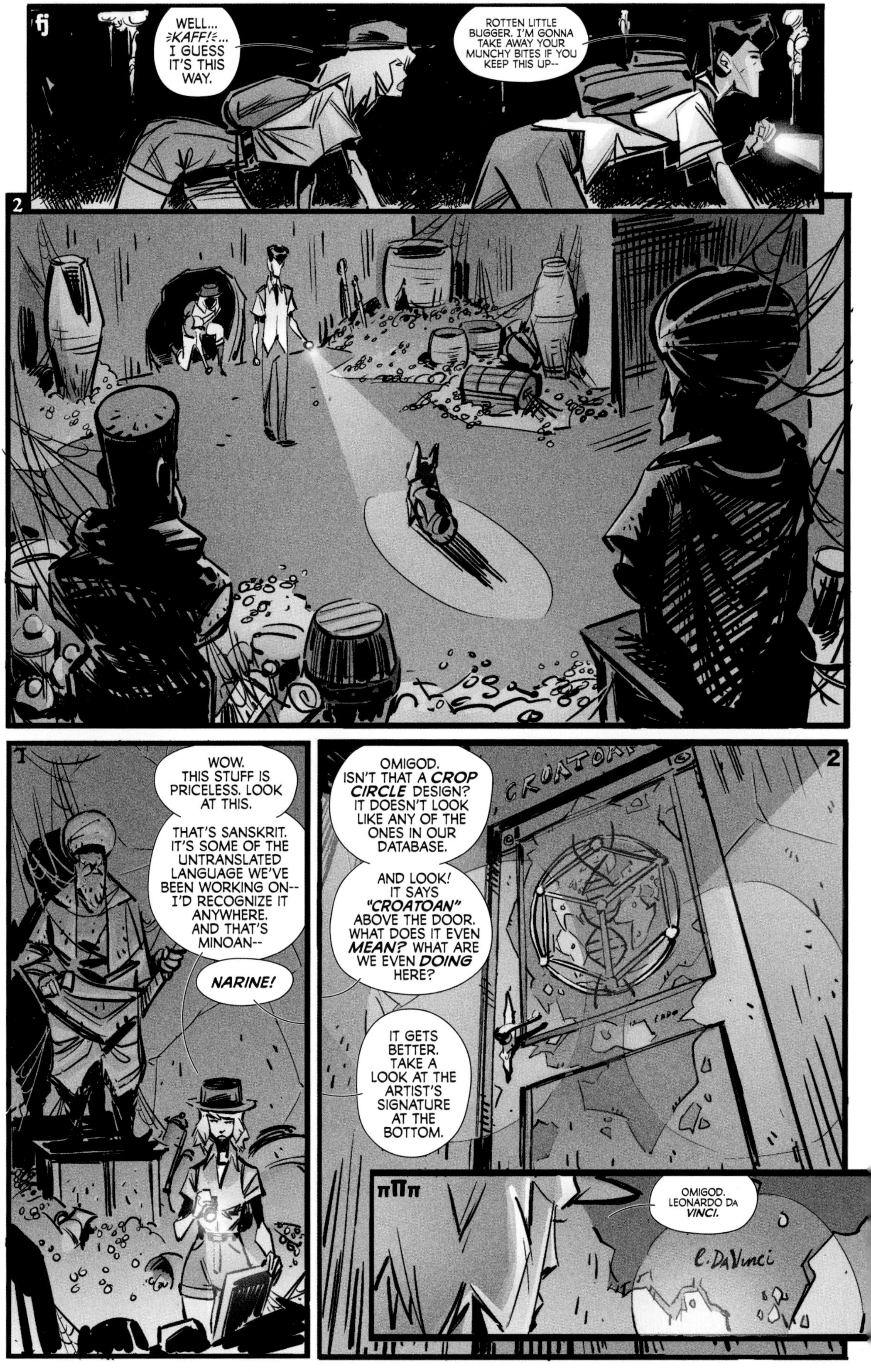
WELL... KAFF!... I GUESS IT'S THIS WAY.
ROTTEN LITTLE BUGGER. I'M GONNA TAKE AWAY YOUR MUNCHY BITES IF YOU KEEP THIS UP--
WOW. THIS STUFF IS PRICELESS. LOOK AT THIS.
THAT'S SANSKRIT. IT'S SOME OF THE UNTRANSLATED LANGUAGE WE'VE BEEN WORKING ON-- I'D RECOGNIZE IT ANYWHERE. AND THAT'S MINOAN--
NARINE!
OMIGOD. ISN'T THAT A CROP CIRCLE DESIGN? IT DOESN'T LOOK LIKE ANY OF THE ONES IN OUR DATABASE.
AND LOOK! IT SAYS "CROATOAN" ABOVE THE DOOR. WHAT DOES IT EVEN MEAN? WHAT ARE WE EVEN DOING HERE?
IT GETS BETTER. TAKE A LOOK AT THE ARTIST'S SIGNATURE AT THE BOTTOM.
OMIGOD. LEONARDO DA VINCI.
L. DaVinci

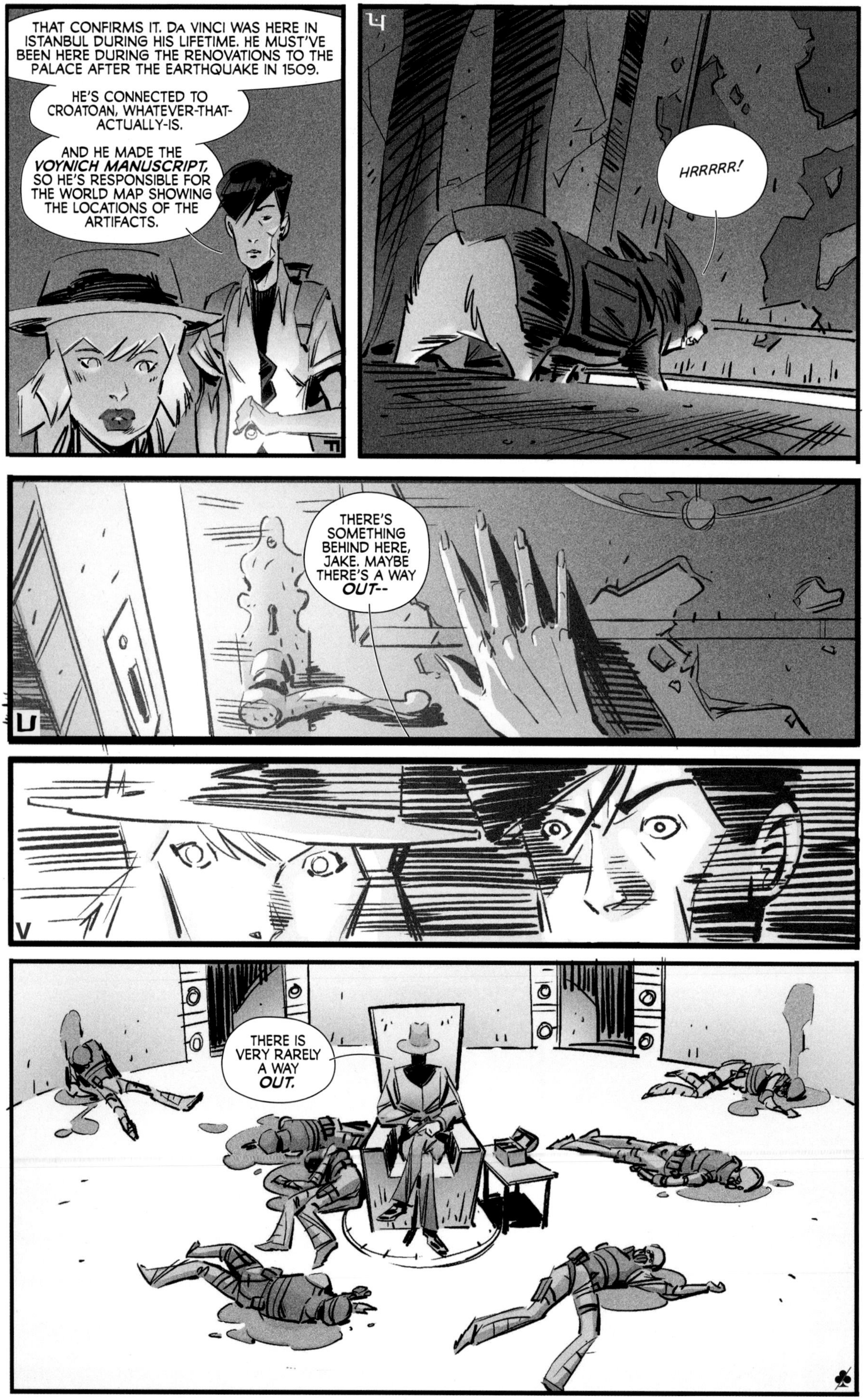
THAT CONFIRMS IT. DA VINCI WAS HERE IN ISTANBUL DURING HIS LIFETIME. HE MUST'VE BEEN HERE DURING THE RENOVATIONS TO THE PALACE AFTER THE EARTHQUAKE IN 1509.
HE'S CONNECTED TO CROATOAN, WHATEVER-THAT-ACTUALLY-IS.
AND HE MADE THE *VOYNICH MANUSCRIPT,* SO HE'S RESPONSIBLE FOR THE WORLD MAP SHOWING THE LOCATIONS OF THE ARTIFACTS.
HRRRRR!
THERE'S SOMETHING BEHIND HERE, JAKE. MAYBE THERE'S A WAY *OUT--*
THERE IS VERY RARELY A WAY *OUT.*

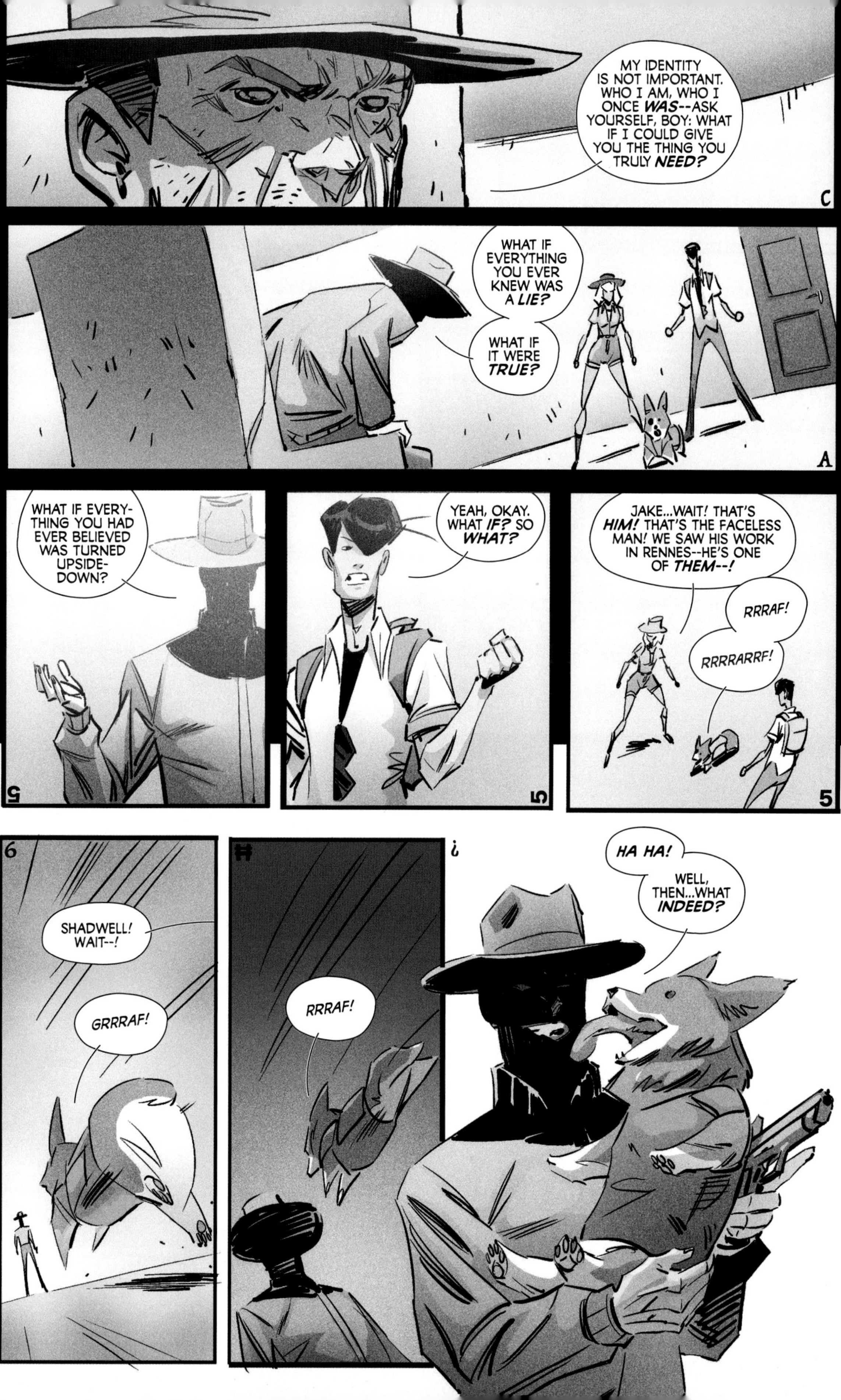
MY IDENTITY IS NOT IMPORTANT. WHO I AM, WHO I ONCE WAS--ASK YOURSELF, BOY: WHAT IF I COULD GIVE YOU THE THING YOU TRULY NEED?
WHAT IF EVERYTHING YOU EVER KNEW WAS A LIE?
WHAT IF IT WERE TRUE?
WHAT IF EVERYTHING YOU HAD EVER BELIEVED WAS TURNED UPSIDE-DOWN?
YEAH, OKAY. WHAT IF? SO WHAT?
JAKE...WAIT! THAT'S HIM! THAT'S THE FACELESS MAN! WE SAW HIS WORK IN RENNES--HE'S ONE OF THEM--!
RRRAF!
RRRRARRF!
SHADWELL! WAIT--!
GRRRAF!
RRRAF!
HA HA!
WELL, THEN...WHAT INDEED?

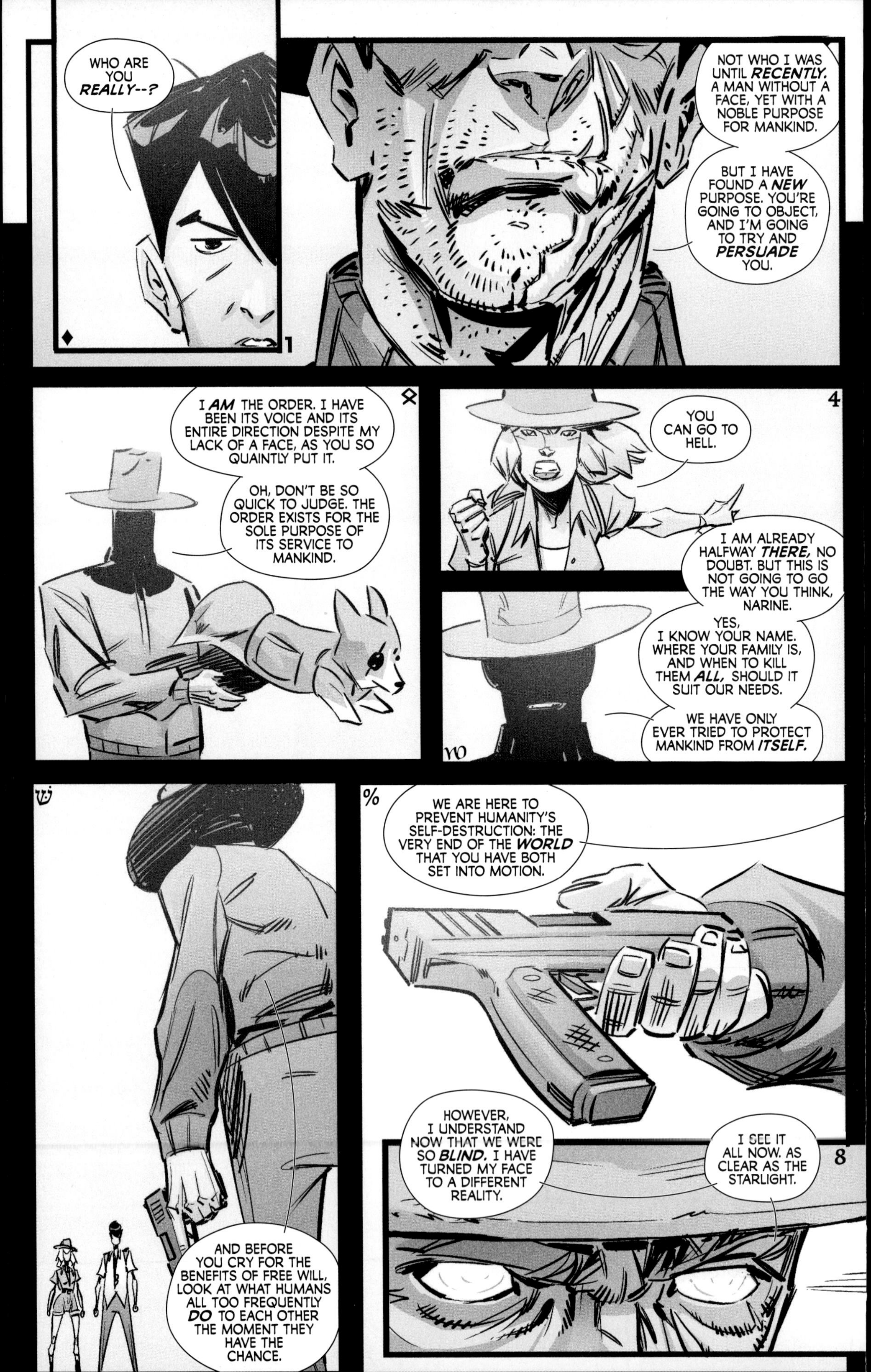

WHO ARE YOU REALLY--?
NOT WHO I WAS UNTIL RECENTLY. A MAN WITHOUT A FACE, YET WITH A NOBLE PURPOSE FOR MANKIND.
BUT I HAVE FOUND A NEW PURPOSE. YOU'RE GOING TO OBJECT, AND I'M GOING TO TRY AND PERSUADE YOU.
I AM THE ORDER. I HAVE BEEN ITS VOICE AND ITS ENTIRE DIRECTION DESPITE MY LACK OF A FACE, AS YOU SO QUAINTLY PUT IT.
OH, DON'T BE SO QUICK TO JUDGE. THE ORDER EXISTS FOR THE SOLE PURPOSE OF ITS SERVICE TO MANKIND.
YOU CAN GO TO HELL.
I AM ALREADY HALFWAY THERE, NO DOUBT. BUT THIS IS NOT GOING TO GO THE WAY YOU THINK, NARINE.
YES, I KNOW YOUR NAME. WHERE YOUR FAMILY IS, AND WHEN TO KILL THEM ALL, SHOULD IT SUIT OUR NEEDS.
WE HAVE ONLY EVER TRIED TO PROTECT MANKIND FROM ITSELF.
AND BEFORE YOU CRY FOR THE BENEFITS OF FREE WILL, LOOK AT WHAT HUMANS ALL TOO FREQUENTLY DO TO EACH OTHER THE MOMENT THEY HAVE THE CHANCE.
WE ARE HERE TO PREVENT HUMANITY'S SELF-DESTRUCTION: THE VERY END OF THE WORLD THAT YOU HAVE BOTH SET INTO MOTION.
HOWEVER, I UNDERSTAND NOW THAT WE WERE SO BLIND. I HAVE TURNED MY FACE TO A DIFFERENT REALITY.
I SEE IT ALL NOW. AS CLEAR AS THE STARLIGHT.

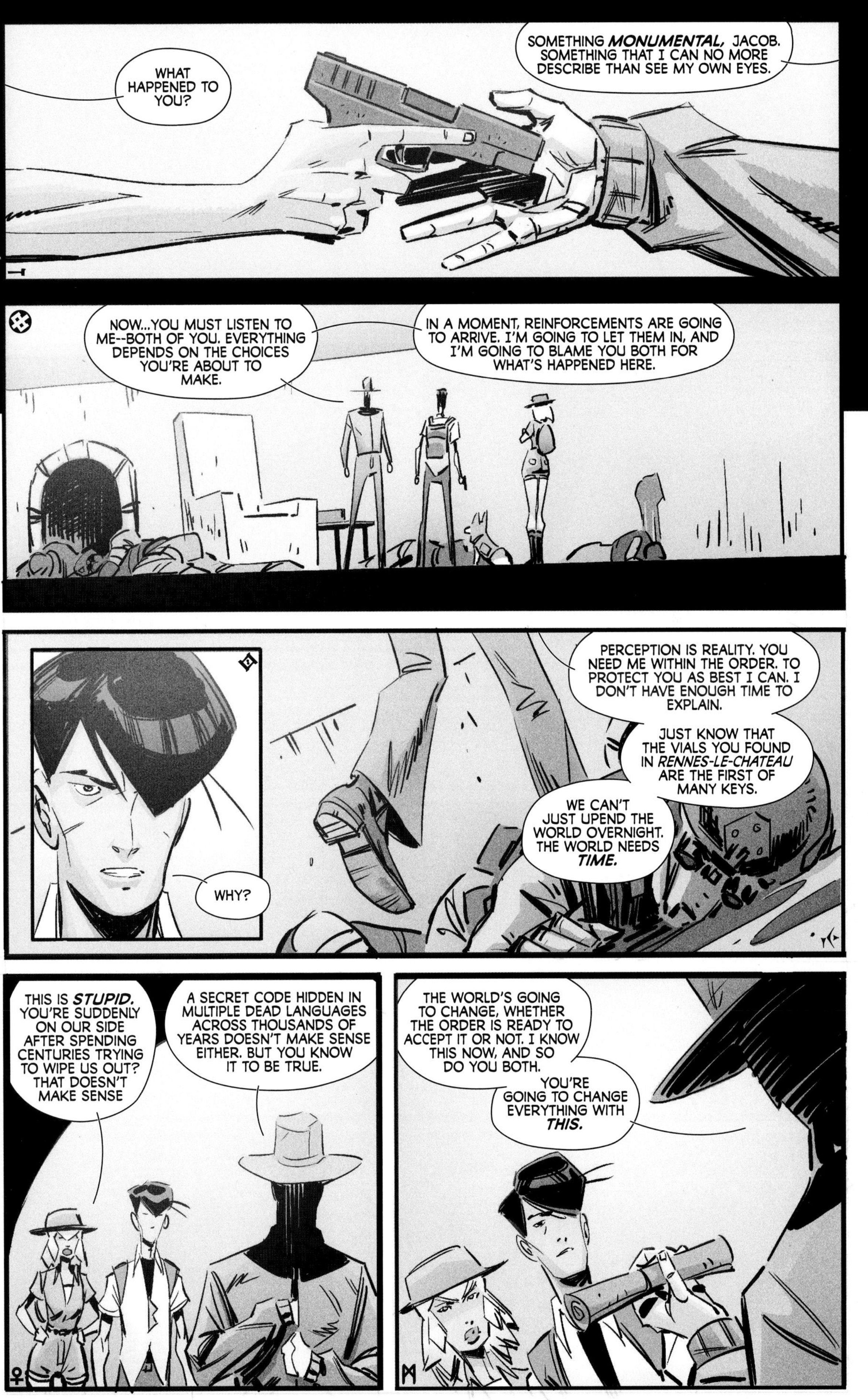
WHAT HAPPENED TO YOU?
SOMETHING ***MONUMENTAL,*** JACOB. SOMETHING THAT I CAN NO MORE DESCRIBE THAN SEE MY OWN EYES.
NOW...YOU MUST LISTEN TO ME--BOTH OF YOU. EVERYTHING DEPENDS ON THE CHOICES YOU'RE ABOUT TO MAKE.
IN A MOMENT, REINFORCEMENTS ARE GOING TO ARRIVE. I'M GOING TO LET THEM IN, AND I'M GOING TO BLAME YOU BOTH FOR WHAT'S HAPPENED HERE.
WHY?
PERCEPTION IS REALITY. YOU NEED ME WITHIN THE ORDER. TO PROTECT YOU AS BEST I CAN. I DON'T HAVE ENOUGH TIME TO EXPLAIN.
JUST KNOW THAT THE VIALS YOU FOUND IN *RENNES-LE-CHATEAU* ARE THE FIRST OF MANY KEYS.
WE CAN'T JUST UPEND THE WORLD OVERNIGHT. THE WORLD NEEDS ***TIME.***
THIS IS ***STUPID.*** YOU'RE SUDDENLY ON OUR SIDE AFTER SPENDING CENTURIES TRYING TO WIPE US OUT? THAT DOESN'T MAKE SENSE
A SECRET CODE HIDDEN IN MULTIPLE DEAD LANGUAGES ACROSS THOUSANDS OF YEARS DOESN'T MAKE SENSE EITHER. BUT YOU KNOW IT TO BE TRUE.
THE WORLD'S GOING TO CHANGE, WHETHER THE ORDER IS READY TO ACCEPT IT OR NOT. I KNOW THIS NOW, AND SO DO YOU BOTH.
YOU'RE GOING TO CHANGE EVERYTHING WITH ***THIS.***

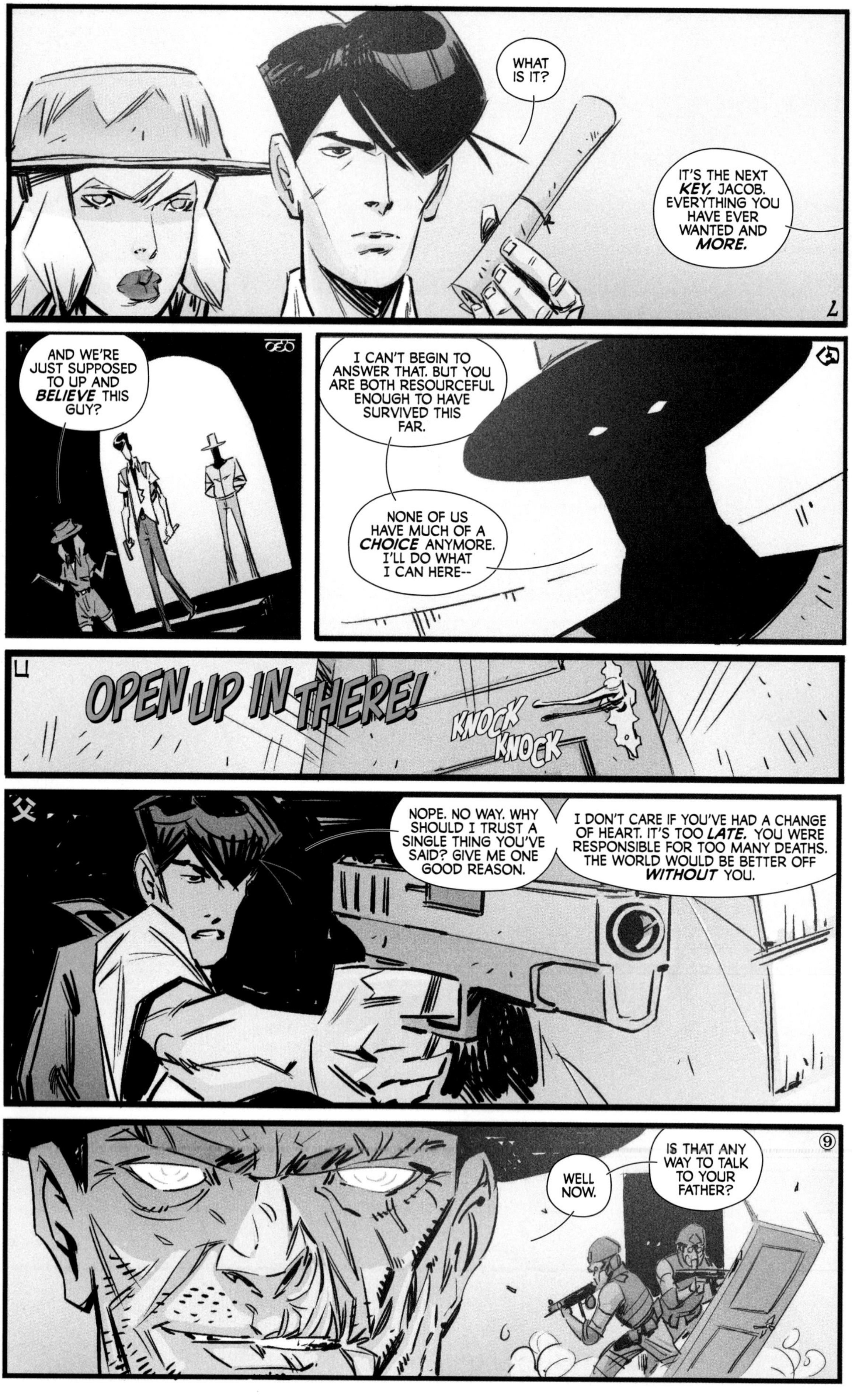
WHAT IS IT?
IT'S THE NEXT KEY, JACOB. EVERYTHING YOU HAVE EVER WANTED AND MORE.
AND WE'RE JUST SUPPOSED TO UP AND BELIEVE THIS GUY?
I CAN'T BEGIN TO ANSWER THAT. BUT YOU ARE BOTH RESOURCEFUL ENOUGH TO HAVE SURVIVED THIS FAR.
NONE OF US HAVE MUCH OF A CHOICE ANYMORE. I'LL DO WHAT I CAN HERE--
OPEN UP IN THERE!
KNOCK KNOCK
NOPE. NO WAY. WHY SHOULD I TRUST A SINGLE THING YOU'VE SAID? GIVE ME ONE GOOD REASON.
I DON'T CARE IF YOU'VE HAD A CHANGE OF HEART. IT'S TOO LATE. YOU WERE RESPONSIBLE FOR TOO MANY DEATHS. THE WORLD WOULD BE BETTER OFF WITHOUT YOU.
WELL NOW.
IS THAT ANY WAY TO TALK TO YOUR FATHER?

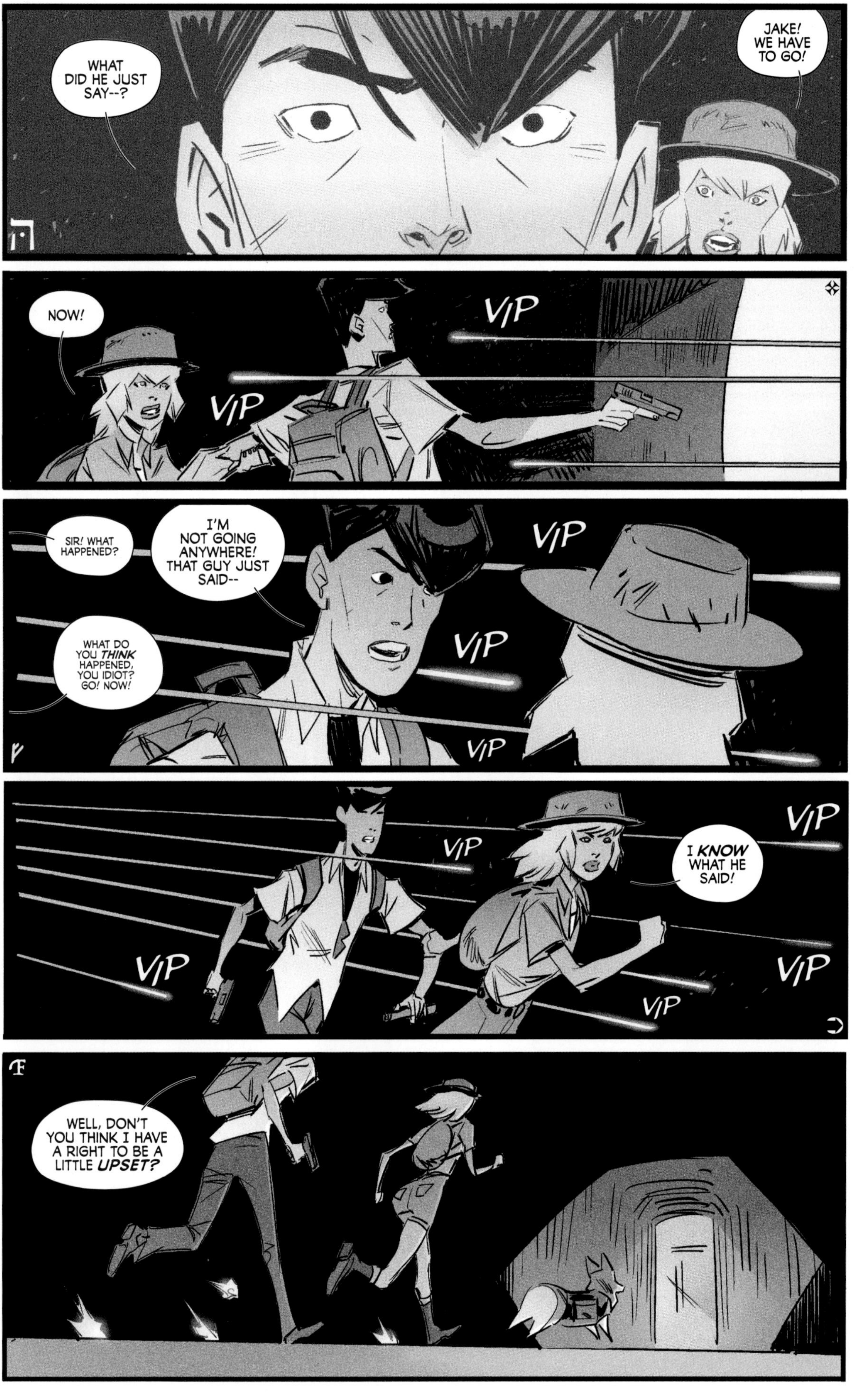
WHAT DID HE JUST SAY--?
JAKE! WE HAVE TO GO!
NOW!
VIP
VIP
SIR! WHAT HAPPENED?
I'M NOT GOING ANYWHERE! THAT GUY JUST SAID--
WHAT DO YOU *THINK* HAPPENED, YOU IDIOT? GO! NOW!
VIP
VIP
VIP
VIP
VIP
I *KNOW* WHAT HE SAID!
VIP
VIP
VIP
WELL, DON'T YOU THINK I HAVE A RIGHT TO BE A LITTLE *UPSET?*

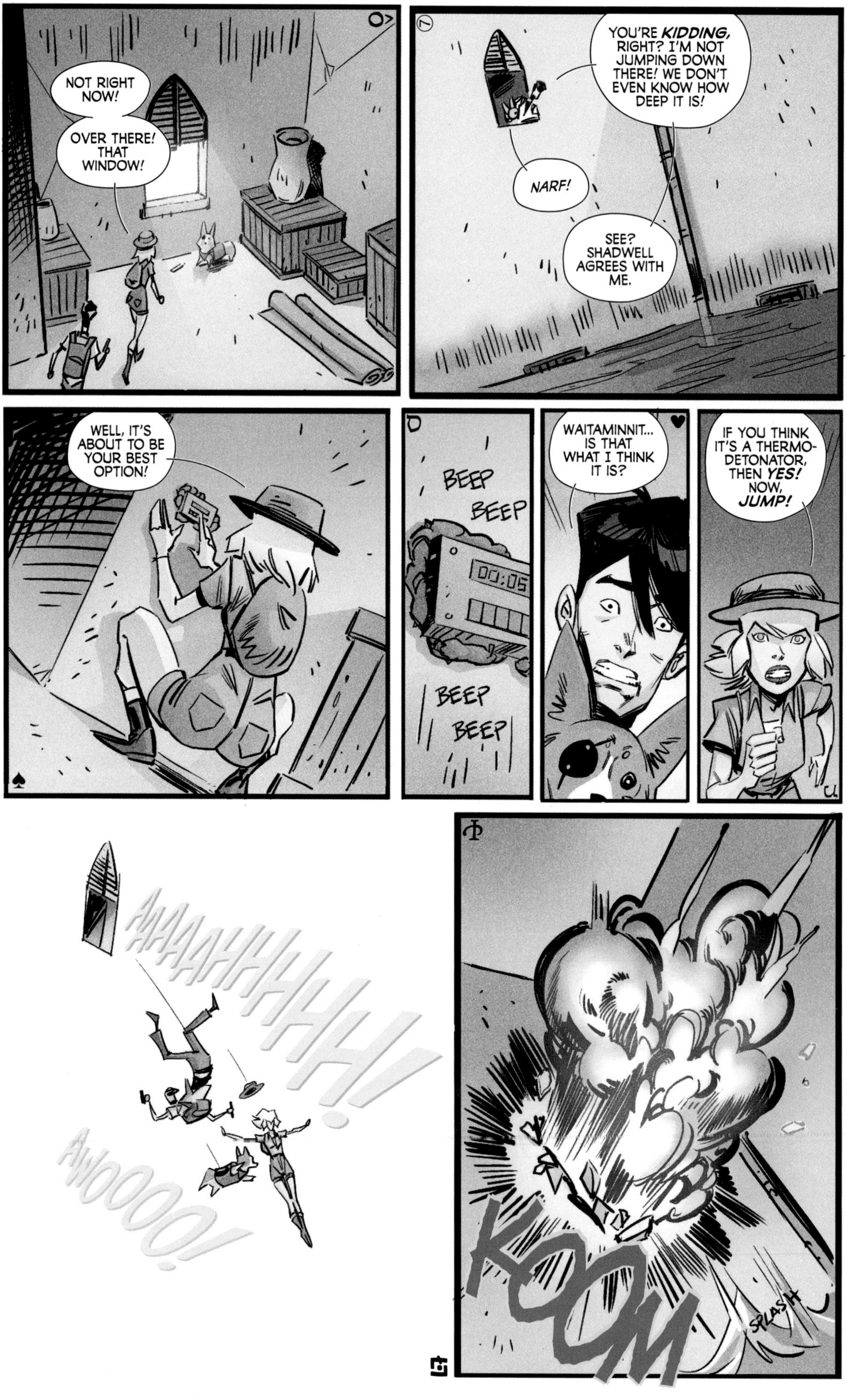
NOT RIGHT NOW!
OVER THERE! THAT WINDOW!
YOU'RE **KIDDING,** RIGHT? I'M NOT JUMPING DOWN THERE! WE DON'T EVEN KNOW HOW DEEP IT IS!
NARF!
SEE? SHADWELL AGREES WITH ME.
WELL, IT'S ABOUT TO BE YOUR BEST OPTION!
BEEP BEEP
00:05
BEEP BEEP
WAITAMINNIT... IS THAT WHAT I THINK IT IS?
IF YOU THINK IT'S A THERMO-DETONATOR, THEN **YES!** NOW, **JUMP!**
AAAAAHHHHHH!
AWOOOO!
KOOM
SPLASH

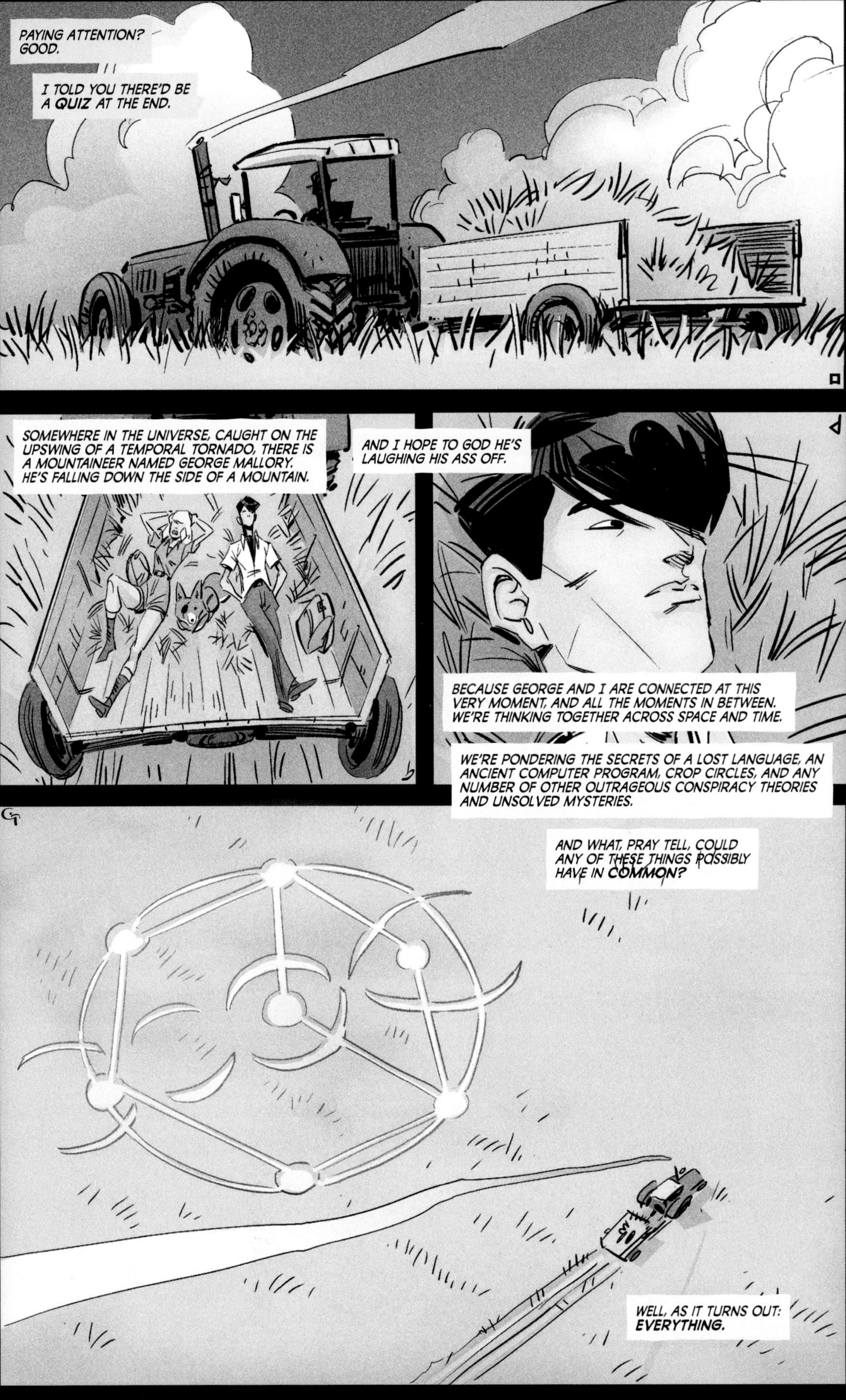
PAYING ATTENTION? GOOD.
I TOLD YOU THERE'D BE A **QUIZ** AT THE END.
SOMEWHERE IN THE UNIVERSE, CAUGHT ON THE UPSWING OF A TEMPORAL TORNADO, THERE IS A MOUNTAINEER NAMED GEORGE MALLORY. HE'S FALLING DOWN THE SIDE OF A MOUNTAIN.
AND I HOPE TO GOD HE'S LAUGHING HIS ASS OFF.
BECAUSE GEORGE AND I ARE CONNECTED AT THIS VERY MOMENT, AND ALL THE MOMENTS IN BETWEEN. WE'RE THINKING TOGETHER ACROSS SPACE AND TIME.
WE'RE PONDERING THE SECRETS OF A LOST LANGUAGE, AN ANCIENT COMPUTER PROGRAM, CROP CIRCLES, AND ANY NUMBER OF OTHER OUTRAGEOUS CONSPIRACY THEORIES AND UNSOLVED MYSTERIES.
AND WHAT, PRAY TELL, COULD ANY OF THESE THINGS POSSIBLY HAVE IN **COMMON?**
WELL, AS IT TURNS OUT: **EVERYTHING.**

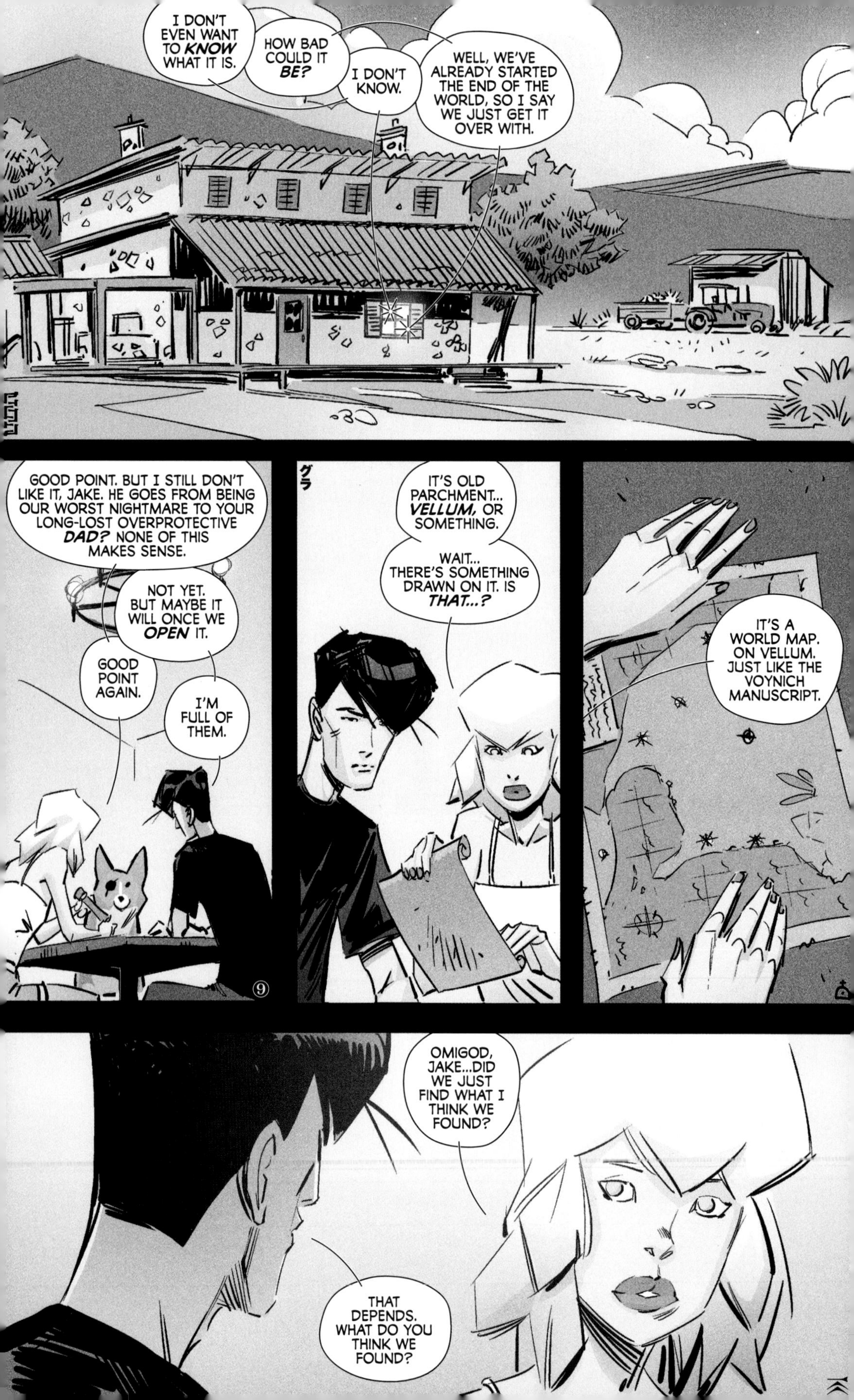
I DON'T EVEN WANT TO *KNOW* WHAT IT IS.
HOW BAD COULD IT *BE?*
I DON'T KNOW.
WELL, WE'VE ALREADY STARTED THE END OF THE WORLD, SO I SAY WE JUST GET IT OVER WITH.
GOOD POINT. BUT I STILL DON'T LIKE IT, JAKE. HE GOES FROM BEING OUR WORST NIGHTMARE TO YOUR LONG-LOST OVERPROTECTIVE *DAD?* NONE OF THIS MAKES SENSE.
NOT YET. BUT MAYBE IT WILL ONCE WE *OPEN* IT.
GOOD POINT AGAIN.
I'M FULL OF THEM.
グラ
IT'S OLD PARCHMENT... *VELLUM,* OR SOMETHING.
WAIT... THERE'S SOMETHING DRAWN ON IT. IS *THAT...?*
IT'S A WORLD MAP. ON VELLUM. JUST LIKE THE VOYNICH MANUSCRIPT.
OMIGOD, JAKE...DID WE JUST FIND WHAT I THINK WE FOUND?
THAT DEPENDS. WHAT DO YOU THINK WE FOUND?

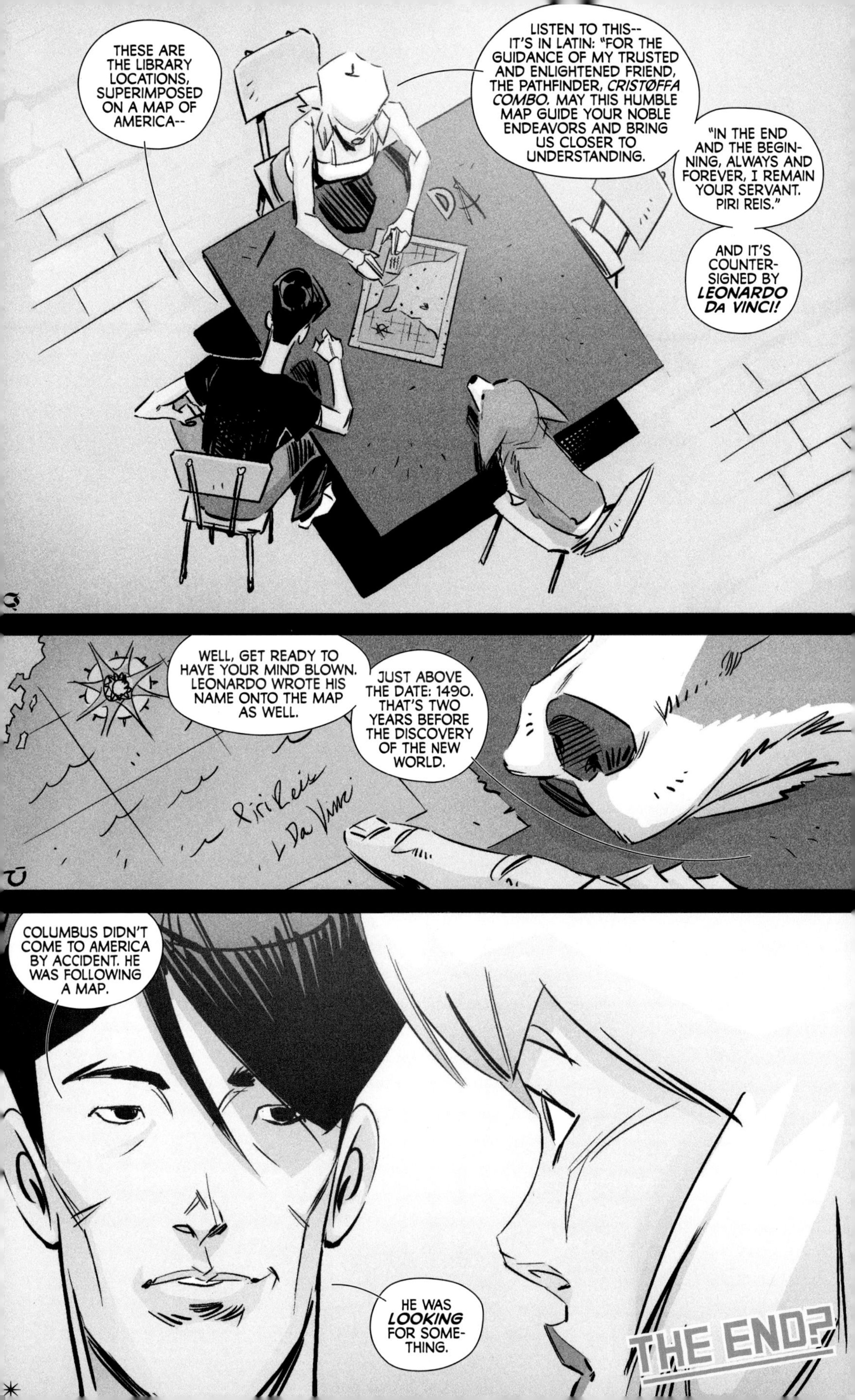
THESE ARE THE LIBRARY LOCATIONS, SUPERIMPOSED ON A MAP OF AMERICA--
LISTEN TO THIS-- IT'S IN LATIN: "FOR THE GUIDANCE OF MY TRUSTED AND ENLIGHTENED FRIEND, THE PATHFINDER, *CRISTØFFA COMBO.* MAY THIS HUMBLE MAP GUIDE YOUR NOBLE ENDEAVORS AND BRING US CLOSER TO UNDERSTANDING.
"IN THE END AND THE BEGINNING, ALWAYS AND FOREVER, I REMAIN YOUR SERVANT. PIRI REIS."
AND IT'S COUNTER-SIGNED BY ***LEONARDO DA VINCI!***
WELL, GET READY TO HAVE YOUR MIND BLOWN. LEONARDO WROTE HIS NAME ONTO THE MAP AS WELL.
JUST ABOVE THE DATE: 1490. THAT'S TWO YEARS BEFORE THE DISCOVERY OF THE NEW WORLD.
Piri Reis
L Da Vinci
COLUMBUS DIDN'T COME TO AMERICA BY ACCIDENT. HE WAS FOLLOWING A MAP.
HE WAS ***LOOKING*** FOR SOME-THING.
THE END?

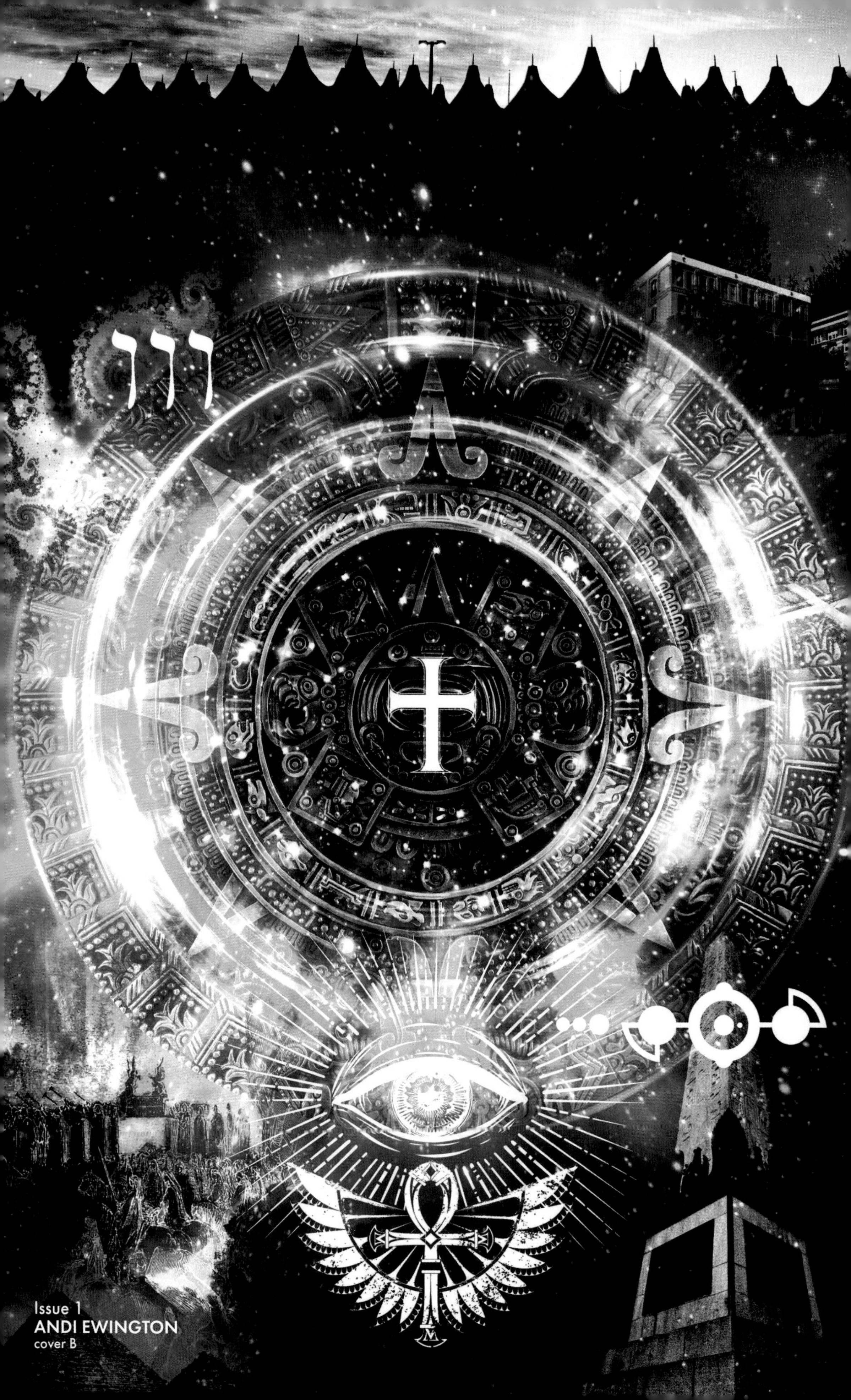
Issue 1
ANDI EWINGTON
cover B

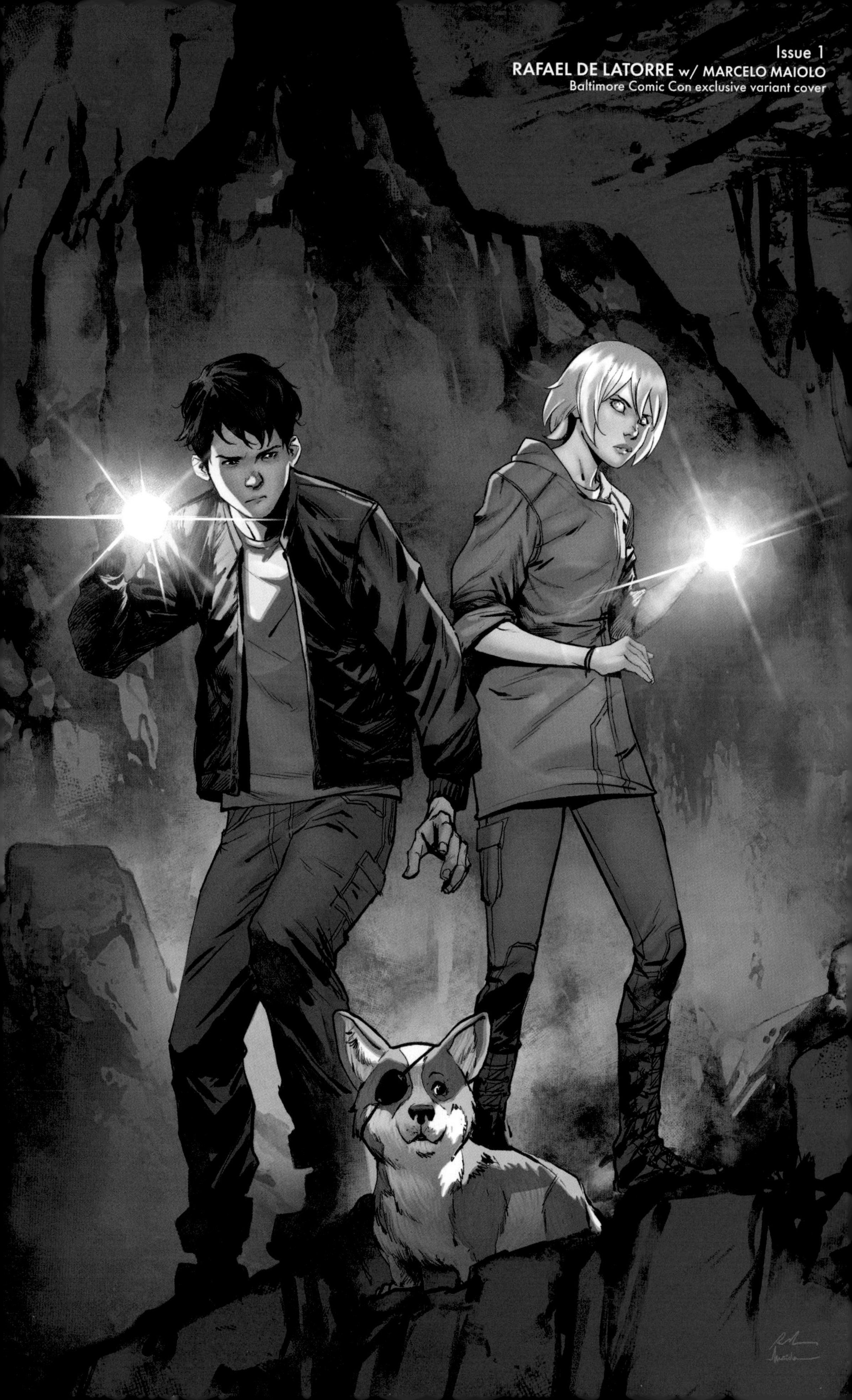

Issue 1
RAFAEL DE LATORRE w/ MARCELO MAIOLO
Baltimore Comic Con exclusive variant cover

Issue 1
JUAN DOE
New York Comic Con exclusive variant cover

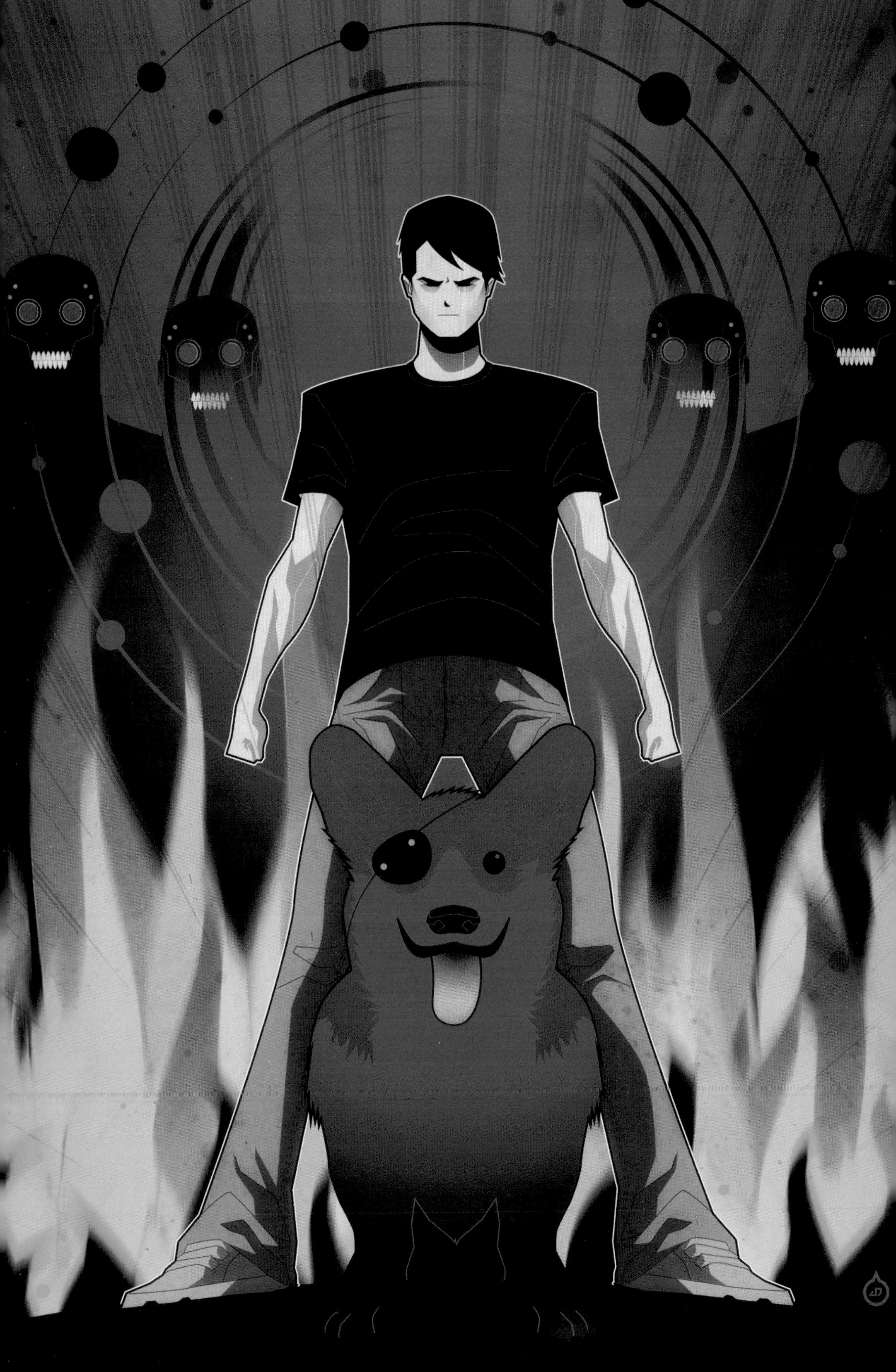

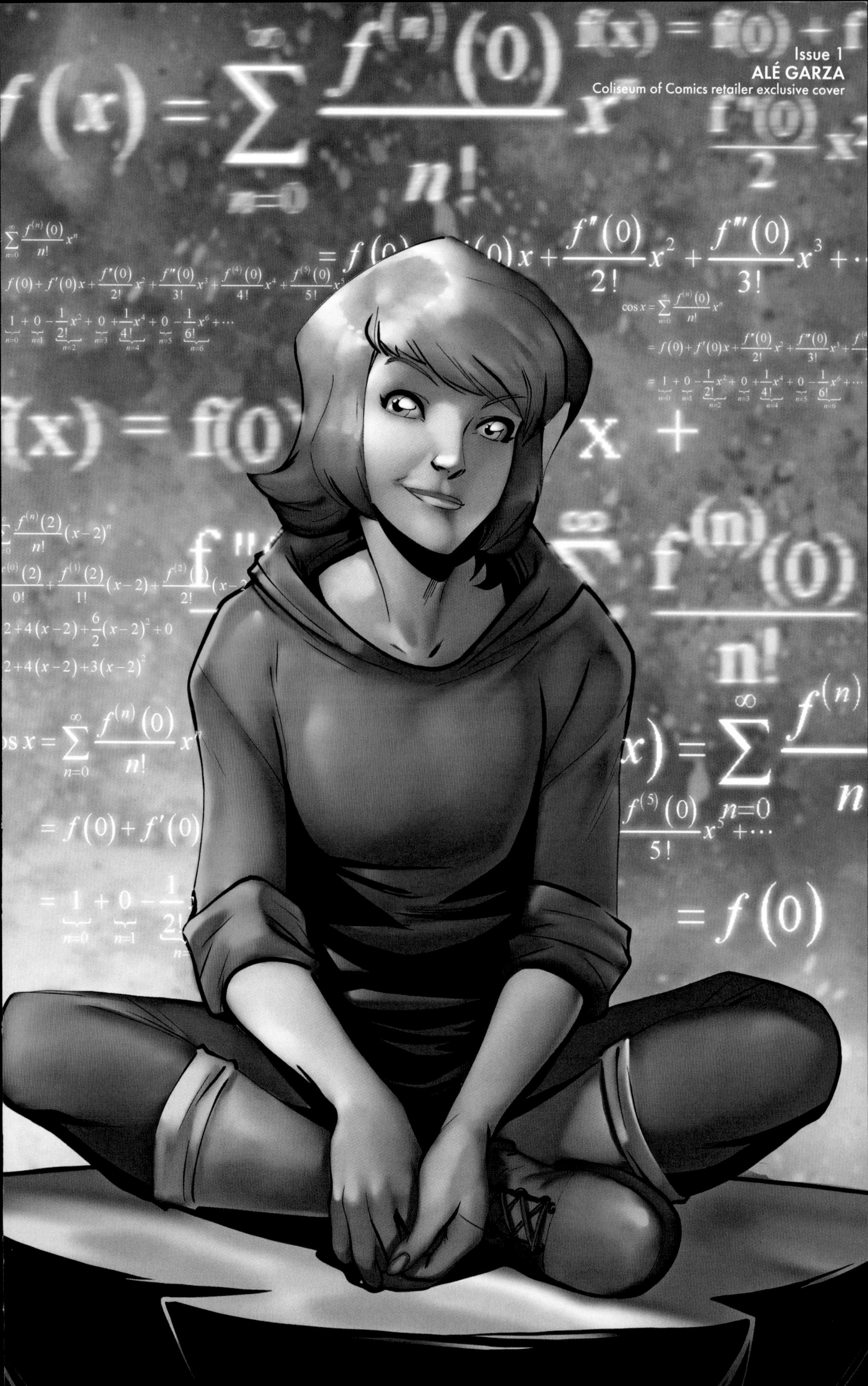

Issue 1
ALÉ GARZA
Coliseum of Comics retailer exclusive cover

Issue 1
WESLEY ST. CLAIRE
Long Beach Comic Con exclusive variant cover

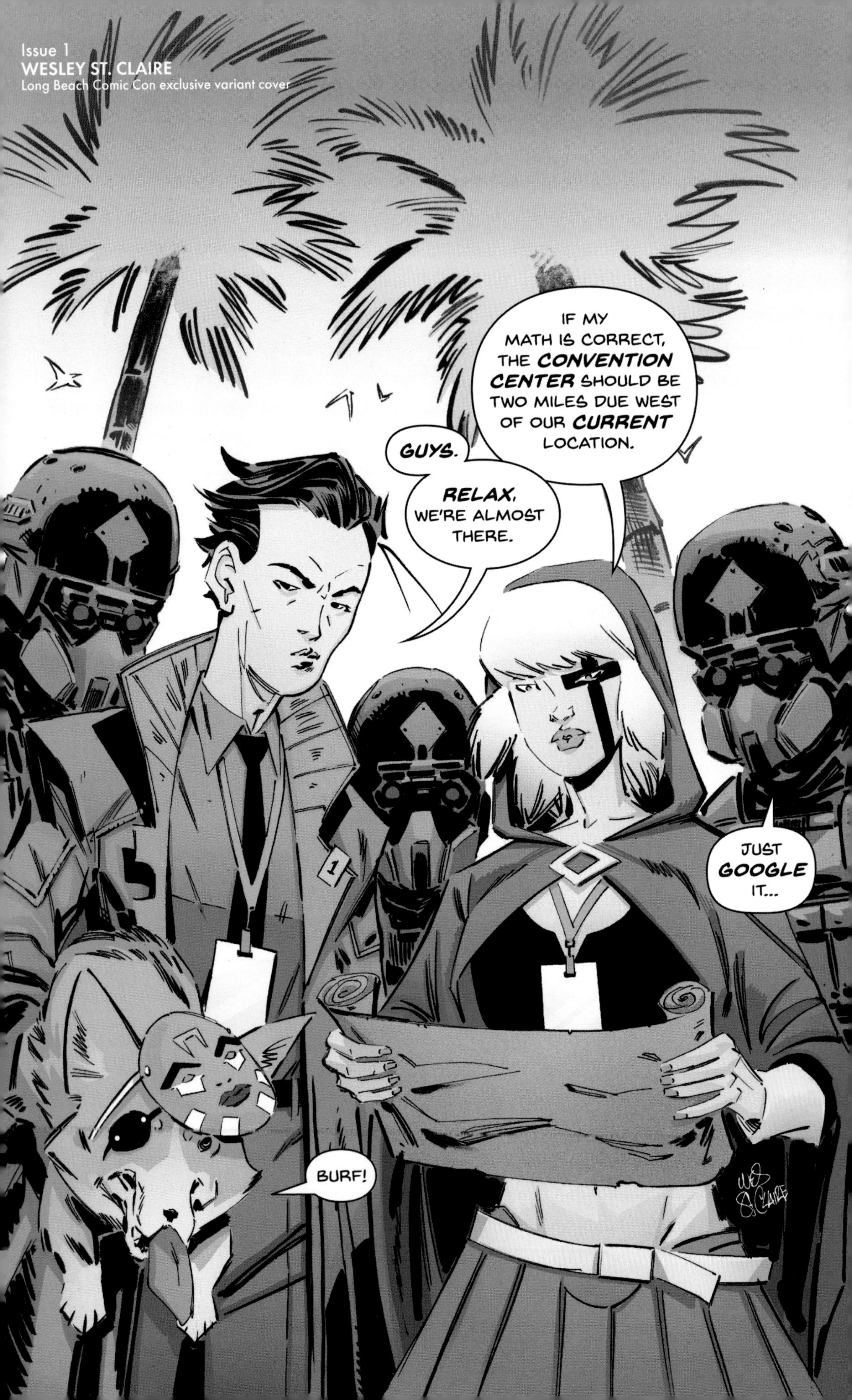
GUYS.
RELAX, WE'RE ALMOST THERE.
IF MY MATH IS CORRECT, THE CONVENTION CENTER SHOULD BE TWO MILES DUE WEST OF OUR CURRENT LOCATION.
JUST GOOGLE IT...
BURF!
WES ST. CLAIRE

BEYONDERS™

BEHIND THE SCENES

BEYONDERS

sketchbook

art by WESLEY ST. CLAIRE

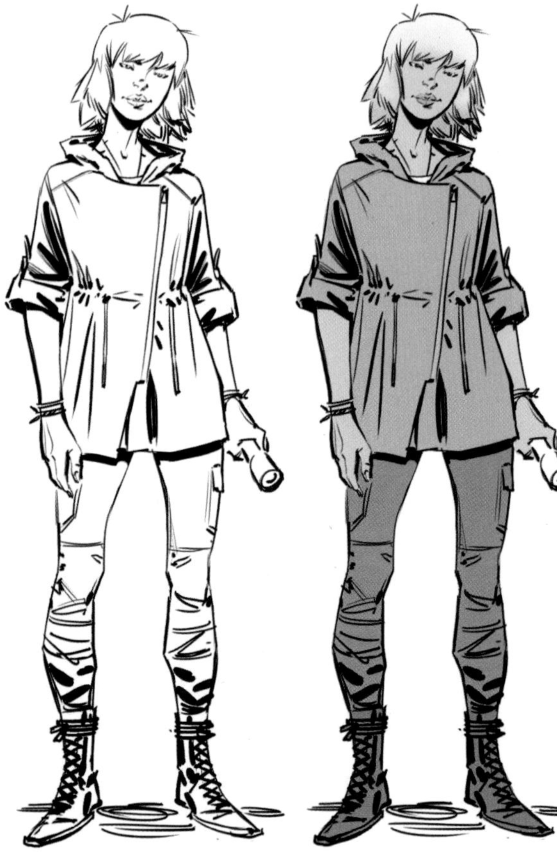

Narine

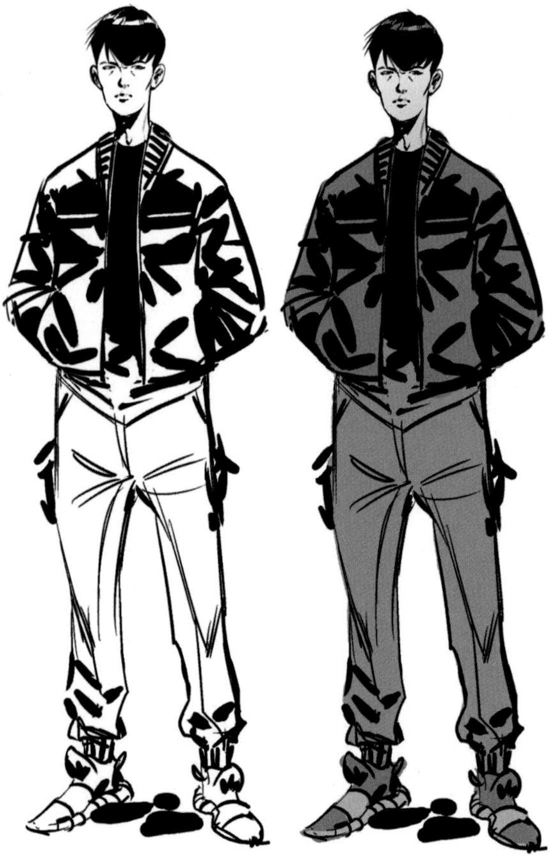

Jake

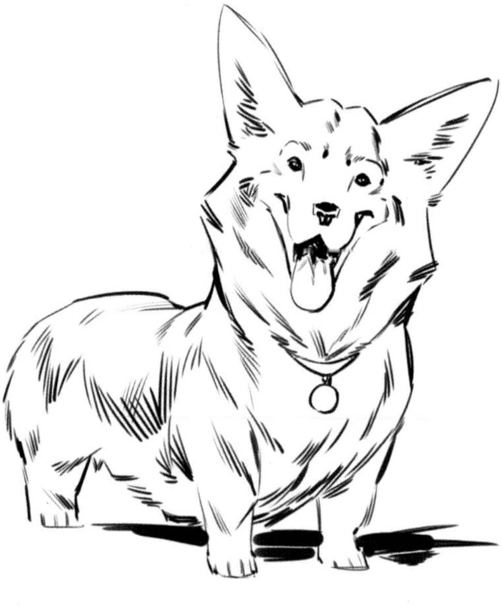

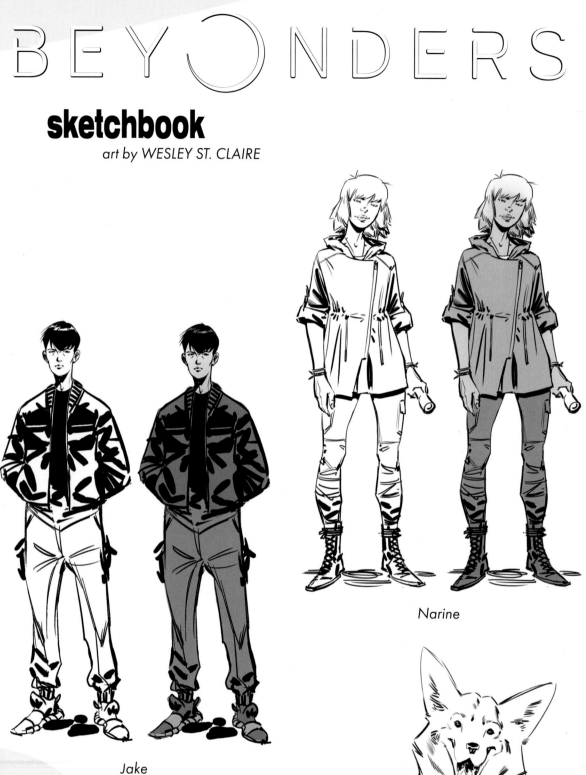

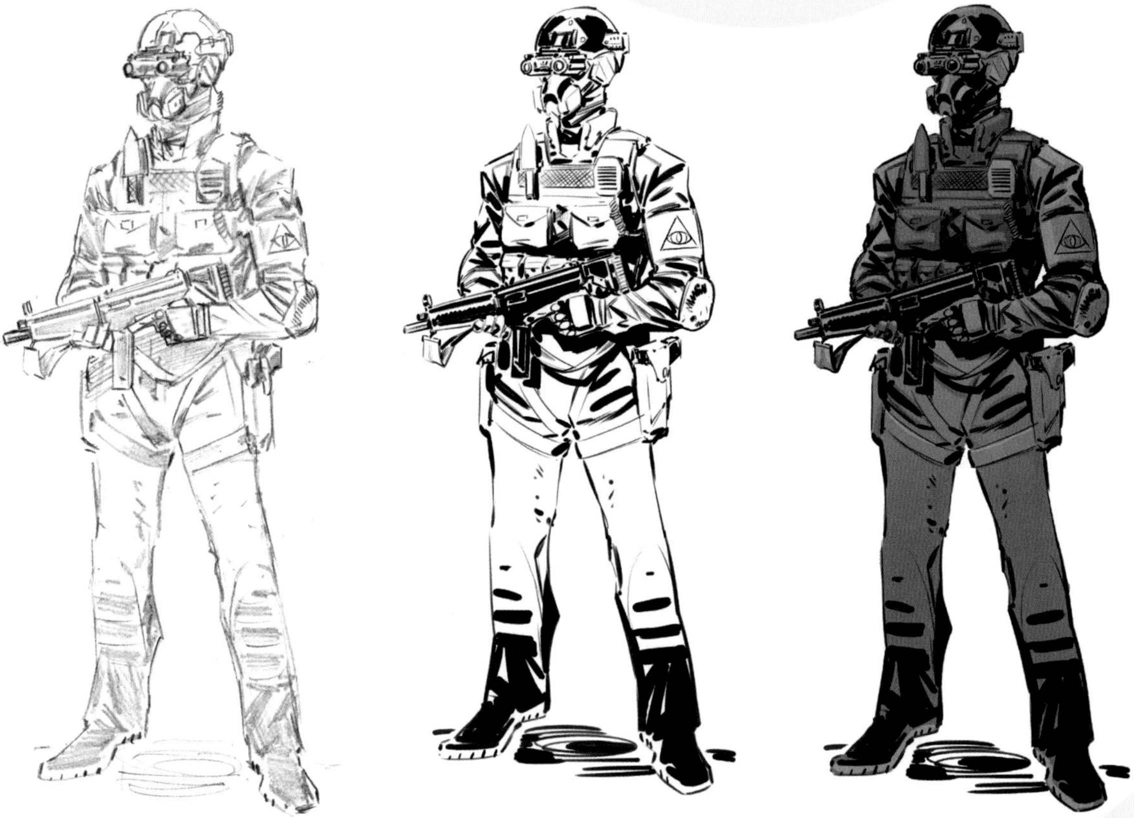

Order Soldier

Shadwell

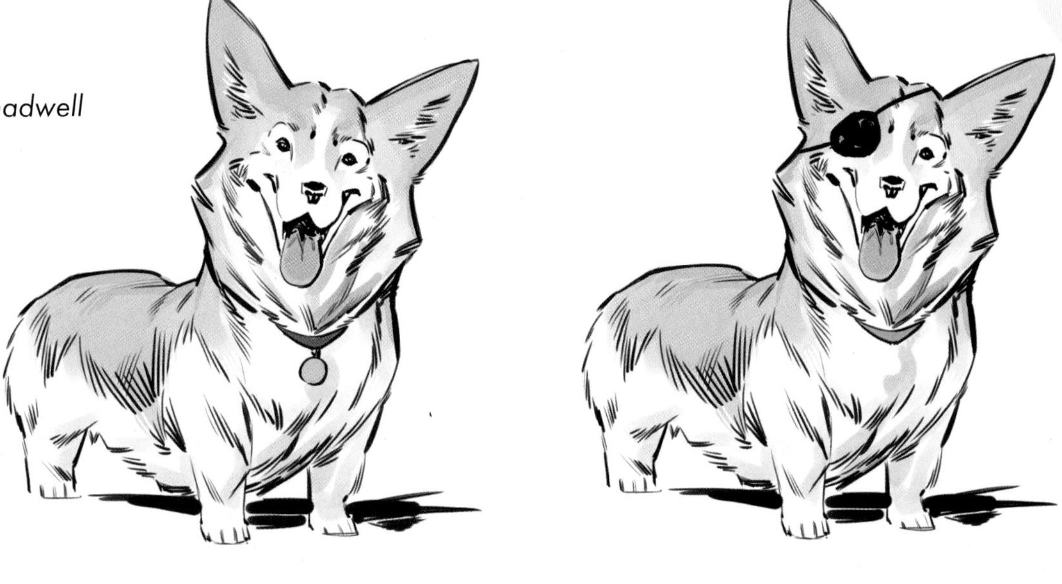

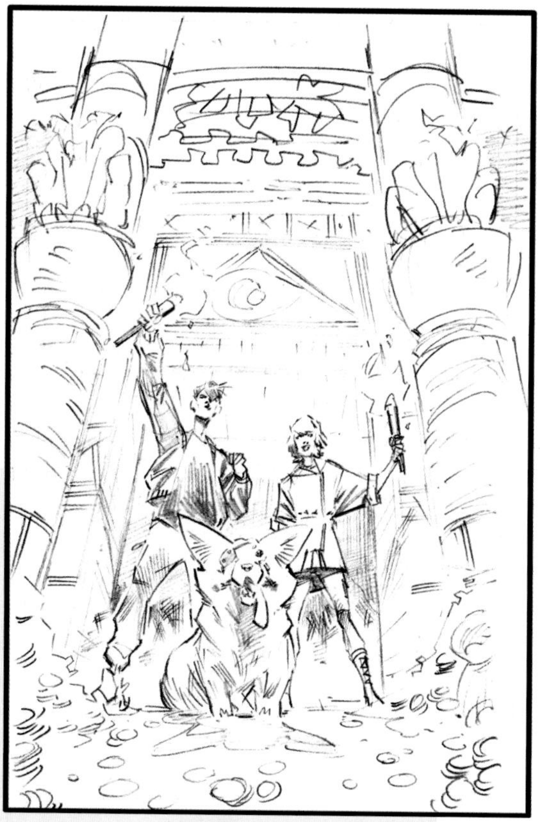

Issue #1 cover layout

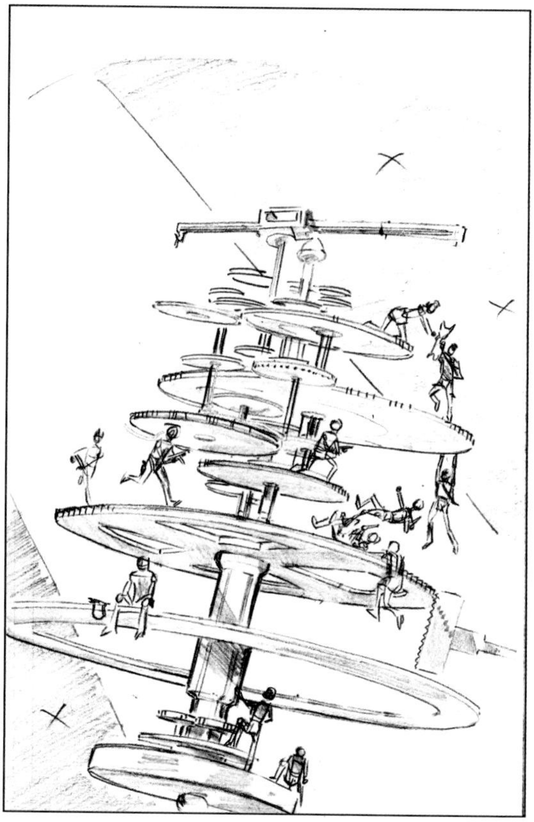

Issue #2 cover layout

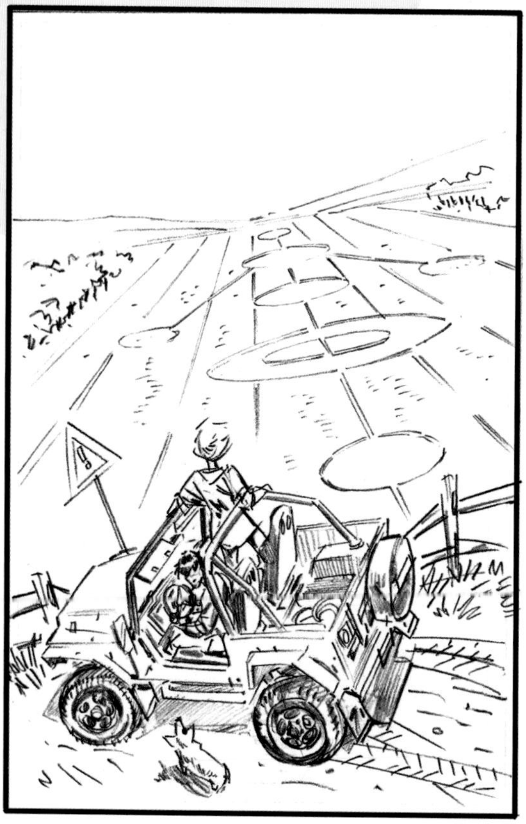

Issue #3 cover layout

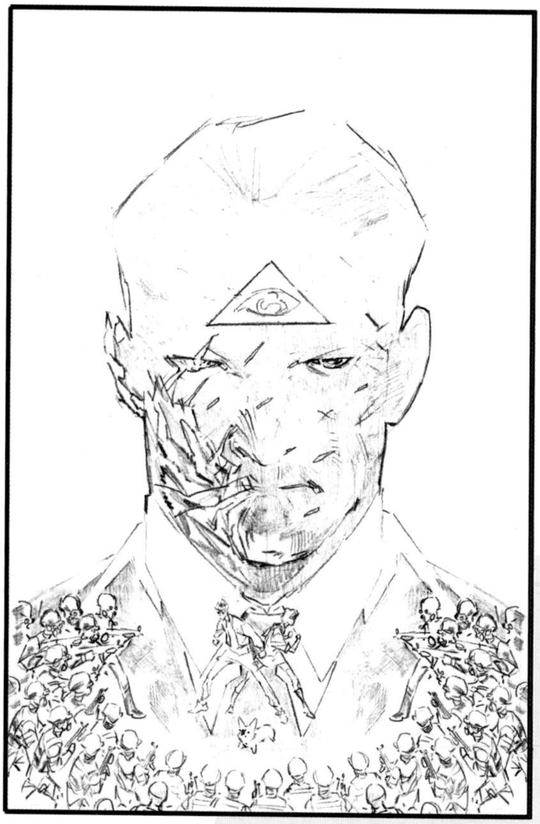

Issue #4 cover layout - unused

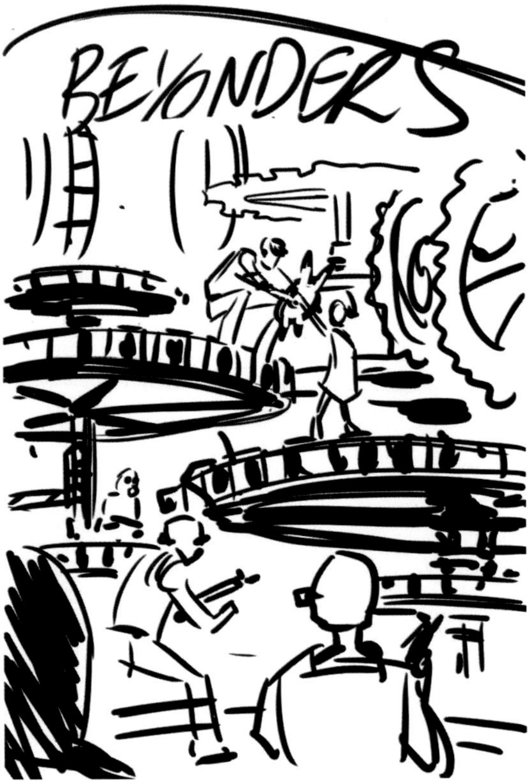
BEYONDERS

Issue #2 cover layout - unused

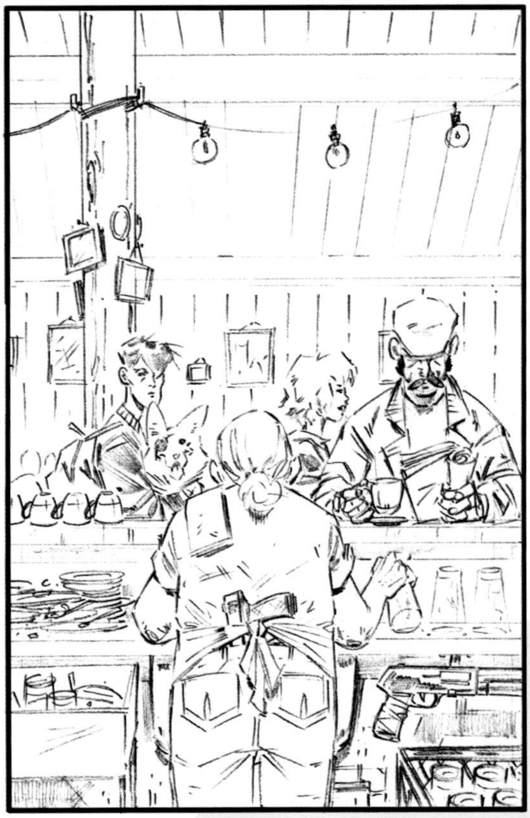

Issue #2 cover layout - unused

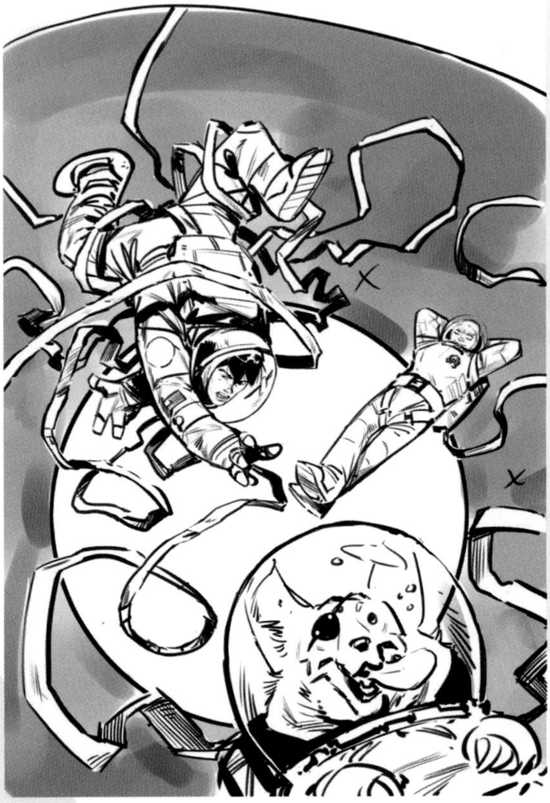

Issue #5 cover layout - unused

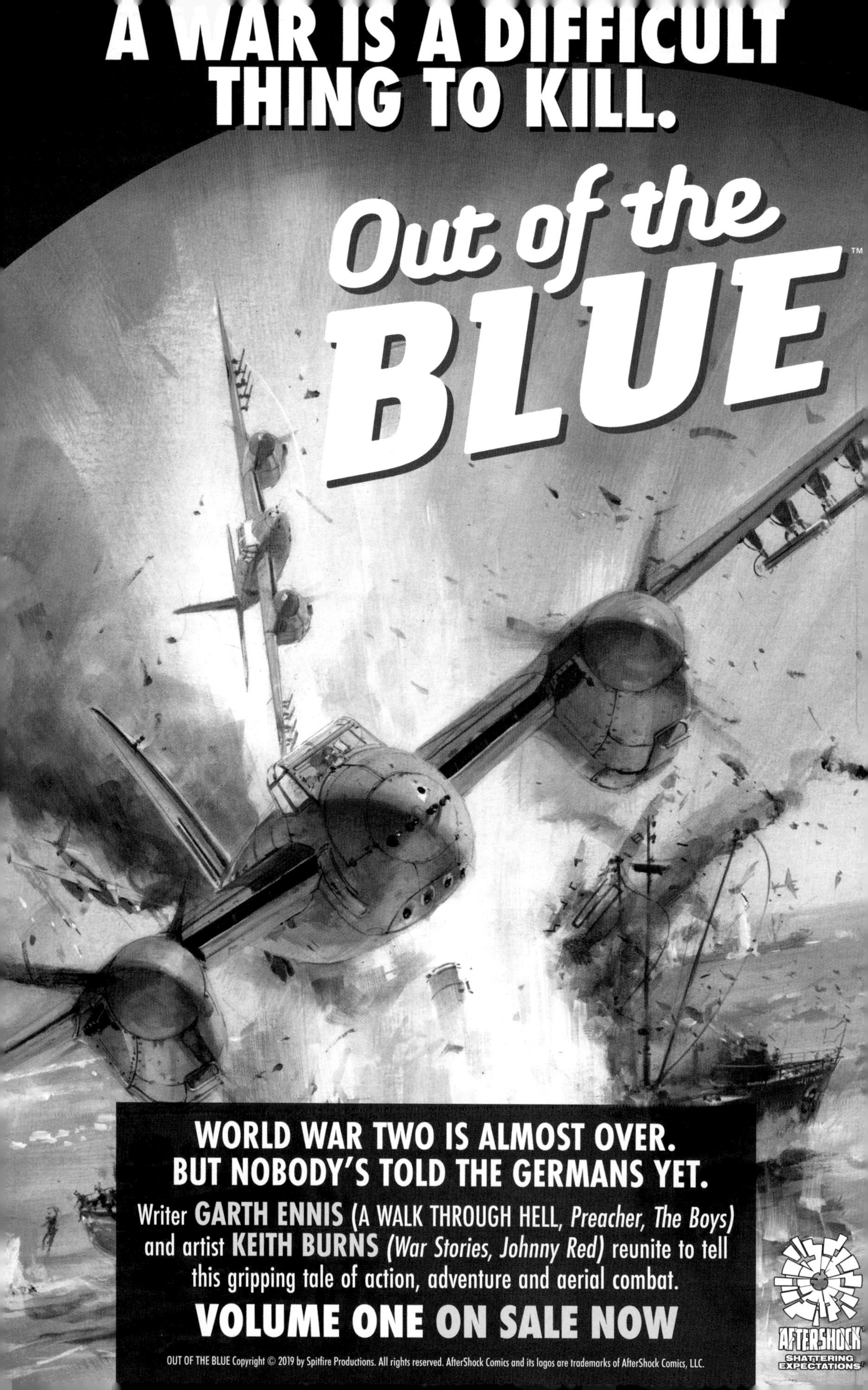
A WAR IS A DIFFICULT THING TO KILL.
Out of the BLUE™
WORLD WAR TWO IS ALMOST OVER.
BUT NOBODY'S TOLD THE GERMANS YET.
Writer GARTH ENNIS (A WALK THROUGH HELL, Preacher, The Boys) and artist KEITH BURNS (War Stories, Johnny Red) reunite to tell this gripping tale of action, adventure and aerial combat.
VOLUME ONE ON SALE NOW
OUT OF THE BLUE Copyright © 2019 by Spitfire Productions. All rights reserved. AfterShock Comics and its logos are trademarks of AfterShock Comics, LLC.
AFTERSHOCK
SHATTERING EXPECTATIONS

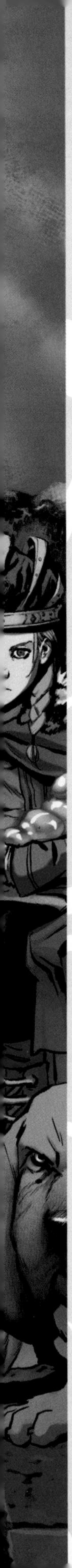

STOCK UP ON THESE GREAT AFTERSHOCK COLLECTIONS!

A WALK THROUGH HELL VOL 1
GARTH ENNIS / GORAN SUDZUKA
SEP181388

ALTERS VOL 1 & VOL 2
PAUL JENKINS / LEILA LEIZ
MAR171244 & APR181239

AMERICAN MONSTER VOL 1
BRIAN AZZARELLO / JUAN DOE
SEP161213

ANIMOSITY YEAR ONE, VOL 1, VOL 2 & VOL 3
MARGUERITE BENNETT / RAFAEL DE LATORRE
FEB181034, JAN171219, AUG171130 & MAY181314

ANIMOSITY: EVOLUTION VOL 1 & VOL 2
MARGUERITE BENNETT / ERIC GAPSTUR
MAR181079 & FEB188089

ANIMOSITY: THE RISE HARDCOVER
MARGUERITE BENNETT / JUAN DOE
AUG178324

ART OF JIM STARLIN HARDCOVER
JIM STARLIN
MAR181077

BABYTEETH YEAR ONE, VOL 1 & VOL 2
DONNY CATES / GARRY BROWN
OCT181328, OCT171087 & APR181225

BETROTHED VOL 1
SEAN LEWIS / STEVE UY
DEC181449161115

BEYONDERS VOL 1
PAUL JENKINS / WESLEY ST. CLAIRE
JAN191468

BLACK-EYED KIDS VOL 1, VOL 2 & VOL 3
JOE PRUETT / SZYMON KUDRANSKI
AUG161115, FEB171100 & JAN181152

BROTHERS DRACUL VOL 1
CULLEN BUNN / MIRKO COLAK
SEP181404

CAPTAIN KID VOL 1
MARK WAID / TOM PEYER / WILFREDO TORRES
APR171231

CLAN KILLERS VOL 1
SEAN LEWIS / ANTONIO FUSO
JAN191469

COLD WAR VOL 1
CHRISTOPHER SEBELA / HAYDEN SHERMAN
JUL181518

DARK ARK VOL 1 & VOL 2
CULLEN BUNN / JUAN DOE
FEB181035 & SEP181394

DREAMING EAGLES HARDCOVER
GARTH ENNIS / SIMON COLEBY
AUG161114

ELEANOR & THE EGRET VOL 1
JOHN LAYMAN / SAM KIETH
DEC171041

FU JITSU VOL 1
JAI NITZ / WESLEY ST. CLAIRE
APR181241

HER INFERNAL DESCENT VOL 1
LONNIE NADLER / ZAC THOMPSON / KYLE CHARLES / EOIN MARRON
OCT181341

HOT LUNCH SPECIAL VOl 1
ELIOT RAHAL / JORGE FORNES
DEC181449

INSEXTS YEAR ONE, VOL 1 & VOL 2
MARGUERITE BENNETT / ARIELA KRISTANTINA
APR181228, JUN161072 & SEP171098

JIMMY'S BASTARDS VOL & VOL 2
GARTH ENNIS / RUSS BRAUN
DEC171040 & JUN181333

MONSTRO MECHANICA VOL 1
PAUL ALLOR / CHRIS EVENHUIS
JUL181517

OUT OF THE BLUE VOL 1
GARTH ENNIS / KEITH BURNS
JAN191460

PESTILENCE VOL 1 & VOL 2
FRANK TIERI / OLEG OKUNEV
NOV171154, OCT181340

REPLICA VOL 1
PAUL JENKINS / ANDY CLARKE
MAY161030

ROUGH RIDERS VOL 1, VOL 2 & VOL 3
ADAM GLASS / PATRICK OLLIFFE
OCT161101, SEP171097 & AUG181474

SECOND SIGHT VOL 1
DAVID HINE / ALBERTO PONTICELL
DEC161186

SHIPWRECK VOL 1
WARREN ELLIS / PHIL HESTER
MAR181078

SHOCK HARDCOVER
VARIOUS
JAN181139

SUPERZERO VOL 1
AMANDA CONNER / JIMMY PALMIOTTI / RAFAEL DE LATORRE
MAY161029

THE LOST CITY EXPLORERS VOL 1
ZACHARY KAPLAN / ALVARO SARRASECA
NOV181434

THE NORMALS VOL 1
ADAM GLASS / DENNIS CALERO
SEP181391

UNHOLY GRAIL VOL 1
CULLEN BUNN / MIRKO COLAK
JAN181151

WITCH HAMMER OGN
CULLEN BUNN / DALIBOR TALAJIC
SEP181387

WORLD READER VOL 1
JEFF LOVENESS / JUAN DOE
SEP171096

www.aftershockcomics.com/collections

ABOUT THE CREATORS OF

BEYONDERS™

PAUL JENKINS writer

@mypauljenkins

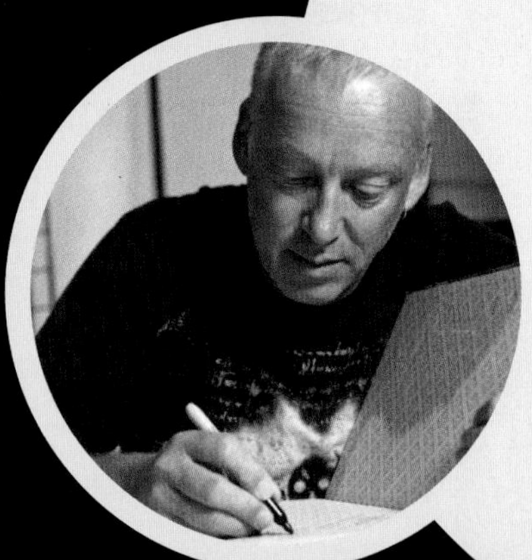

Paul Jenkins has been creating, writing and building franchises for over twenty years in the graphic novel, film and video game industries. Over the last two decades Paul has been instrumental in the creation and implementation of literally hundreds of world-renowned, recognizable entertainment icons.

From his employment with the creators of the *Teenage Mutant Ninja Turtles* at the age of 22 to his preeminent status as an IP creator, Paul has provided entertainment to the world through hundreds of print publications, films, video games, film and new media. With six Platinum-selling video games, a Number One MTV Music Video, an Eisner Award, Five Wizard Fan Awards, and multiple Best Selling Graphic Novels, Paul Jenkins is synonymous with success. He has enjoyed recognition on the New York Times bestseller list, has been nominated for two BAFTA Awards, and has been the recipient of a government-sponsored Prism Award for his contributions in storytelling and characterization.

Paul's extensive list of comic book credits include *Batman* and *Hellblazer* for DC Comics; *Inhumans, Spider-Man, The Incredible Hulk, Wolverine: Origin, Civil War: Frontlines, Captain America: Theater of War* and *The Sentry* for Marvel Comics; and *Spawn* for Image Comics.

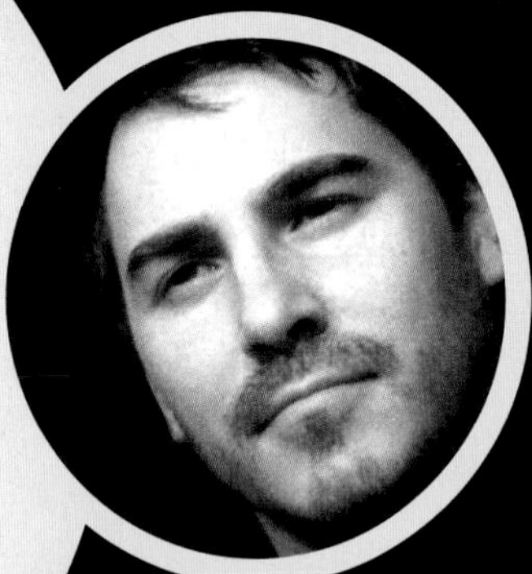

WESLEY ST. CLAIRE artist

@wesstclaire

Wes St. Claire began his passion for comics and storytelling at a young age, selling mini-comics to classmates in his fifth grade economy class for Monopoly money. As a teen he spent four years taking college-level art classes, and eventually went on to three semesters at Montgomery College's School of Art & Design. After a few years off from school, Wes set out to study cartoon illustration at The Kubert School of Cartoon and Graphic Art in 2009. Once graduated from The Kubert School, Wes pursued his career in the narrative arts and achieved his first major publication with DC Comics penciling for the 2015 *Teen Titans Annual*. He now resides in New Jersey and has been working with AfterShock since his debut on FU JITSU.

MARSHALL DILLON letterer

@MarshallDillon

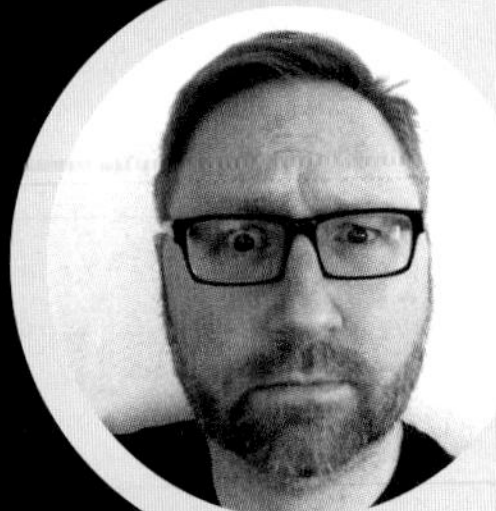

A comic book industry veteran, Marshall got his start in 1994, in the midst of the indie comic boom. Over the years, he's been everything from an independent self-published writer to an associate publisher working on properties like *G.I. Joe, Voltron,* and *Street Fighter*. He's done just about everything except draw a comic book, and worked for just about every publisher except the "big two." Primarily a father and letterer these days, he also dabbles in old-school paper and dice RPG game design. You can catch up with Marshall at firstdraftpress.net.